# The Haynes Automotive
# Electrical Manual

**by Ken Freund, Jon LaCourse, Mike Stubblefield, Bob Worthy and John H Haynes** Member of the Guild of Motoring Writers

## The Haynes Automotive Repair Manual for chassis electrical systems

*(11U1 – 1654)*

ABCDE FGHIJ KLMNO P 2

**Haynes Publishing Group**
Sparkford Nr Yeovil
Somerset BA22 7JJ England

**Haynes North America, Inc**
861 Lawrence Drive
Newbury Park
California 91320 USA

# Acknowledgements

We wish to thank The Auto Parts Store in Camarillo, California for providing the alternators and starters seen in Chapters 4 and 5.

Equus Products Inc., 17291 Mt. Hermann, Fountain Valley, CA 92708 provided the dashboard gauges used in Chapter 7, and the driving lights installed in Chapter 6 were provided by KC HiLites, P.O. Box 155, Williams, AZ 86046.

In addition, thanks are due to The Chrysler Corporation, Ford Motor Company, General Motors Corporation, Mazda Motor Corporation, Mitsubishi Motors Corporation, Nissan Motor Company and Toyota Motor Corporation for the provision of technical information and certain illustrations.

© **Haynes North America, Inc.** **1989**

With permission from J.H. Haynes & Co. Ltd.

A book in the **Haynes Automotive Repair Manual Series**

**Printed in the USA**

**ISBN 1 85010 654 1**

**Library of Congress Catalog Number 89-82240**

**While every care is taken to ensure that the information in this manual is correct, no liability can be accepted by the authors or publishers for loss, damage or injury caused by any errors in, or omissions from, the information given.**

# Contents

# Haynes electrical manual

# Preface

Not too long ago, the average automotive electrical system consisted of a battery, a generator, a few motors and a bunch of switches, relays, fuses and lights. Not anymore.

In the last two decades, automobile electrical systems have become increasingly elaborate. The rate at which electrical/electronic systems are evolving outpaces development on other parts of the automobile. As you're probably aware, there's a lot of electrical complexity in even the simplest new automobiles.

The best automotive electricians are sometimes baffled by modern electrical systems, and you, the home mechanic, may not feel qualified to work on them.

We at Haynes think we can restore your confidence. In this book, we have tried to take a practical approach to diagnosing and repairing problems related to the chassis electrical system. You'll find a minimum of electrical theory and a maximum of diagnostic and repair information. You don't have to be an electrician to use this book, and you don't have to spend a king's ransom on special tools and test equipment; the equipment you'll need to perform the procedures in this book should pay for itself after the first few repairs.

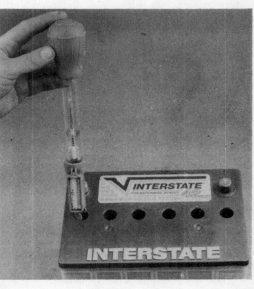

# Haynes electrical manual

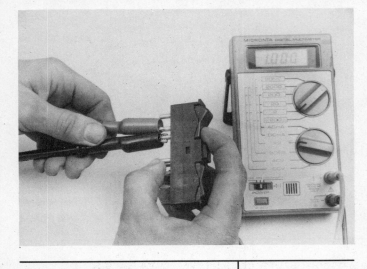

As with all automotive work, the keys to success are patience and clear, careful thinking. Obviously, the procedures in this book can't lead you step-by-step through every electrical problem you'll encounter. Chapters 1, 2 and 3 are designed to give you a basic understanding of automotive electrical systems and introduce you to logical troubleshooting procedures. This knowledge will prepare you to deal with all types of electrical problems. Even if you've done some work on electrical systems before, it's a good idea to review the information in these Chapters, especially the information on test equipment in Chapter 3.

In Chapters 4 through 8, you'll find detailed troubleshooting procedures as well as component replacement and overhaul information for starting, charging, lighting, gauge and accessory circuits. The individual procedures in these Chapters discuss any special equipment needed to carry out the procedure.

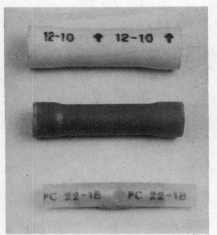

Since this book cannot detail all variations of all vehicles, we recommend you supplement the information in this book with the Haynes Automotive Repair Manual written for your particular vehicle. Using these two books, some patience and a minimum of test equipment, you should be able to handle most repairs on chassis electrical systems.

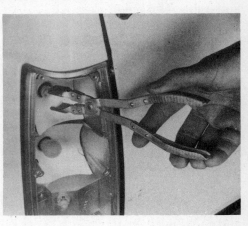

Mike Forsythe, editor

**Caution:** *The procedures in this manual are written for vehicles with negative-ground electrical systems. Some older (mostly British) vehicles have positive-ground systems. If you're working on a vehicle with a positive-gound system, you may have to reverse references to "positive" and "negative" in some procedures.*

# 1 Basic automotive electricity

## Electricity and the automobile

Without electricity, modern automobiles could not function. Electrical devices start your car, charge the battery, monitor the engine, play music, roll the windows up and down, lock the doors, adjust the mirrors, wipe the windshield, illuminate the road, tell other drivers when you're stopping or turning and perform a host of other tasks. You probably never give one of these components a second thought, unless, of course, it malfunctions . . .

People spend their entire lives studying the mysteries of the phenomenon known as electricity. Unless you're planning to become an electrical engineer, we assume you don't have the time to do that. You want to learn enough about electricity and electrical theory so you can understand how the components and systems on your vehicle function. That's this Chapter's focus.

*This (greatly simplified) wiring harness illustrates the automobile's dependence on electricity for nearly everything*

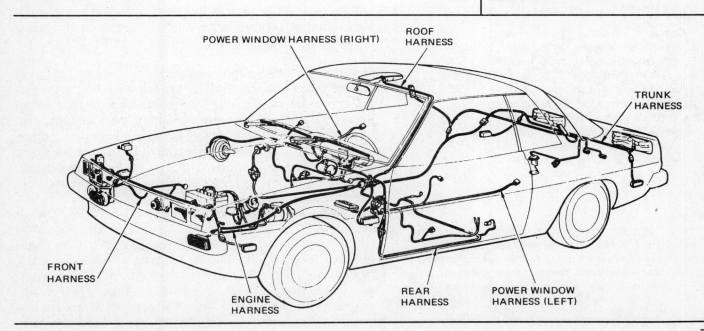

POWER WINDOW HARNESS (RIGHT)

ROOF HARNESS

TRUNK HARNESS

FRONT HARNESS

ENGINE HARNESS

REAR HARNESS

POWER WINDOW HARNESS (LEFT)

# Haynes electrical manual

## What is electricity?

No one actually knows, but after several hundred years of trying to figure it out, we do know some of its characteristics:

*It has positive and negative charges.*
*It's invisible*
*It can be controlled*
*It flows (in a complete circuit)*
*It can be stored.*

You may remember something about positive and negative charges from high school physics. And you probably have at least a vague sense of some of the other characteristics of electricity. Let's review some of those ideas briefly.

### Polarity

Remember those experiments you did with magnets in grade-school science class? Every magnet has a North pole and a South pole. On some magnets, these poles are marked + (positive) and – (negative). If you place the + pole of one magnet near the – pole of another magnet, they attract each other. If you put both + poles or both – poles near each other, they repel each other. We call this attraction of opposites and repulsion of likes polarity. Polarity causes electrons (and thus electrical current) to act as it does.

### Electrons

Why is electricity invisible? Because it operates on an atomic level. Atoms are the building blocks of the universe; everything is made of atoms. They can't be seen because they're very small. It would take millions of them to dot each i in this sentence. Amazingly, atoms themselves still aren't the smallest parts of matter. Each atom is composed of particles – protons, neutrons and electrons. Protons have a positive charge, electrons have a negative charge and neutrons, as the name implies, have no charge. Electrons, like tiny planets, orbit around the atom's neuclus (composed of protons and neutrons). They are held in their orbit because they are attracted to the positively charged protons in the nucleus (remember from our earlier discussion that positive and negative charges attract each other).

In the atom of a good conductor (like copper), some of the electrons are not strongly attracted to the protons in the nucleus and are free to float from one atom to another. If an extra electron is introduced into the orbit of an atom, one of the electrons already there is forced to leave, since there is now an excessively negative charge in the atom. We can harness this phenomenon, known as electron drift, to produce electrical current. The trick is to put excess electrons into orbit in the atoms of a conductor.

So where do these excess electrons come from? On automobiles, they come from the battery or alternator. We will discuss these two components in depth in later chapters, but for now, just think of them as devices that crank out zillions of excess electrons. At one terminal of the battery, or alternator, there are too many electrons; at the other, there aren't enough. Attach a copper wire between

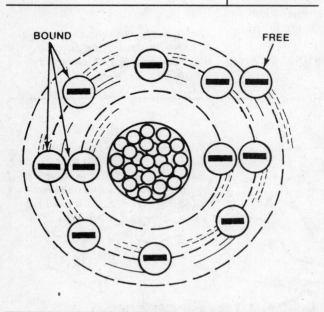

BOUND

FREE

*Electrons closest to the nucleus are called "bound" electrons because they're tightly controlled by the nucleus – electrons farthest from the nucleus are referred to as "free" electrons because they're free to leave*

the two terminals of a battery or an operating alternator and free electrons start pushing into the copper wire. What was random electron drift begins to assume a pattern of more or less continuous movement. As long as there are too many electrons behind, and not enough ahead, the electrons travel in a semi-orderly way in one direction. This directional flow of electrons in the wire is called electrical *current*.

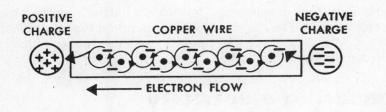

POSITIVE CHARGE     COPPER WIRE     NEGATIVE CHARGE

← ELECTRON FLOW

*When you attach a wire between the two terminals of a battery (or an alternator), free electrons start pushing into the wire and random electron drift assumes a pattern of movement from the negative to positive terminals – we call this behavior current flow*

## Current flow and conductors

Current flow only occurs in materials with lots of free electrons. Such materials are called conductors. Copper is a good conductor, but it isn't the only one. Other metals, including aluminum, lead and even gold are sometimes used as electrical conductors.

When electrons flow through a conductor, the effect of the flow is available instantaneously at the other end of the conductor. The speed of the electrons is actually less than a few inches per second, but the energy applied to one end of the circuit is transmitted at the speed of light. The way it works is illustrated by the following example:

Imagine several billiard balls placed in a line, each touching the next. Drive another ball into the first ball in line and what happens? A ball simultaneously pops off the other end of the line. Electrons behave in the same way, only much faster. This movement of electrons along a conductor is called *amperage* and is directly related to the voltage (the electrical pressure that causes the current to flow) applied to the conductor.

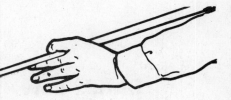

*Current travels at the speed of light using a principle that's similar to this billiard-table example – think of the force from the cue ball as voltage and the balls striking each other as current flow*

## Resistors

In some materials, like iron, nickel and nichrome, electron drift isn't as active as it is in a good conductor. When a free electron drifts to another atom, some of its energy is absorbed, and the electron pushed out has less energy than the one that displaced it. Materials made of these atoms are called *resistors* because, even though they conduct, they resist (slow down) current flow.

# Haynes electrical manual

### Insulators

In some materials, there's no electron drift at all, so they can't conduct electricity. These materials are sometimes referred to as dielectric, but more often are simply called *insulators.* Typical insulating materials include air, rubber, glass, wood, plastics, bakelite and porcelain. Note that insulators are all some sort of non-metallic material; conductors and resistors are usually made of metal.

### Semiconductors

Semiconductors, or solid-state devices, are the basic building blocks of electronic circuits. They're made from a material (usually silicon) that doesn't conduct in its pure form, but will behave like a conductor under certain conditions.

## Measuring electricity

So far, we've been talking about electricity from a theoretical standpoint. But when you're working on your car, it's critical that you know the relationship between voltage, amperage and resistance. We've already touched on two of these three terms. Now let's define them.

### Volts

Volts are units of electrical pressure – how much pressure is pushing the electrons through the circuit. The symbol used for volts is V. Smaller voltages are measured in millivolts (1/1000th of a volt); larger voltages are measured in kilovolts (1,000 volts).

### Amps

Amps, or amperes, are units of electron flow – how fast the electrons are passing through the conductor. The symbol for Amps is A. Smaller current flow is measured in milliamps (ma) (1/1,000th of an amp).

### Ohms

Ohms are units of resistance – how much the conductor or resistor resists the flow of electric current. The symbol for ohms is the Greek letter Omega (aX). Smaller resistances are measured in milliohms (maX) (1/1,000th of an ohm). Larger resistances are measured in megohms (MaX) (1,000 ohms).

### Ohm's Law

In the early 1800s, a German physicist named George S. Ohm described the link between voltage, amperage and resistance in a simple electrical circuit. He said that:

The current in a circuit is directly proportional to the applied voltage and inversely proportional to the resistance in the circuit.

It is important that you understand this relationship between volts, amps and ohms. If you study Ohm's Law, as it's called, carefully, you will see that it can be broken down into three simple statements:

**1** When the voltage goes up or down, current flow also goes up or down (as long as the resistance stays the the same).

**2** When resistance goes up, current goes down (as long as voltage stays the same).

**3** When resistance goes down, current goes up (as long as voltage stays the same)

Unless you'll be designing circuits, That's all you really need to know about Ohm's law. and you'll be able to understand what any voltage, resistance or amperage is telling you about the other two values.

## Electrical circuits

Now that you know a little about how electricity behaves in general, let's look at how it behaves in a typical automobile circuit. First, we need to look at what makes up a circuit. Then we'll describe how it works and discuss the three basic types of automotive circuits.

In its simplest terms, the circuit is the basis for current flow. Without a circuit, there can be no current flow. The circuit is also what ties the components of an electrical system together. Without a circuit to connect them, electrical components would be just that – components. When they're connected in a circuit, they become a system.

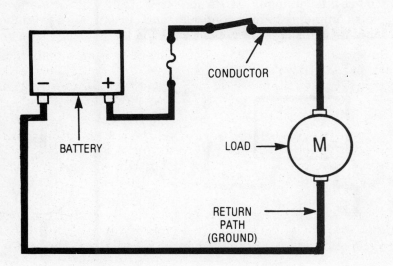

*A complete circuit has a feed or power side (the conductor) and a return path to the voltage source (the battery) – the device being powered (the load) is the dividing point between the two sides of the circuit*

For a circuit to exist, two conditions must be present:

**1** There must be a complete, unbroken path through which the current can flow. It must be able to flow from the source of the voltage, through all the various wires, connectors, switches and components and back to the voltage source. When this condition exists, the circuit is said to have continuity.

**2** There must be a difference in voltage between two points of the circuit. In automobiles, these points are the two battery terminals. This difference is called *potential*.

Automotive circuits have two sides: The feed (power) side (attached to the positive [+] battery terminal on most vehicles), and the return (ground) side (attached to the negative [–] battery terminal on most vehicles). In a simple circuit that has only one load (component being powered by the current flow), the load is the dividing point between the two sides.

## Single-wire circuits

Automobiles use *single-wire* circuits. They have a feed wire to each load, but do away with the return wire back to the source. Instead, components are connected, individually or in groups, to the chassis, which acts as a big return conductor back to the battery. This chassis return path is known as *ground*. The battery itself is connected to ground by cables from the negative terminal (on most vehicles) to the chassis.

# Haynes electrical manual

## Voltage difference

Before we look at the three basic types of circuits found on automobiles, there are two other concepts you should understand – voltage difference (which we've briefly touched upon already) and voltage drop.

Look at the accompanying illustration. The switch is open, so current can only flow from the battery positive terminal to the switch. This side of the circuit has what is known as *potential voltage* – it's got 12 volts from the battery ready to use. On the other side of the switch, there are zero volts available. So there's a difference of 12 volts between the two sides of the switch. We call this the *voltage difference.*

Now close the switch: Current flows across the switch and the voltage difference vanishes. Voltage on either side of the switch is equal. The switch has little or no resistance and there are 12 volts on either side. The circuit is complete; there is continuity and current flows from the source through the wires and the switch to the load, then back to the battery.

*In this circuit, the switch is open, so there's a 12-volt potential on one side of the switch and no voltage on the other side.*

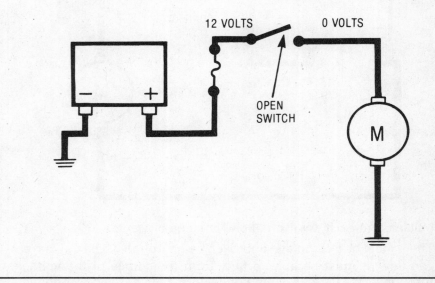

12 VOLTS       0 VOLTS

OPEN SWITCH

M

## Voltage drop

When the current passes through a load, the process is slightly different. A potential of 12 volts is applied to the positive side of the component, but this time it has to overcome a resistance to generate the required current flow. Because the resistance of the component is designed to provide just the number of amps needed by the component, the voltage is almost entirely used up in the process. We have a *voltage drop.*

We could say that the voltage is being used up as it pushes current across a resistance. It's important that you understand the concept of voltage drop because, practically speaking, it means that there's no voltage on the ground return side of the circuit. Voltage drop across the load is essentially equal to voltage supplied.

In the real world of real circuits, of course, things aren't quite as neat as the above description of voltage drop. There's a tiny voltage drop in the switches and feed wires of a circuit, so the load receives a fraction less than full source voltage. There's also a very small voltage drop in the ground return circuit, so that also affects the actual voltage drop across the load.

We'll show you how voltage potential and voltage drop can be applied in automotive electrical diagnosis and troubleshooting in Chapter 3. Now lets look at the three basic types of circuits – series, parallel and series/parallel – which you'll encounter in automotive electrical systems.

# Basic automotive electricity

A series circuit has two or more loads in sequence. Current has to pass through each load to complete its path back to the battery. A break at any point in the circuit, either on the feed side or the ground side, whether it's a break in the wire or a failure of a component, stops all current flow in the circuit.

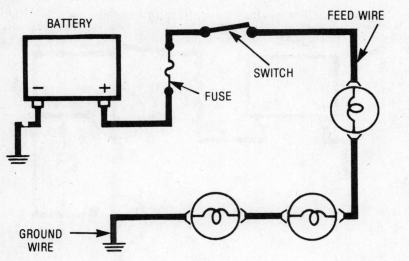

*In a series circuit, current must pass through each load on its way back to the battery*

A series circuit has the following important characteristics:

**1** Current (amperage) is the same everywhere in the circuit.

**2** Voltage drop varies in proportion to the resistances.

**3** Circuit resistance is the total of all the resistances in the circuit.

The easiest way to understand these three charateristics of a series circuit is to visualize a bunch of water pipes forming a continuous loop. Now let's put a water pump in there somewhere to create current flow (the "water pump" in an actual automotive electrical circuit is, of course, the battery). Okay. Start up the pump and what happens? The water starts circulating through the pipes. It just goes round and round, through the pipes, back to the pump, through the pump, back through the pipes, etc. If the pipes have the same internal diameter throughout the entire circuit, the flow rate of the water (amperage in an electrical circuit) is the same everywhere too. But the push delivered by the pump (voltage) diminishes as it gets farther from the pump. If the diameter of the pipes is the same throughout, the push from the pump diminishes at a constant rate. If some of the pipes have smaller diameters, the resistance to flow goes up in these areas and the push delivered by the pump (voltage) dimishes more quickly; if some of the pipes have larger diameters than the others, the push from the pump doesn't go down as much.

## Parallel circuit

The accompanying illustration shows a parallel circuit. Each load in the circuit has a separate feed wire and a return path to ground. In a parallel circuit, current doesn't have to pass through all the components to complete the circuit; the circuit is completed through each one separately. A break in an individual ground wire, or a component failure, will not affect the operation of the other components.

# Haynes electrical manual

## Parallel circuit (continued)

*In a parallel circuit, each load has a separate feed wire – current doesn't have to pass through all the components to complete the circuit*

A parallel circuit has the following important characteristics:

**1** Current at a branch of the circuit varies if the resistance of that branch's loads varies.

**2** Voltage drop across all the loads is the same.

**3** Circuit resistance is less than any single resistance.

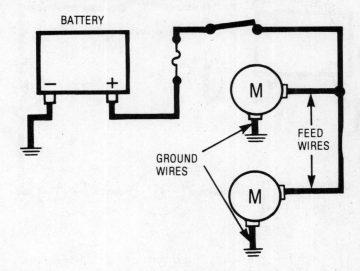

Now, let's look at our analogy again: Visualize a parallel circuit of water pipes with a pump circulating water through them. In this circuit, it's the water flow rate (current) – not the push (voltage) – that varies. Why? Think of one of those Y-splitters that allow you to attach two garden hoses to a single faucet. Turn on the valve for one hose and turn off the valve for the other hose, then turn on the faucet full blast; a healthy stream of water comes out of the hose that's attached to the On valve. Now open the valve for the other hose; water also comes out the second hose, but it's only half as strong in force as the stream from the first hose, and the stream from the first hose is itself only half what it was. The force, or push, from the water pressure in the line (voltage) is the same, but when you open the second valve, the total resistance goes down (because total hose area increases). Flow (amperage) through either of the two hoses is less than it would be through a single hose. The actual rate of flow through each hose depends on that hose's internal diameter (resistance). If both hoses have the same diameter, the current flow through each is the same; if one hose is bigger or smaller than the other, the current flow is proportionally bigger or smaller.

## Series-parallel circuit

The series-parallel circuit is a combination of the previous two types. In this type of circuit, one load is in series with two or more other loads, which are in parallel with each other.

A series-parallel circuit has two important characteristics:

**1** The voltage drop across the loads in parallel with each other will be the same.

**2** The sum of the voltage drop at the first load and the drop across either of the other two loads equals the source voltage.

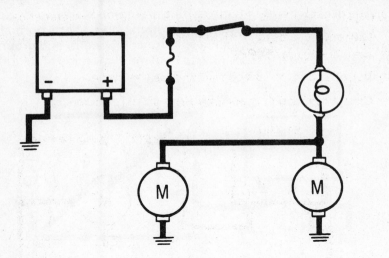

*In a series-parallel circuit, one load is in series with two or more other loads in parallel with each other*

When you're looking at wiring diagrams for your vehicle, you'll find circuits are often neither series nor parallel, but series-parallel. The trick is to figure out just what part of the circuit it is that you're checking (the series part or the parallel part).

## Circuit malfunctions

In Chapter 3 we'll familiarize you with electrical troubleshooting techniques. Here we'll discuss the three basic types of malfunctions that can occur in an electrical circuit.

An open is a physical break anywhere in the circuit. It can occur in the wiring, at connections, or even within a component. When an open occurs, there is no longer any current flow, either because it's unable to reach the load at all or can't return through the ground path to the source.

## Opens

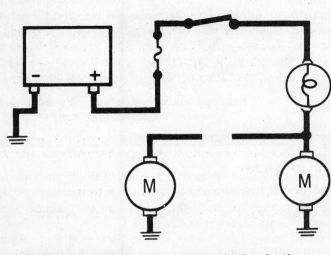

*Opens are physical breaks anywhere in the circuit . . .*

*. . . and can occur in wires, as shown here, or at components*

## Shorts

Shorts occur when damage to wiring or a component causes a circuit to find a new path back to the source. In automobiles, shorts normally occur between two wires or between a wire (or component) and ground.

In Chapter 3, we'll discuss how to read the symptoms of a short and locate it.

*A short (indicated by the lightning bolt symbol in this drawing) causes current to find a new path to the source – in this example, the two motors (marked "M") will operate rapidly even when the switch is open – when the switch is closed, the motors will slow down slightly and the light bulb (the load in series) will glow dimly*

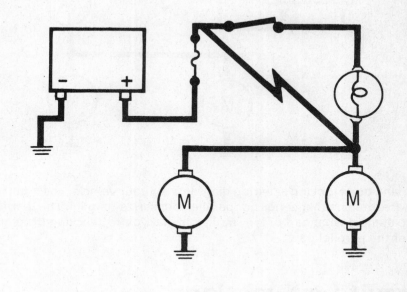

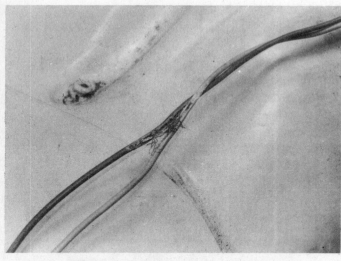

*Shorts can occur between wires, . . .*

*. . . between a wire and ground (as shown here) or even within a component*

## Excessive resistance

When there is excessive resistance in a wire or load, the load(s) try to draw the same current, which in turn causes a higher than normal voltage drop. If resistance increases enough, the effect can be the same as an open: No current at all gets through to the load.

Normally, excessive resistance causes components in the circuit to operate at reduced efficiency: lights are dim, electric motors run at slower than normal speed, etc.

*Corrosion like this on a battery terminal can cause enough resistance to prevent the engine from starting – always check carefully for corrosion, loose connections and chafed or partly broken wires when you suspect excessive resistance in a circuit*

The cause of this type of symptom is usually dirty or corroded contacts or terminals. Dirt or corrosion acts like insulation between two parts of the circuit. Another common cause is a chafed or partly broken wire, which reduces the available cross-sectional area through which current can flow.

## Switches

Automotive electrical circuits are almost always controlled by a switch of some sort. Switches do two things: Allow current into a circuit and direct the flow of current within a circuit. Switches come in a wide variety of configurations, and some look pretty complicated. But they all perform one, or both, of the above functions.

The following describes the types of switches (classified by electrical function) you are likely to find on your vehicle.

*Automotive switches are actuated in a variety of ways – top, left to right: toggle, rocker, push-pull knob, rotary knob, pushbutton and door jamb (actuated by the opening and closing of a door) – bottom: slide and pushbutton combination switch – this terminology tells you how to operate the switch, but it doesn't tell you how it functions electrically*

# Haynes electrical manual

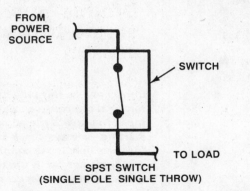

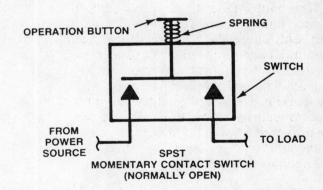

*The single-pole, single-throw (SPST) switch has only two positions – On and Off*

*On a momentary contact SPST switch, a spring-loaded contact keeps the switch from making contact until pressure is applied to the button*

## Single-pole, single-throw switch

The single-pole, single-throw (SPST) switch is the simplest design. The "throws" refer to the number of output circuits; the "poles" refer to the number of circuits completed by the switch. The SPST has only two positions – On and Off. It either completes or "breaks" the circuit. The back-up light switch on vehicles with a manual transmission is a typical example: Put the transmission in Reverse; the switch closes the circuit to the back-up lights and they come on. Put the transmission back in Neutral or a forward gear – the switch opens and the lights go out.

The momentary contact switch is another type of SPST switch. A spring-loaded contact on this switch keeps it from completing the circuit until pressure is applied to the button. Because the spring holds the contacts open, this switch is sometimes designated as a *normally open* type. The horn switch is a good example of the normally open design. Another variation is the *normally closed* switch, which has closed contacts until the button is pressed.

## Single-pole, double-throw switch

The single-pole, double-throw (SPDT) switch has three terminals (one wire in and two wires out). One goes to the battery, the other two go to separate circuits or loads. Either load can be connected to the battery, depending on the position of the switch. The high beam switch is an SPDT switch. Some SPDT switches are known as *center-off* switches because they have three positions – On, Off and On. They control one load in each of the On positions and break both circuts when the control actuator is in between.

*The singe-pole, double-throw (SPDT) switch has three terminals – one goes to the battery and the other two go to separate circuits or loads*

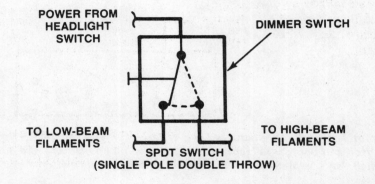

The double-pole, single-throw (DPST) switch has only two positions – On and Off. But, unlike the SPST switch, it has two independent poles, each connected to its own circuit. Each pole has two terminals. Think of the DPST as two SPST switches in one housing, with a common control actuator. The DPST can operate two separate loads at the same time. Headlight/running light switches are sometimes a DPST design.

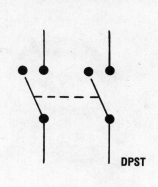

## Double-pole, single-throw switch

*The double-pole, single-throw (DPST) switch has two positions (On and Off), but the the switch actuator controls two circuits*

The double-pole, double-throw (DPDT) switch has two independent poles, each with two On positions. Think of the DPDT switch as two SPDT switches in one housing, operated by one control actuator. The DPDT switch has six terminals: three for each pole.

*The double-pole, double-throw (DPDT) switch has a pair of poles, each with two On positions – think of the DPDT as two SPDT switches in one housing and operated by one actuator*

## Double-pole, double-throw switch

The single-pole, multiple-throw (SPMT) switch allows you to select various settings for a device, such as a heater fan. This type of switch is usually wired to a series of resistors that control the current being fed to the device. Typical settings are Off, Low, Medium and High.

## Single-pole, multiple-throw switch

Switches can be designed with a large number of poles and throws. For instance, one type of neutral start switch (allows you to start vehicles with an automatic transmission only in Neutral or Park) has two poles and six throws. It's referred to as a multiple-pole, multiple-throw (MPMT) switch. It has two movable wipers that move in unison across two sets of terminals (when you see a dotted line between the wipers on an MPMT symbol, it indicates that the wipers are mechanically linked).

## Multiple-pole, multiple-throw switch

*This Ford neutral start switch is an example of a multiple pole, multiple throw (MPMT) switch*

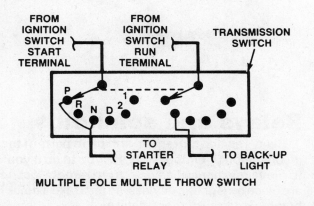

MULTIPLE POLE MULTIPLE THROW SWITCH

## Rheostats

*This back-side view of a rheostat shows the coiled resistance wire used to vary the resistance in the switch*

Have you ever wondered how the illumination intensity of the instrument panel is adjusted from dim to bright? It's a rheostat, also known as a variable resistor, that makes this possible.

Here's how a rheostat works: One end of a piece of coiled resistance wire is connected to the battery feed wire. The other end of the wire isn't attached to anything. The wire from the rheostat to the load is attached to a movable element called a *wiper*. The wiper is mounted so it rubs against the resistance wire. When the wiper is close to the battery-feed-wire-end of the resistance wire, the rheostat imposes little additional resistance to the circuit. But as you slide the wiper to the far end of the resistance wire, current flows through increasingly more resistance to get to the wiper, reducing current flow to the load. You can dial in any amount of resistance you want – from zero to high. This feature gives you precise control over the amount of current being fed to the load.

## Heater blower fan switches

*This Ford resistor assembly is pretty typical of heater blower motor resistors – the coiled resistance wires are used to control blower motor speed*

Rheostats aren't usually capable of carrying high current without burning out. High current circuits which need variable resistance are usually equipped with a single-pole, multiple-throw slide switch. The typical three-speed blower switch for a heater is the most common example of this application. Fan motor speed is determined by the position of the switch. Depending on the switch position, the current is routed through different resistors in series with the motor. In the Low position, all the resistors are used. As the switch is turned to the next higher speed, a resistor is

bypassed; as it's turned to the next speed, another resistor is bypassed, and so on. In the High position, all the resistors are bypassed, providing full current to the motor. Unlike the coiled resistance wire in a rheostat, these resistors are capable of taking higher current without damage (but they do get hot, so they're often located right in the blower airstream).

## Relays and solenoids

Relays switch current on and off in parts of the circuit where it would be inconvenient, or impossible, for you to do it yourself. Solenoids allow you to move mechanical devices from remote locations. Relays and solenoids are electromagnetic devices, so let's take a quick look at electromagnetism before we discuss these devices.

**VIEW B**

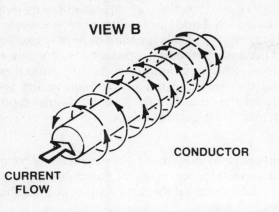

CURRENT
FLOW

CONDUCTOR

*When current flows through a conductor, an electromagnetic field is produced around it – this field remains as long as the current continues to flow through the conductor*

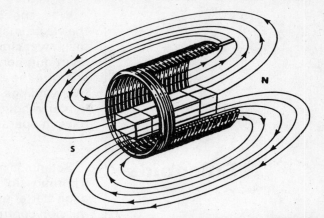

*If you wrap a conductor around an iron core, the field surrounding the wire will induce electromagnetism in the core – the more coils wrapped around the core, the greater the magnetism induced in the core*

## Electromagnetism

When current flows through a conductor, an electromagnetic field around the conductor is produced. This field remains as long as the current continues to flow through the conductor.

If you wrap this conductor around an iron core and flow current through the wire, the electromagnetic field surrounding the wire will induce electromagnetism in the core.

As a general rule, the more times the wire is wrapped around the core, the greater the magnetism induced in the core. Again, the magnetism will remain in the core only as long as current flows through the wire.

## Relays

A relay is an electric switch that allows a small current to control a much larger one. It consists of an electromagnetic coil, a fixed core and a movable armature. The armature, attracted by magnetism in the core, moves whenever the coil is energized. The relay has a control circuit (the small current which activates the relay) and a power circuit (the large current that is switched on or off by the relay). When the control circuit switch is open, no current flows to the coil, so the coil has no magnetism. When the switch is closed, the coil is energized, making the soft iron core into an electromagnet, which draws the armature down. This closes the power circuit contacts, connecting power to the load(s).

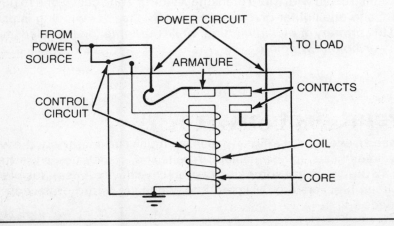

POWER CIRCUIT

FROM
POWER
SOURCE

TO LOAD

ARMATURE

CONTROL
CIRCUIT

CONTACTS

COIL

CORE

*Cutaway of a typical relay*

When the control switch is opened, the current stops flowing in the coil, the electromagnetism disappears and the armature is released, breaking the power circuit contacts. Relays of this type are generally used only for short duration contact because of the high amount of current needed to energize the coil. For relays that remain in operation for longer periods, two windings are provided – one to pull the armature down and a second, lighter winding that breaks the circuit on the first winding and holds the relay in operation with much less current drain.

## Solenoids

Solenoids provide mechanical movement in areas on the vehicle where it is impossible, or inconvenient for you to reach. Solenoids are used to engage starter motors, lock and unlock doors and actuate engine and transmission control devices.

*Cutaway of a typical solenoid*

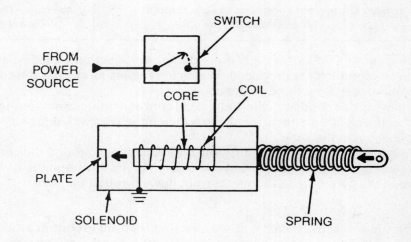

A solenoid consists of an electromagnetic coil surrounding a movable metal core, or plunger. When the coil is energized, the magnetic field pulls the core until it's centered in the coil. Usually, a return spring pulls the core back to its uncentered position when power to the coil is shut off. The movable core provides the mechanical movement. Solenoids are also sometimes used to close contacts, acting as a relay at the same time.

Solenoids that may remain in use for long periods of time are sometimes constructed with more than one winding – one heavy one to pull the core in, and one lighter one to hold it in. The heavier winding is usually called the *primary* or *pull-in* winding, while the lighter one is called the *secondary* or *hold-in* winding.

## Circuit protection

When an overload in a circuit cause too much current to flow, the wiring in the circuit heats up, the insulation melts and, sometimes, a fire starts – UNLESS the circuit has some kind of protective device. Fuses, fusible links and circuit breakers are designed into circuits to afford protection from overloads.

# Basic automotive electricity

*Fuse panels are often located under the driver's side of the dash panel – check the owner's manual for the location on your vehicle*

*Typical methods of installing in-line fuses*

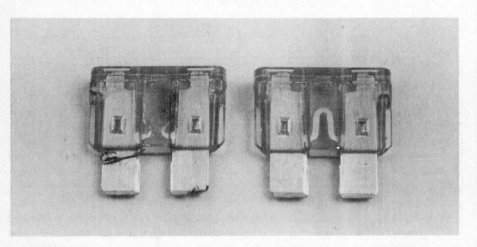

*Modern miniature fuse (good fuse on the right, blown fuse on the left)*

## Fuses

*Traditional fuse (good fuse on the top, blown fuse on the bottom)*

Fuses are the most common form of circuit protection used in automobiles. They're mounted either in a fuse panel or in-line. Early designs use a strip of low-melting-point metal enclosed in a glass tube or placed on a ceramic insulator. A newer "miniature" type has spade connectors and is enclosed in a plastic housing. In operation, they both work exacly the same way: If an excessive current flows through the circuit, the fuse element melts at the narrow portion, opening the circuit and preventing damage.

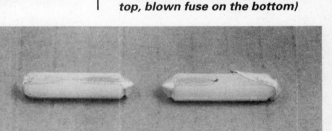

*Ceramic fuses are often used on European cars (good fuse on the left, blown fuse on the right)*

Fuses are designed to carry a preset maximum current, and to "blow" when that maximum is exceeded. The maximum current flow in amps is marked on the fuse. Always replace a blown fuse with a new fuse of the correct rating, both in type and current capacity.

Usually, a visual check of a fuse will suffice. Sometimes, however, a fuse can have an open in it even when it's not obviously blown. In Chapter 3, we'll show you how to check that kind of condition.

## Fusible links

While fuses protect individual circuits, fusible links are designed to protect the entire electrical system. Fusible links are short lengths of smaller gauge wire usually installed between the battery and the ignition switch, or between the battery and the fuse panel. Because they're a lighter gauge wire (and a different material) than the main conductor, they'll melt and open the circuit before damage can occur in the rest of the circuit. Fusible link wire is covered with a special insulation that bubbles when it overheats, indicating the link has melted. To replace a fusible link, you simply cut it out of the conductor and replace it with a new one. We'll show you how in Chapter 3.

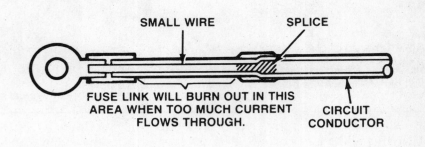

*Cutaway of a typical fusible link*

## Circuit breakers

Circuit breakers are used in circuits where temporary overloads are not uncommon, and in circuits where power must be rapidly restored (headlights, windshield wipers, etc.). The typical circuit breaker is made of a set of contacts controlled by an arm made of two kinds of metals that expand at different rates. When too much current flows in the circuit, this *bimetal arm* becomes overheated and opens the contacts – and the circuit – because of the uneven expansion of the two metals. When the current stops flowing, the bimetal arm cools, once again closing the circuit. If the overload is still present, the circuit breaker once again "cycles." If the overload is gone, the circuit continues to function in a normal manner. This type of circuit breaker is known as a *cycling,* or *self-resetting* design because – after opening the circuit to protect it against overload – it automatically reconnects the circuit each time.

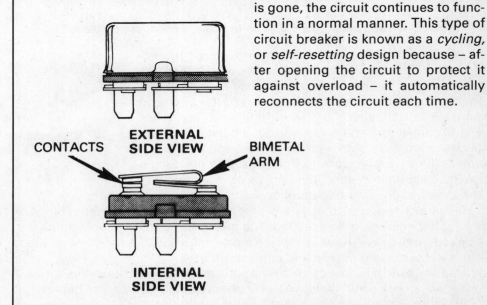

*A typical self-resetting circuit breaker*

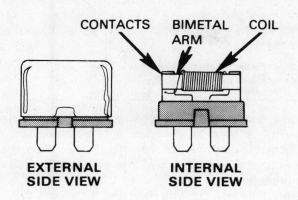

CONTACTS  BIMETAL  COIL
ARM

EXTERNAL
SIDE VIEW

INTERNAL
SIDE VIEW

Another type of circuit breaker is referred to as *non-cycling* or *manually resettable.* In this type, there's a coil wrapped around the bimetal arm. When an overcurrent exists and the contacts open, a small current passes through the coil. This current through the coil isn't large enough to operate the load, but it's sufficient to heat up both the coil and the bimetal arm. That keeps the arm in the open position until power is removed from the coil. On this type of circuit breaker, you'll see a button somewhere on the case or housing. To reset the breaker (shut off the power to the coil), you simply push in on the button.

# 2 Understanding wiring diagrams

## General information

Wiring diagrams are useful tools when troubleshooting electric circuits. Electrical systems on modern vehicles have become increasingly complex, making a correct diagnosis more difficult. If you take the time to fully understand wiring diagrams, you can take much of the guesswork out of electrical troubleshooting.

If you have an older vehicle, you may find the wiring diagrams difficult to decipher. Frequently, older diagrams give no information on component location, operation or how to read the diagram. Many of them are organized in ways that make tracing wires difficult.

Today's wiring diagrams tend to be more carefully organized, and the cross-references between each portion of the diagram are clearly explained. They often have component locators and some are even in color (to show wire colors).

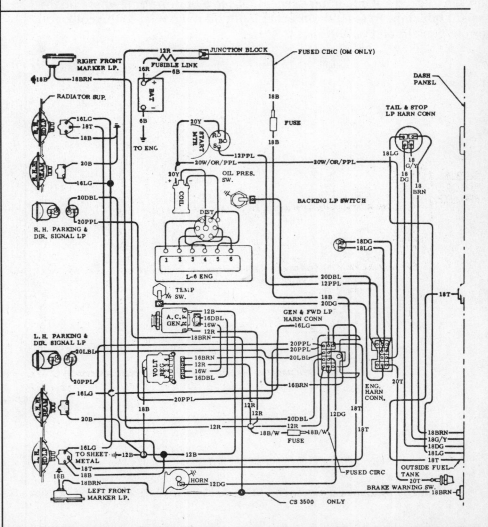

*A diagram from the late 1960's – many older diagrams have little information on where the components are located, how they work or how to read the diagram*

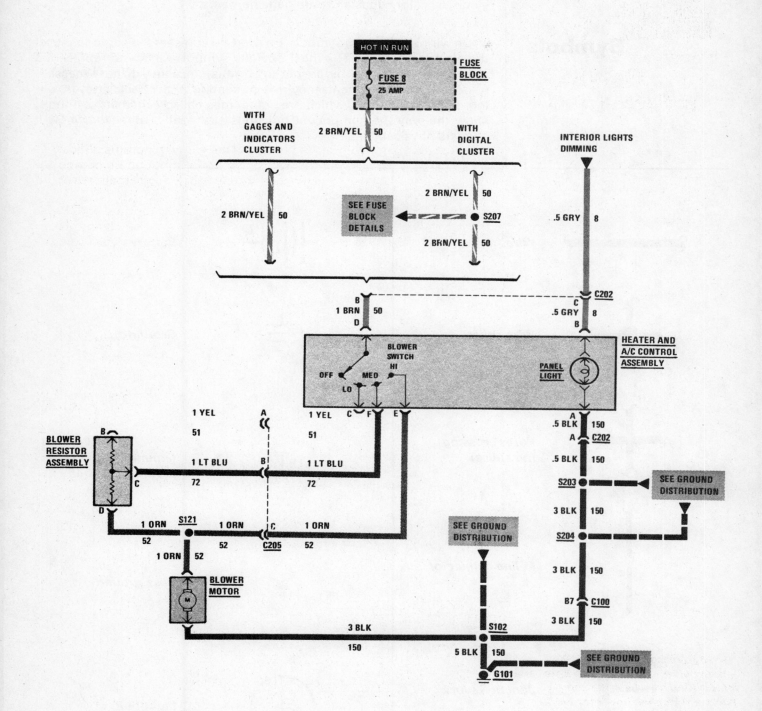

*Many modern diagrams like this one show individual circuits – this is a heater blower motor circuit*

## Components of a wiring diagram

Wiring diagrams can be broken down into three main components: symbols, color codes and wire gage numbers.

### Symbols

On wiring diagrams, symbols are used to represent the components of the electrical system. The most obvious symbol is a line to represent a wire. Some other symbols are not so obvious, since they do not necessarily look like the components they're representing. That's because most wiring diagram symbols, which are sometimes called *schematic* symbols, show the way the component functions electrically rather than how it appears physically.

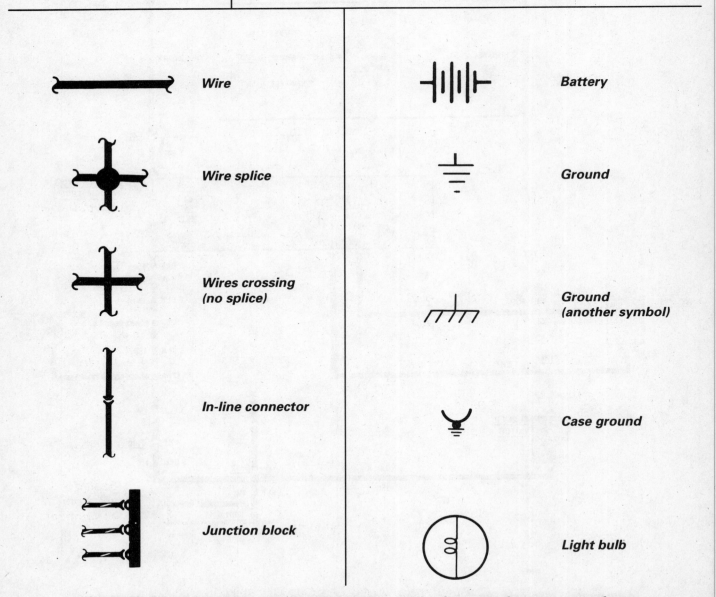

| | |
|---|---|
| Wire | Battery |
| Wire splice | Ground |
| Wires crossing (no splice) | Ground (another symbol) |
| In-line connector | Case ground |
| Junction block | Light bulb |

*Typical wiring diagram symbols – these symbols vary somewhat from manufacturer to manufacturer*

# Understanding wiring diagrams

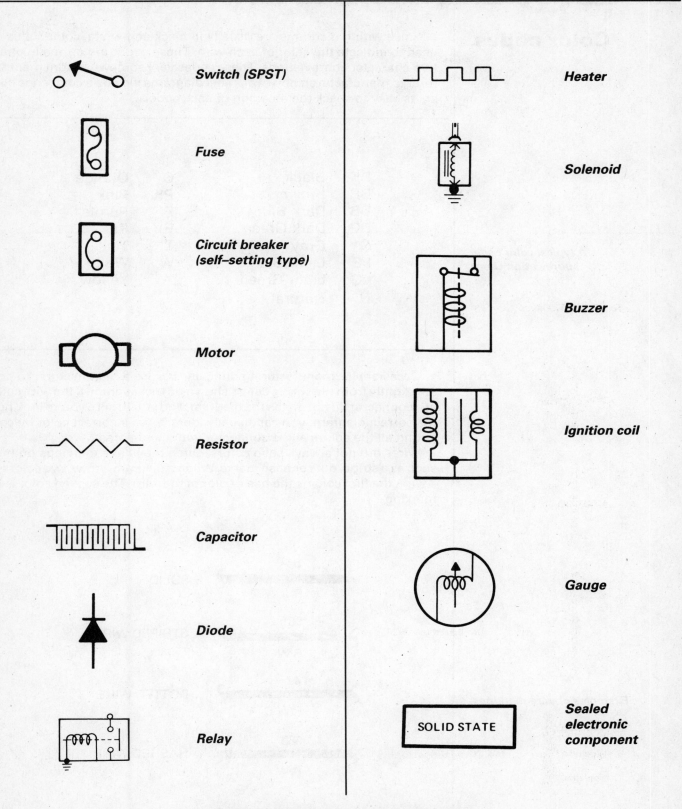

| Symbol | Label | Symbol | Label |
|--------|-------|--------|-------|
| | Switch (SPST) | | Heater |
| | Fuse | | Solenoid |
| | Circuit breaker (self–setting type) | | Buzzer |
| | Motor | | Ignition coil |
| | Resistor | | |
| | Capacitor | | Gauge |
| | Diode | | |
| | Relay | SOLID STATE | Sealed electronic component |

*Typical wiring diagram symbols (continued)*

# Haynes electrical manual

## Color codes

Since wiring diagrams are usually in black-and-white, color codes are used to indicate the color of each wire. These codes are normally one or two-character abbreviations. These codes vary somewhat from manufacturer to manufacturer; however, most diagrams include a color code chart so its easy to check the meaning of each code.

*A typical color code abbreviation chart*

| | | | |
|---|---|---|---|
| BK | Black | O | Orange |
| BR | Brown | PK | Pink |
| DB | Dark Blue | P | Purple |
| DG | Dark Green | R | Red |
| GY | Gray | T | Tan |
| LB | Light Blue | W | White |
| LG | Light Green | Y | Yellow |
| N | Natural | | |

Occasionally, manufacturing difficulties cause a manufacturer to deviate slightly from the wiring colors shown on the diagram. If the wire colors at a connector do not match the diagram, and you're sure you're looking at the correct diagram, you can usually identify the incorrect color by comparing all the colors at the connector with the diagram.

Wires are not always solid colors. Often they have markings on them such as a stripe, dots or hash marks. When a diagram shows two colors for a wire, the first color is the basic color of the wire. The second color is the marking.

*Examples of wire markings*

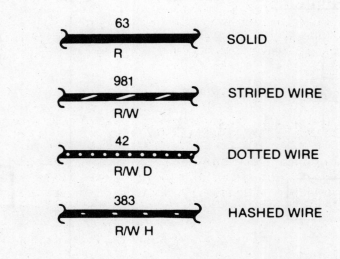

Example: 1.25F - GB

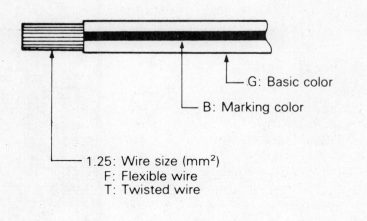

└─ G: Basic color

└─ B: Marking color

└─ 1.25: Wire size (mm²)
F: Flexible wire
T: Twisted wire

*This example code is for a green wire with a black stripe – the 1.25 is the metric wire gage number*

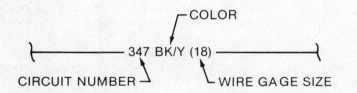

┌─ COLOR

┤ 347 BK/Y (18) ├

CIRCUIT NUMBER ┘  └─ WIRE GAGE SIZE

*This code indicates the color of the wire (black with a yellow marking), the wire gage number (in AWG) and the circuit number*

The wire gage number represents the wire thickness. (We'll tell you more about wire gage in Chapter 3). In a wiring diagram, the gage number for each wire is usually listed either before or after the color code.

## Wire gage numbers

## Reading wiring diagrams

Wiring diagrams either show the entire electrical system on one page, or they split up the electrical system onto multiple pages and have cross-references which tie them all together. When a diagram is split up, there are usually charts with the diagram that explain the cross-referencing system.

Most diagrams show the power source at the top of the page and the grounds at the bottom.

The accompanying illustrations show examples of wiring diagrams from various manufacturers and the methods they use to cross-reference and show components.

# Haynes electrical manual

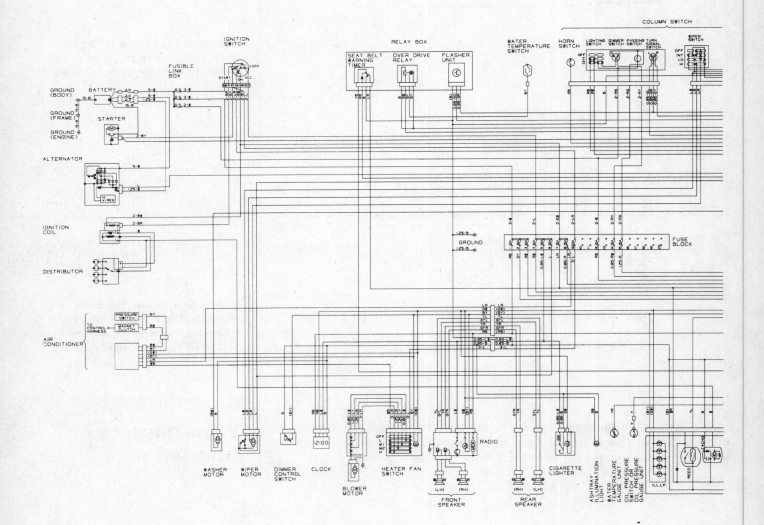

*This Mitsubishi diagram shows the vehicle's entire electrical system (1 of 2)*

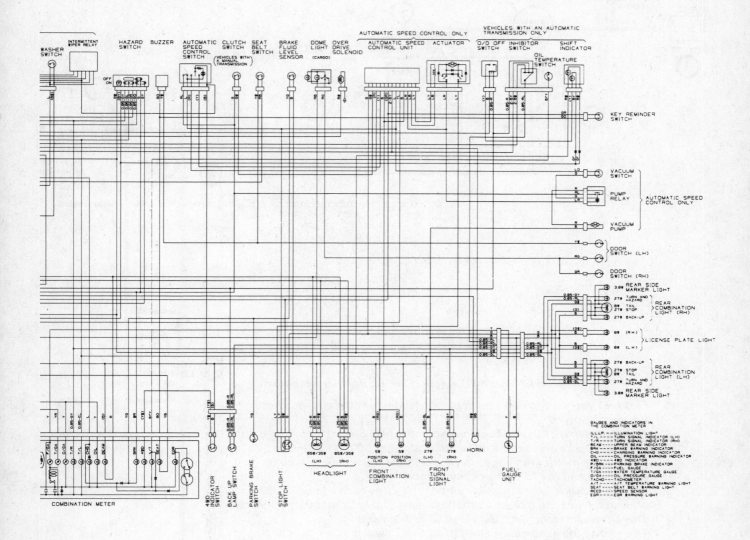

*Mitsubishi wiring diagram (2 of 2)*

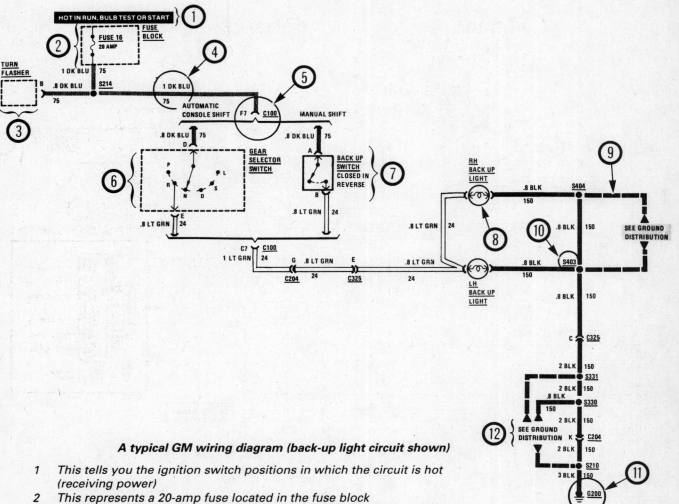

**A typical GM wiring diagram (back-up light circuit shown)**

1　This tells you the ignition switch positions in which the circuit is hot (receiving power)
2　This represents a 20-amp fuse located in the fuse block
3　This represents another circuit which is also run off the same fuse
4　The 1 is the metric wire gage size, the DK BLU is the dark blue color of the wire and the 75 is the circuit number
5　The C100 stands for connector number 100 – this code can be cross-referenced to a diagram that will show the location of the connector
6　This shows the schematic details of an SPMT switch
7　This shows the schematic details of an SPST switch
8　This is the symbol for a light bulb
9　This indicates the wire may have one or more splices before it is grounded
10　This splice number code can be cross-referenced to a diagram that will show you where the splice is located
11　This ground number code can be cross-referenced to a diagram that will show you where the ground is located
12　This is a cross-reference to a diagram that shows the circuit grounds

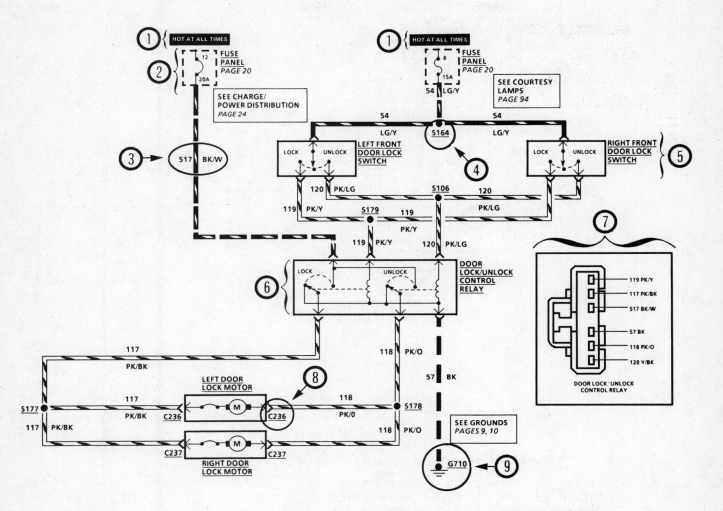

**A typical Ford diagram (power door lock circuit shown)**

1  This tells you the circuit is hot (receiving power) at all times
2  This is a 20-amp fuse located in the fuse panel
3  The 517 is the circuit number and the BK/W stands for a black wire with a white marking
4  This splice number code can be cross-referenced to a chart that will tell you where the splice is located
5  This symbol shows the schematic details of an SPDT switch
6  This symbol shows the schematic details of a dual relay unit
7  This shows the details of a connector, indicating the colors of its wires, their associated circuit numbers and locations in the connector.
8  The C236 stands for connector number 236 – this code can be cross-referenced to a chart that shows a diagram of the connector
9  This ground number code can be cross-referenced to a chart that tells where the ground is located

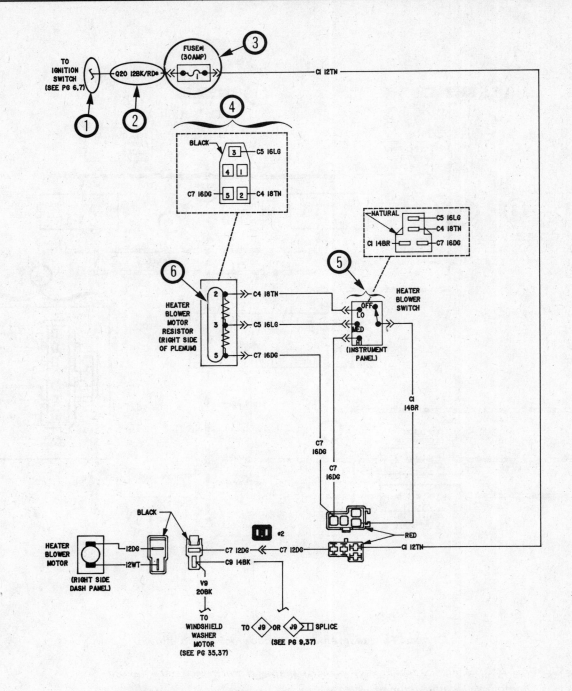

*A typical Chrysler diagram (heater blower motor circuit shown)*

1   This symbol indicates the wire continues to another circuit
2   Q20 is the circuit code, 12 is the wire gage size and BK/RD stands for a black wire with a red marking
3   This indicates a 30-amp fuse
4   This is a diagram of the connector for the blower motor resistor, showing the color codes and circuit numbers of its wires and the color of the connector
5   This symbol shows the schematic details of an SPMT switch
6   These numbers correspond to the numbers on the connector diagram above, so you can more easily find the wires in the connector

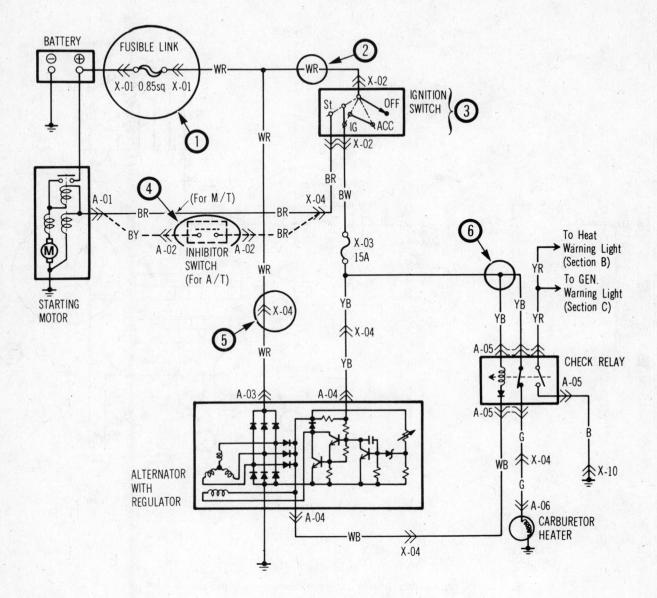

**A typical Mazda diagram (charging and starting circuits shown)**

1   This is the symbol for a fusible link with connectors – the X-01 code can be cross-referenced to a chart that tells where the fusible link is located – the 0.85 is the fusible link's metric wire gage size

2   This color code is for a white wire with a red marking

3   This symbol shows the schematic details of an SPMT switch – the switch is in the Off position, and the dashed lines show the other possible switch positions

4   This symbol shows the schematic details of an SPST switch – the dashed lines mean the switch may or may not be installed on the vehicle

5   This is a wire connector with a location code that you can cross-reference to a chart to find the location of the connector

6   This is a wire splice

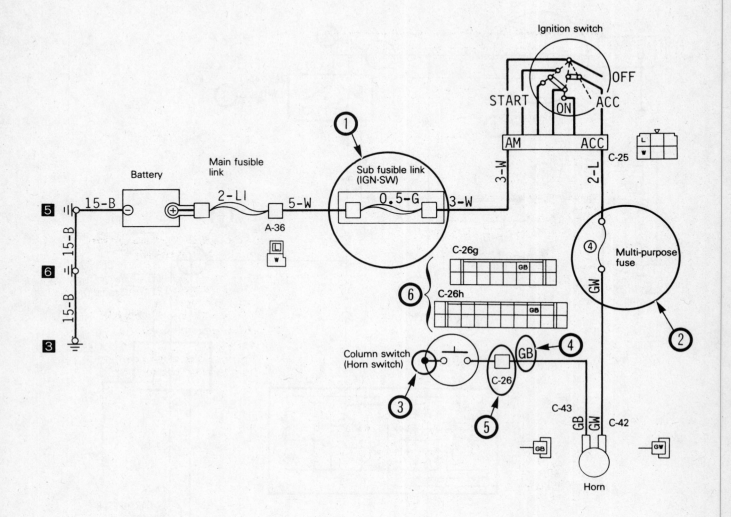

**A typical Mitsubishi diagram (horn circuit shown)**

1   This is a fusible link with connectors, 0.5 metric wire gauge and green in color
2   This is a symbol for a fuse – the 4 is a location code
3   This indicates the switch grounds directly to the body
4   This is a color code for a green wire with a black marking
5   This is the symbol for a connector – the C26 stands for connector number 26
6   This diagram shows the C-26 connector and the location of the green/black wire within the connector

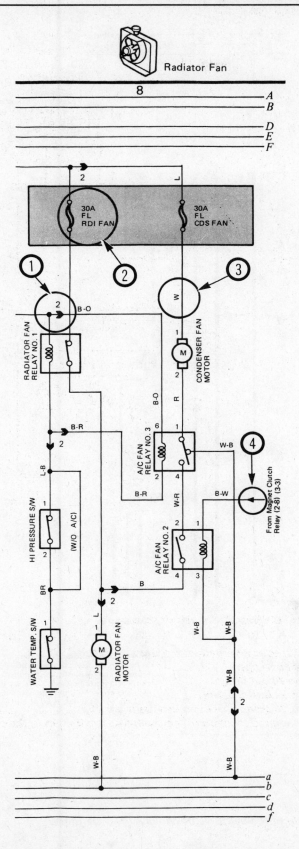

Radiator Fan

**A part of a typical Toyota diagram (radiator fan circuit shown)**

1  This is a connector – the 2 is a location code
2  This is a 30-amp fusible link
3  This is a color code for a white wire
4  This indicates a wire coming from another circuit

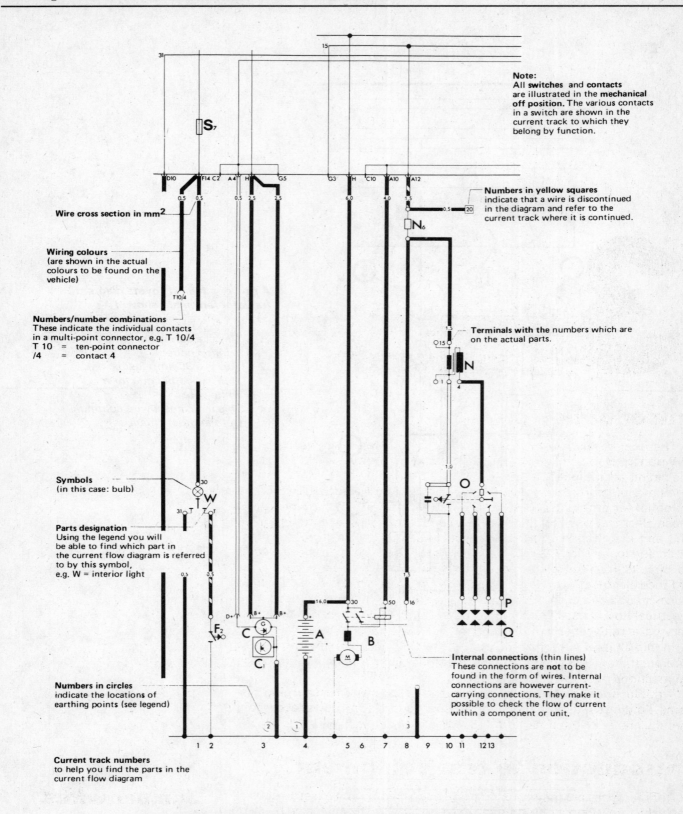

**Note:**
All **switches** and **contacts** are illustrated in the **mechanical off position**. The various contacts in a switch are shown in the current track to which they belong by function.

**Wire cross section in mm²**

**Numbers in yellow squares** indicate that a wire is discontinued in the diagram and refer to the current track where it is continued.

**Wiring colours** (are shown in the actual colours to be found on the vehicle)

**Numbers/number combinations**
These indicate the individual contacts in a multi-point connector, e.g. T 10/4
T 10 = ten-point connector
/4 = contact 4

**Terminals with the numbers which are on the actual parts.**

**Symbols** (in this case: bulb)

**Parts designation**
Using the legend you will be able to find which part in the current flow diagram is referred to by this symbol, e.g. W = interior light

**Internal connections** (thin lines) These connections are **not** to be found in the form of wires. Internal connections are however current-carrying connections. They make it possible to check the flow of current within a component or unit.

**Numbers in circles** indicate the locations of earthing points (see legend)

**Current track numbers** to help you find the parts in the current flow diagram

*This illustration explains some of the symbols on Volkswagen diagrams*

# Diagnosing and correcting circuit faults

## Introduction

The goal of any electrical diagnosis is to determine where the faulty component is located which prevents the current from flowing through the circuit as originally designed.

As manufacturers load up modern vehicles with electrical devices, the potential for problems increases dramatically. Due to the complexity of these electrical systems and the high cost of many replacement parts, a "hit and miss" approach to troubleshooting is unsatisfactory. An organized and logical approach to diagnosis is essential to repair these electrical circuits in a prompt and cost effective manner.

Since electricity is invisible, specialized test equipment is necessary to trace circuits and check components. An accurate method of measuring electrical flow is essential if the problem is to be found without unnecessary parts replacement and wasted time.

In this Chapter we will show you how to select test equipment, how to operate it, how to troubleshoot electrical problems and how to make the connections necessary to repair wiring.

Troubleshooting procedures specific to starting systems, charging systems, lighting systems, gauge/indicator light circuits and power accessory circuits are located in Chapters 4, 5, 6, 7 and 8, respectively.

## Introduction to test equipment

Jumper wires are mainly used to find open circuits and excessive resistance by bypassing a portion of an existing circuit. They can also be used for testing components off the vehicle. They may be purchased already assembled or fabricated from parts purchased at an automotive or electronics supply store.

**Jumper wires**

Jumper wires may be equipped with various types of terminals for different uses. Jumper wires used to carry current from the battery to a component should have an in-line fuse installed to avoid an overload and should also have insulated boots over the terminals to prevent accidental grounding.

**Warning:** *Never use jumpers made of wire that is thinner (of lighter gage) than the wiring in the circuit you are testing. Always use a fuse with the same (or lower) rating as the circuit had originally.*

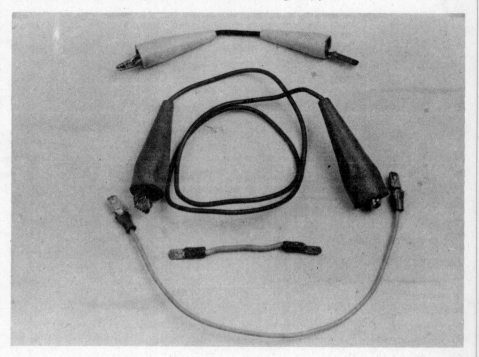

*Jumper wires may be equipped with various types of terminals for different uses*

## Test lights

Test lights are used to check for voltage in a circuit while power is connected to the circuit. Test lights are among the least expensive testing devices available and should be included in every tool box. They may be purchased already made-up or fabricated from parts purchased at an automotive or electronics supply store. Test lights come in several styles, but all have three parts in common; a light bulb, a test probe and a wire with a ground connector. Six, 12, or 24-volt systems may be tested by changing the bulb to the appropriate voltage. Although accurate voltage measurements aren't possible with a

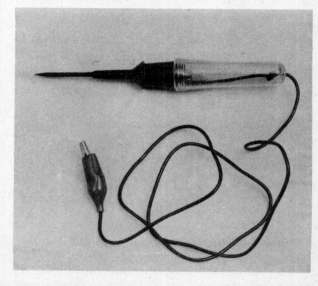

*A Test light is a must for automotive electrical testing*

# Diagnosing and correcting circuit faults

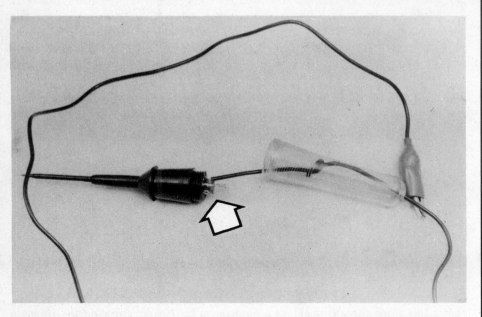

*The test light bulb (arrow) may be changed to match the voltage of the vehicle being tested*

test light, large differences may be detected by the relative brightness of the glowing bulb.

**Note:** *Before using a test light for diagnosis, check it by connecting it to the battery, ensuring the bulb lights brightly.*

## Test buzzers

Test buzzers work the same way as test lights; however they offer the advantage of remote operation. For example, one person working alone may test the brakelight circuit by stepping on the brake pedal and listening for the sound of the buzzer connected to the brakelight bulb socket. A test buzzer may be fabricated at home from parts purchased at an electronics store or made with jumper wires and a key reminder buzzer.

Test buzzers are used in the same manner described for test lights. Additionally, they may be used to find shorts to ground. The procedure for this is covered in the Section entitled *Using test equipment.*

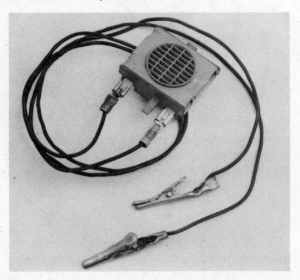

*This test buzzer was made from a key reminder buzzer salvaged from a junked car*

## Continuity testers

Continuity testers (also known as self-powered test lights) are used to check for open or short circuits. They consist of a light bulb, battery pack and two wires combined into one unit. They may be purchased from an auto parts or electronics store. Continuity testers must only be used on

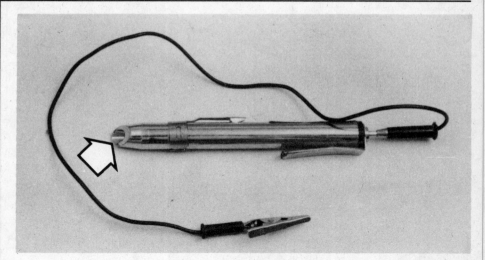

*This continuity tester uses its own batteries to power the light bulb located in its tip (arrow)*

non-powered circuits; vehicle battery voltage would burn out the low-voltage tester bulb.

**Caution:** *Never use a self-powered continuity tester on circuits that contain solid state components, since damage to these components may occur.*

## Short finders

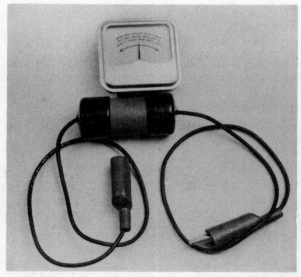

*Short finders consist of a pulse unit and a separate hand-held meter*

Short finders are electromagnetic devices designed to trace short circuits quickly and easily. One part of the short finder is a pulse unit which is installed in place of the fuse for the circuit where a short is suspected. The other part of the short finder is a hand-held meter which is moved along the faulty wiring harness. Meter deflections indicate the area in the harness where the short is located. Short finders are available from major tool manufacturers for a moderate price. The savings from one use can often offset the purchase price.

## Analog (gauge-type) multimeters

Analog multimeters are suitable for a variety of test functions requiring the measurement of volts, ohms and amperes. Many brands and varieties are available at tool and electronics supply stores and by mail order. The units offering the most features and scales are usually the costliest. Analog multimeters can't be used to test solid state circuits, such as computers and electronic ignition control modules. If you already have one of these units, by all means use it for performing the tests described in this book.

# Diagnosing and correcting circuit faults

However, if you intend to purchase a new multimeter, consider getting a digital model. They can perform all the tests an analog unit is capable of plus they are compatible with solid state devices.

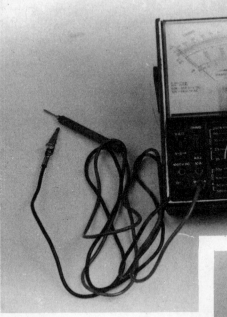

*Analog multimeters can be used to measure volts, amps and ohms in non-solid state circuits*

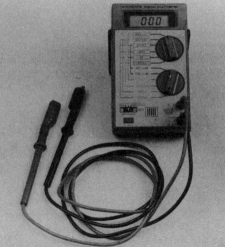

Digital multimeters are used for measuring volts, ohms and amperes with a high degree of accuracy. They are normally available where analog multimeters are sold. Although more expensive than analog units, digital multimeters are compatible with solid state circuits, so you only need to buy one type of tester.

## Digital multimeters

*Digital multimeters can be used for testing all types of circuits*

## Using test equipment

Before you can go chasing electrical gremlins, you have to know how to use test equipment. In this Section we will explain how to use the various testers introduced previously.

**Note:** *Most testers come with instructions. If they differ from the general procedures described here, follow the specific instructions provided by the manufacturer of the tester.*

**Caution:** *Never connect solid state circuits to battery voltage and never test them with any device other than a digital multimeter.*

## Checking for a bad ground

Connect the jumper wire between the component case (or ground terminal) and a clean bare metal spot on the vehicle chassis. If a circuit works properly with the jumper wire in place, but doesn't work when the jumper wire is removed, the ground circuit has an open (or high resistance)

*Here a jumper wire is used to complete a ground circuit on a windshield wiper motor*

which needs repair – check for loose connections, corrosion and broken component ground straps.

## Checking the operation of a component designed to operate on full battery voltage

Ground the component with a jumper as described above and connect a fused jumper wire from the positive battery terminal to the positive terminal on the component being tested. If it now works normally, remove the ground jumper wire. If the device stops working, the ground connection is definitely faulty, but the other side of the circuit may also be bad. Repair it. If the device continues working with the ground jumper removed, look for an open in the positive side of the circuit. If the device won't work, even with both jumper wires in place, the component is faulty. Replace it.

*Components may be tested by connecting them directly to the battery with jumper wires*

# Diagnosing and correcting circuit faults

To use a test light, connect the ground wire to a clean, bare metal ground which is connected to the vehicle chassis. With the circuit switched on, insert the probe into the terminal or socket to be checked. If necessary, the probe can be pushed through the insulation to make contact with the wire. If the bulb lights, voltage is present, meaning the part of the circuit between the test light and the battery is free of opens. After testing is complete, tape over any wires punctured by the probe. Test lights are not sensitive to polarity and can be connected with either the probe or the ground wire connected to positive or negative.

Test buzzers may be connected and used the same way as test lights. Their main advantage is that they allow one person to perform tests which normally require an assistant. For directions on using test buzzers for finding shorts, see *Tracing shorts* below.

Set the voltmeter scale selector switch to the appropriate range (this normally should be higher than battery voltage) and check to see if the test leads are connected to the correct terminals on the tester. The negative lead is black and the positive lead is red. When measuring the voltage in a portion of a circuit, the voltmeter must be connected in parallel with the portion of the circuit to be measured. To avoid damage to the meter, always connect the negative lead to the negative side of the circuit (ground) and connect the positive lead to the positive side of the circuit (the power source side).

## Checking for voltage

### With a test light

*The test light probe can be pushed through a wire's insulation – be sure to wrap electrical tape around the puncture after testing is complete*

### With a test buzzer

### With a voltmeter

*Be sure the test leads are connected properly – positive to positive and negative to negative!*

# Haynes electrical manual

## Checking for continuity

Continuity may be checked with a number of devices. If the circuit has power to it, a voltmeter, test light or test buzzer may be used as described above. If the circuit is not powered, an ohmmeter or self-powered continuity tester should be used.

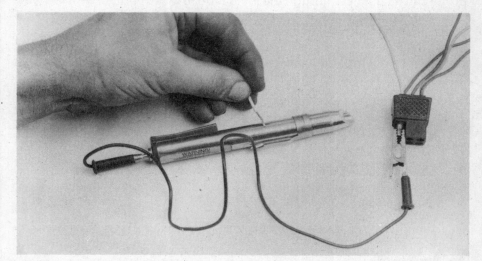

*Here a wire and connector plug is being checked for continuity – if the bulb in the tester lights, the circuit is complete*

**Caution:** *Do not attempt to use a self-powered continuity tester or ohmmeter on a powered circuit. The test device will be damaged.*

To use a continuity tester, first isolate the circuit by disconnecting the battery or removing the fuse or circuit breaker. Select two points along the circuit through which there should be continuity. Connect one lead of the tester to each point. If there is continuity, the tester will light.

**Note:** *The procedure for checking continuity with an ohmmeter is similar to the procedure using a continuity tester. If there is continuity, the ohmmeter will read close to zero ohms (no or very low resistance). The procedure for checking resistance below points out some other special considerations when using an ohmmeter.*

## Checking resistance

Resistance is checked with an ohmmeter. Turn the scale selector switch to the proper ohms range for the device you will be measuring. Make sure the wires are connected to the proper plugs on the meter and turn the meter on. Check that the meter reads "infinity" before testing is begun, then touch the test probes together to ensure the meter goes to zero. Connect one test lead to the positive terminal of the device being tested and connect the other lead to the negative terminal or housing (ground). After testing, switch the ohmmeter off to conserve the batteries.

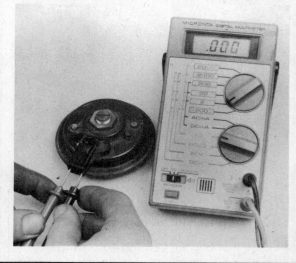

*This horn is being tested for resistance – note the zero ohm reading which indicates an internal short*

# Diagnosing and correcting circuit faults

Shorts to ground are most easily found with a short finder, although a test buzzer is also effective. If you use a buzzer and discover the short is not at a component (meaning it is somewhere in the wiring harness), inspect the exposed portions of the wiring harness for obvious evidence of a short (burned wire insulation, chafing, etc.). If you still can't find the wiring harness short, we strongly recommend you borrow or purchase a short finder. Finding a hidden short in a wiring harness without this device can be very time consuming.

**1**    Remove the blown fuse, leaving the battery connected.

**2**    Connect the pulse unit of the short finder across the fuse terminals.

**3**    Close (turn on) all switches in series with the circuit you are troubleshooting.

**4**    Operate the short finder. The short finder will pulse current to the short. This creates a pulsing magnetic field surrounding the circuit wiring between the fuse panel and the short.

**5**    Beginning at the fuse panel, slowly move the short finder meter along the circuit wiring. The meter will show current pulses through the sheet metal and body trim. As long as the meter is between the fuse block and the short, the needle will move with each current pulse.

**6**    When you have moved the meter past the point of the short, the needle will stop moving. Examine the wiring in that area for the short to ground and repair as needed.

*The short finder pulse unit (arrow) is connected to the fuse terminals in place of the fuse*

**Note:** *A test light or voltmeter may be substituted for the buzzer. However, an assistant will be needed to watch the light or meter while you disconnect components and wiggle the wiring harness.*

**1**    Remove the blown fuse, leaving the battery connected.

**2**    Attach the alligator clips of the test buzzer to the fuse terminals.

## Tracing shorts

### With a short finder

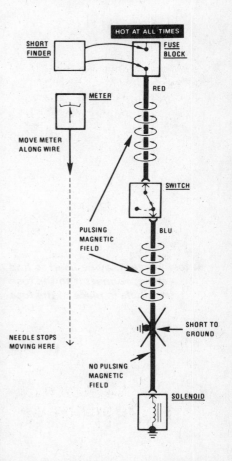

*Move the meter along the wiring harness until the needle pulsations cease; look for the short in that area*

### With a test buzzer

**3** Close (turn on) all the switches that are in series with the circuit you are troubleshooting.

**4** If the circuit is still shorted to ground, the buzzer will sound.

**5** Beginning at the load (the component that is operated by the circuit), disconnect each component in the circuit. Work your way backwards along the circuit until the buzzer stops sounding. Also, wiggle the wiring harness from side-to-side in areas where it's exposed.

**6** When the buzzer stops, carefully check the portion of the circuit you just disconnected (or the part of the wiring harness you were wiggling) for a short. If disconnecting a switch, relay or harness connector caused the buzzer to stop sounding, the short is either at that component or somewhere between the component and the load.

**7** Repair or replace components or wiring as needed.

*A test buzzer may be used to find a short; connect it to the fuse terminals in place of the fuse*

## Checking voltage drop

This test checks for voltage being lost along a wire, or through a connection or switch while current is flowing.

**1** Connect the positive lead of a voltmeter to the end of the wire (or to the side of the connection or switch) which is closer to the battery.

**2** Connect the negative lead of the voltmeter to the other end of the wire (or the other side of the connection or switch).

**3** Select the voltmeter range just above battery voltage.

**4** Switch on the circuit.

**Note:** *When no current is flowing, there can be no voltage drop.*

**5** The voltmeter will show the difference in voltage between the two points. A difference (or drop) of more than about 0.2 to 0.3 volt indicates a problem (except when the voltmeter is connected across a load, in which case a substantial voltage drop is normal).

**6** Clean and repair the connections as needed or replace any faulty components.

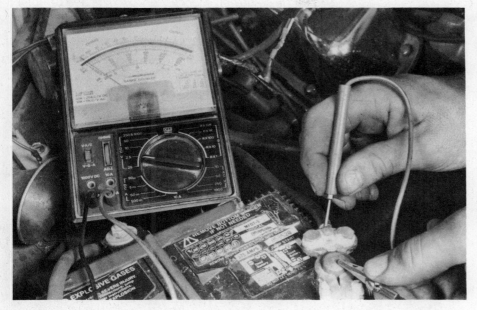

*Note:* Ammeters are always connected in series with the circuit being tested (except units with inductive pickups).

**1** To connect an ammeter into a circuit, unplug a fuse or connector and attach the test leads to the exposed terminals. Remember, the ammeter must always be hooked up in series with the circuit.

**2** Switch on the circuit and read the amperage shown on the meter. If it shows a negative reading, reverse the test lead connections. No reading at all indicates an open (incomplete) circuit.

**3** The reading should be less than (but not substantially less than) the circuit's fuse rating. If the reading is substantially less than the fuse rating, there's excessive resistance somewhere in the circuit. If the reading is higher than the fuse rating, there's a short to ground.

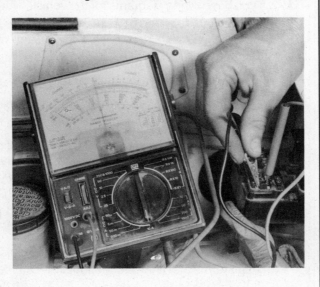

*Here a battery terminal is being checked for voltage drop – in this case, a drop greater than 0.1 volt means the terminal and clamp should definitely be cleaned!*

## Checking current flow with an ammeter

*Current flow (amperage) in a circuit may be checked by connecting an ammeter to the fuse terminals (with the fuse removed)*

# Haynes electrical manual

## Testing relays

**Note 1:** *Chapter 1 covers the general operating principles of relays and the terminology of their parts. The information that follows does not apply to polarity-reversing relays, which are used in some power accessory circuits. See Chapter 8 for more information on these relays.*

**Note 2:** *Some circuits on some newer vehicles use solid-state (electronic) relays. This procedure applies only to electro-mechanical (non-electronic) relays. Electronic relays must be tested by a dealer service department.*

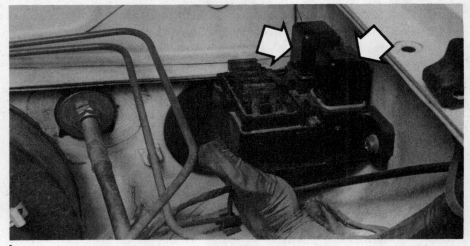

*The relays (arrows) are often mounted on or near the fuse panel*

**1**     We recommend using the correct wiring diagram for your vehicle to determine the proper hook-ups for the relay you're testing. However, if wiring diagrams are not available, you may be able to determine the test hook-ups from the information that follows.

### Relays with four terminals

**2**     On most relays with four terminals, two of the four terminals are for the relay's control circuit (they connect to the relay's coil). The other two are for the relay's power circuit (they connect to the armature contact and the fixed contact).

**3**     If you have wiring diagrams for the vehicle, you can figure out which terminals hook up to which parts of the relay (see Chapter 2 for information on wiring diagrams). Often, relay terminals are marked as an aid.

**4**     As a general rule, the two thicker gage wires connected to the relay are for the power circuit; the two thinner gage wires are for the control circuit.

**5**     Remove the relay from the vehicle and check for continuity between the relay's power circuit terminals. There should be no continuity.

**6**     Connect a fused jumper wire between one of the two control circuit terminals and the positive battery terminal. Connect another jumper wire between the other control circuit terminal and ground. When the connections are made, the relay should click. On some relays, polarity may be critical, so, if the relay doesn't click, try swapping the jumper wires on the control circuit terminals.

**7**     With the jumper wires connected, check for continuity between the power circuit terminals. Now there should be continuity.

**8**     If the relay fails any of the above tests, replace it.

# Diagnosing and correcting circuit faults

**9** If the relay has three terminals, it's a good idea to check the vehicle's wiring diagram to determine which terminals connect to which of the relay's components. Most three-terminal relays are either case-grounded or externally-grounded.

**10** On a case-grounded relay, one side of the relay's control circuit grounds through the relay case, eliminating the need for the fourth terminal. This type of relay requires the case to be securely connected to a good chassis ground. Check this type of relay the same way you would a four-terminal relay, noting that one of the control circuit's terminals is actually the relay case.

**11** On an externally-grounded relay, one of the relay's terminals is connected to a positive power source. We'll call this the *battery power* terminal. Inside the relay, the battery power terminal is connected to one side of both the relay's power and control circuits. Another terminal is connected to the other side of the control circuit; the circuit is completed through a switch to ground. The third terminal is connected to the other side of the power circuit; it's grounded at the circuit's load component. This type of three-terminal relay is sometimes a plug-in type with no connection between the case and ground.

**12** To check an externally-grounded relay, remove it from the vehicle and check for continuity between the relay's battery power terminal and it's power circuit terminal. There should be no continuity.

**13** Hook up a fused jumper wire between the battery power terminal and the positive battery terminal. Connect another jumper wire between the relay's control circuit terminal and ground. The relay should click.

**14** With the jumper wires in place, connect a test light between the relay's power circuit terminal and ground. The test light should light. If the relay fails any of these tests, replace it.

## General troubleshooting strategies

Before you begin troubleshooting a circuit, it is imperative that you formulate a plan of action. Check for simple problems first, such as blown fuses, corroded or loose connections, burned out bulbs or broken, frayed, chafed or burned wires – these are also the most common problems.

The previous two Sections acquainted you with test equipment and the procedures for using it properly. Now let's take a look at some of the methods professionals use when tracking down problems.

Operate the problem circuit in all modes. Determine what components, if any, in the circuit still work. Is it a complete or partial failure? What other circuits are affected? When does it occur? Is the problem intermittent or

## Relays with three terminals

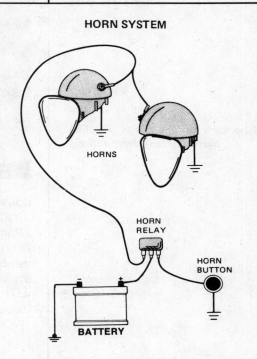

*This diagram shows how an externally-grounded three-terminal relay (a horn relay in this case) is connected to a vehicle's electrical system*

## Identify the problem

## Identify the problem
### (continued)

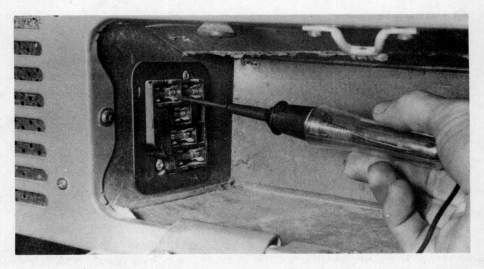

*Check for simple things first, like corroded fuse connections*

does it happen all the time? Be sure to check the operation of all other electrical components on the vehicle. Sometimes what seems to be a problem affecting only one component is also causing (or being caused by) a problem in another circuit. If necessary, make notes of all the affected components and the specific symptoms. This will help you figure out the problem after you've looked at the wiring diagrams and had a chance to think about it. Think carefully about all the electrical components which have been disturbed or worked on recently. These are prime suspects.

## Problems affecting a single component

If a single component of a circuit is affected, start to test at that component and work back toward the fuse panel. Use a logical process of elimination to narrow down the problem. For example, if you find that only one side marker light is inoperative, you have eliminated the fuse, switch and main wiring harness as potential sources of the problem.

Here are four conditions that cause single component failures and how to check for them:

### 1 The component is not receiving current

With the circuit switched on, test for voltage at the component. If there's no voltage, continue to test for voltage in the circuit, working backward toward the fuse panel. When you reach a point where there is voltage, you know the problem lies between that point and your last test point.

### 2 The component is not grounded properly

This condition can be tested two ways: 1) With power to the component, you can test for a voltage drop between the component and ground. The drop should be less than 0.2 to 0.3 volt. 2) With power removed from the component, you can check for resistance between the component and ground. The reading should be zero (or very close to zero) ohms.

### 3 The component itself is faulty

For components designed to operate on full battery voltage, check the operation using a fused jumper wire, as described in the previous Section. For components that operate on less than battery voltage, measure the resistance or check for a voltage drop.

# Diagnosing and correcting circuit faults

**4**  *The wiring is faulty*

This can be checked two ways: 1) With no power to the circuit, check continuity. 2) With power to the circuit, check for a voltage drop in the wiring.

**Problems affecting multiple components**

If the fault affects multiple components, start to test at the point where the circuit gets its power (usually the fuse panel or fusible link). Check the fuses, circuit breakers and/or fusible links (see Chapter 1, if necessary). If the circuit protection devices are blown, look for a short circuit; if they are intact, look for an open circuit or wires from different circuits contacting each other.

Obtain the wiring diagrams for the specific vehicle you are working on whenever possible.

Read about the various types of circuits described in Chapter 1 and learn how to tell which type you are working on.

Familiarize yourself with the current flow in the circuit by tracing the path in the wiring diagram (see Chapter 2). Determine where the circuit receives current, what the circuit protection is, what switches and/or relays control current flow and how the components operate.

Identify each component in the wiring diagram for the circuit you are testing and find the components on the vehicle.

Sometimes, multiple components can be affected by two wires from different circuits contacting each other. Take, for example, two simple circuits, each having one light bulb and an SPST switch. If the wires between each switch and each bulb come into contact with each other, closing either one of the switches will light both bulbs, but one or both bulbs will light more dimly than normal. Closing the other switch will alter the relative brightness of the two bulbs. In complicated circuits, there may be many symptoms, affecting several components, all related to such a problem.

**Intermittent problems**

The most difficult type of electrical problem to diagnose is an intermittent one. Intermittent opens or shorts are usually caused by something rubbing or a component that changes resistance when it heats up or cools down. Corroded and loose connections are also frequently the cause of such problems.

Note when the problem occurs and try to discover how to duplicate the problem during diagnosis. For example, if it only happens when you're going around a corner or over a rough railroad crossing, wiggling the wiring harness may duplicate the problem. If it only happens after the engine is completely warmed up, heating the suspected faulty parts with an electric hair dryer may duplicate the problem. If the problem only occurs during wet weather conditions, a water misting bottle may help you duplicate the problem. Once you can duplicate the problem, follow the test procedures applicable, based on the symptoms.

**Make the repair**

Once the diagnosis has been made, replace the faulty component or repair the wiring as necessary. After the repair has been made, operate the system and confirm that your repair has removed all the symptoms and has not caused any new problems.

## Types of connectors

## Electrical connections

Automobiles typically have many types of electrical connectors for different purposes. With the increasing complexity of modern automobile electrical systems and the advent of computer control systems, many special connector types have made their appearance. Before we show you how to make your own electrical connections, let's take a look at the types of connectors commonly used on automobiles.

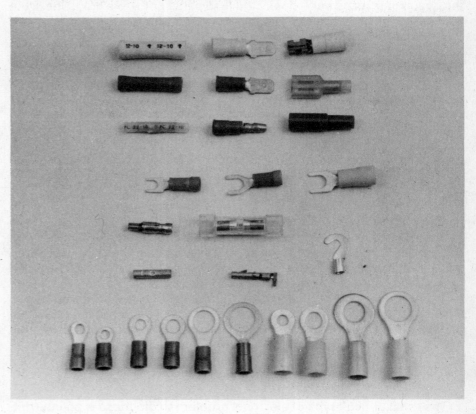

*Many types of connectors are used on modern cars and trucks*

## Crimp connectors

To make their own electrical connections, many professional electrical technicians pick from the variety of crimp connectors available. Crimp connectors are not as weatherproof as soldered connections, but, when

you use a special tool, making these connections is quick and easy. If you choose the uninsulated variety of these connectors, you can ensure a weatherproof connection by soldering it after you make the crimp, then insulating it with heat shrink tubing. Later in this Section we'll show you how to make crimp connections, solder and use heat shrink tubing.

*Crimp connectors are available with and without insulation*

# Diagnosing and correcting circuit faults

Butt connectors may be used to join two stripped wire ends together permanently.

*Butt connectors are available in a variety of diameters to fit different wire gages, as follows:*

*1  10 to 12 gage*
*2  14 to 16 gage*
*3  18 to 22 gage*

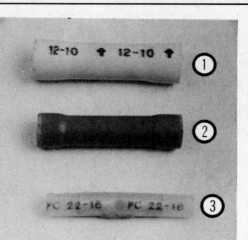

Ring terminals go completely around a stud or screw. They make good electrical and mechanical contact and don't come loose from terminal blocks easily.

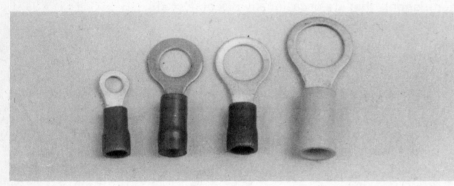

**Ring terminals**

*Ring terminals are available for different wire gages and stud sizes*

Spade and hook terminals are similar to ring terminals, but they have an open side. Their advantage is they may be quickly connected to a terminal block. Their disadvantage is they come loose easier than ring-types. They're best suited to temporary installations.

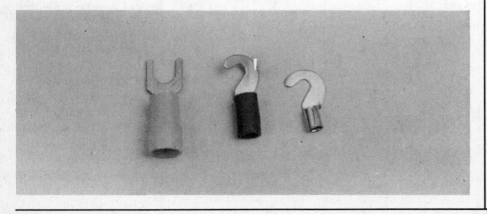

**Spade and hook terminals**

*Spade and hook terminals – from left-to-right: insulated spade terminal, insulated hook terminal, uninsulated hook terminal*

# Haynes electrical manual

### Bullet connectors

*Two types of bullet connectors*

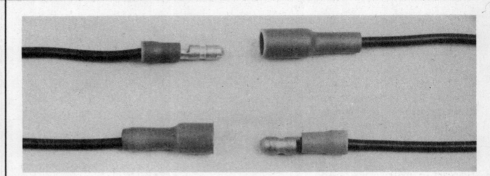

*When used in pairs, the male and female ends of bullet connectors should be staggered like this to prevent incorrect connections*

Bullet connectors are available in male and female types. When used in pairs, they may be installed with male and female ends on adjacent wires to prevent improper connections. Bullet terminals are generally used for components that are occasionally disconnected.

### Flat blade connectors

Also known as quick disconnect or push-on connectors, they are used on many fuse panels and accessories. They are also generally used for components that are occasionally disconnected.

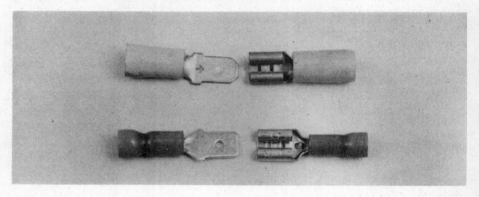

*Male and female ends of flat blade connectors – 10-12 gage wire size (top) 14-16 gage wire size (bottom)*

### Snap-splice connectors

These connectors are frequently supplied with trailer wiring kits and other accessory kits. The main advantage with this type of connection is that you don't have to cut the original wire to make a connection. However, they are not as reliable as soldered connections and have a low current capacity. To make a connection, place the two wires to be connected into position in the "V" grooves in the metal portion of the connector. Close the flap, clamp the unit together with pliers and you are done.

*3.31   Two brands of snap-splice connectors showing top and bottom views*

# Diagnosing and correcting circuit faults

These connectors are made to connect two or more wires simultaneously and are designed so they can only be installed one way. This protects you from reconnecting it improperly after you've disconnected it.

Multi-wire connectors that were installed on the vehicle at the factory are available through a dealer parts department; aftermarket type connectors may be found in auto parts and electronics stores.

Many types of special electrical connectors are used on modern computerized cars. Replacements for most of them are available from a dealer or auto parts store. Prior to starting any repairs, obtain the necessary parts to complete the repair.

On many of these special connectors, it's possible to remove a single terminal from the connector so you can replace a component or repair a wire. To do so, separate the connector halves and remove any terminal covers or retainers. Depress the terminal locking tang using a small pick. Place the pick between the locking tang of the terminal and the plastic of the connector body and ease the wire back enough to release the locking tang. Gently pull the wire out the back of the connector plug.

Inspect the condition of the terminal and lead. If they are reuseable, bend the tang back into shape with the pick. If the terminal needs replacement, attach a new one using the procedures described later in this Section under *Installing crimp connectors.*

Before inserting the lead, make certain that the terminal is shaped correctly. Gently insert the lead from the back of the connector plug. The terminal should stop or "catch" about halfway into the connector body. Push back and forth gently on the lead to be sure the terminal is secure in both directions. Apply silicone grease to the terminal end to prevent corrosion and install the connector.

## Multi-wire connectors

*This is one half of a multi-wire connector – the notched corner allows the terminal to be connected only one way; other designs of multi-wire connectors have tabs and slots on the connector housings for the same purpose*

## Special connectors

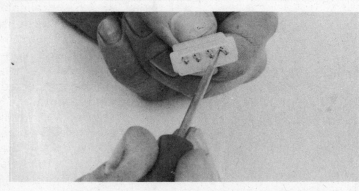

*Depress the terminal locking tang with a small pick tool*

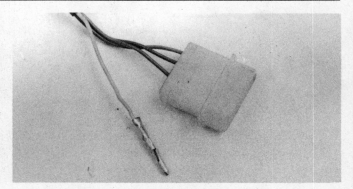

*The wire and terminal should slip out the back of the connector plug*

## Making Connections

### Stripping wires

Now that you're familiar with the types of connectors available, we'll show you how you can make your own connections to repair the electrical system or add accessories.

Unless you're using snap-splice connectors (discussed earlier), the first step to making a connection is stripping the insulation off the wire(s) where the connection will be made.

If you are unsure of the wire size, begin with an opening in your wire stripper/crimper that barely cuts into the insulation and work down in size until the wire strips clean. If you intend to solder the wires together, strip about 1/2-inch of insulation off. If you are using crimp-type butt connectors, cut off just enough insulation (about 1/4-inch) so the wire will fill one side of the connector. Don't nick or cut any of the strands. Inspect the stripped end for nicks and cuts. If the wire is damaged, cut off the stripped end and repeat the process. Twist the strands about one-half turn to keep them together.

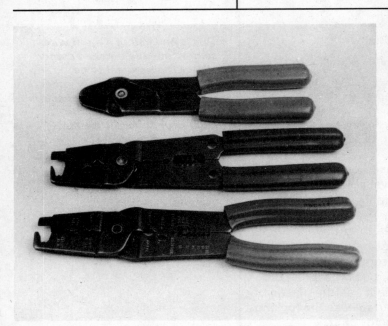

*Wire stripper tools are available at most tool supply, auto parts and electronics stores – many, like the ones shown here, can also be used to install crimp connectors – be sure to buy a good quality tool*

*Be sure the strands of wire aren't damaged when the insulation comes off*

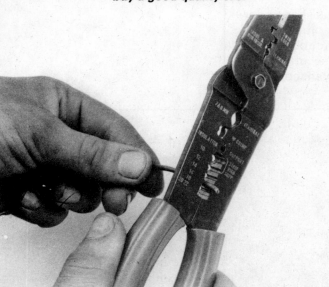

*Find the size opening that cuts the insulation but not the wire*

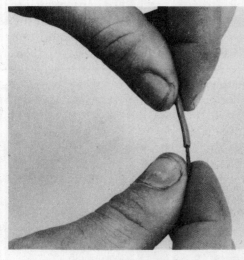

*Twist the strands to keep them together*

# Diagnosing and correcting circuit faults

Wires enclosed in a harness must be separated to expose the individual wire during repair. If the harness is in a plastic conduit that has a lengthwise slit, simply slip the wire out. If the harness is taped, carefully cut and unwind the tape until the damaged portion of the wiring is exposed.

Cut the ends of the wire off cleanly, removing as little wire as possible. Strip the wire ends as described above.

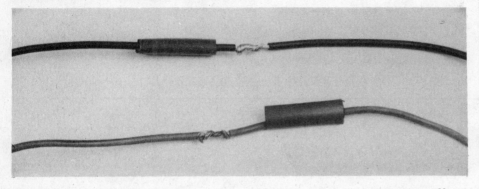

**Note:** *If more than one adjacent wire is being spliced, stagger (or offset) the splices to avoid a thick lump in the harness.*

At this point, you must choose between the various methods of joining wires. Most splices are made with crimp-type butt connectors. The insulated type should be used. If the splice will be exposed to the weather, the preferred method is soldering. Soldered joints can be insulated with heat shrink tubing or tape. The heat shrink tubing is recommended because it is more permanent and secure. Refer to the specific procedures in this Section for further information.

Crimp connectors are available in a number of sizes which correspond to the wire gage. The popular sizes use color-coded insulation to make identification easier:

> *Red for 18 to 22 gage*
> *Blue for 14 to 16 gage*
> *Yellow for 10 to 12 gage*

If you're installing ring connectors, you must also select the proper stud size. These are commonly #6, #8, #10, 1/4-inch, 3/8-inch and 1/2-inch.

*Caution:* Always use insulated connectors on the positive side of the circuit. Most connectors are designed to be used with copper wire; to avoid dissimilar metal corrosion, use connectors that are compatible with the wire being used.

Select the proper size and type of connector to be installed. Strip the insulation from the wire for a distance equal to the length of the connector barrel (usually about 1/4-inch).

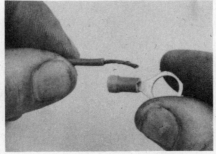

**Splicing wires**

*Stagger the splices to avoid a thick lump in the harness*

**Installing crimp connectors**

*Strip away only enough insulation to fit the wire through the connector (usually about 1/4-inch)*

61

Slip the connector onto the wire. Position the crimping tool on the spot to be crimped. Squeeze the handles of the crimping tool together until the terminal barrel is fully crimped to the wire without excessive distortion. Check the security of the crimp by pulling on the terminal.

*Insert the stripped wire end(s) into the connector, . . .*

*This butt connector has been securely crimped onto the wires – note the indentations left by the tool*

*. . . then crimp the terminal securely onto the wire*

## Soldering

Before you can begin, you will need a soldering iron or gun and solder. For automotive electrical systems, a dual-heat soldering gun of 100/140 watts capacity is very handy. Soldering irons are less expensive but take longer to heat up. If you buy one, get it with about a 50 watt rating.

Solder is sold with various proportions of tin alloyed into it, most commonly 40/60, 50/50 and 60/40, with the percentage of tin listed first. 60/40 works well for wiring. Always use a rosin core solder or rosin flux. This cleans the joint, removing oxides and other materials that would prevent a good connection.

*Soldering guns and irons are available from tool supply, auto parts and electronics stores in a variety of brands and ratings*

# Diagnosing and correcting circuit faults

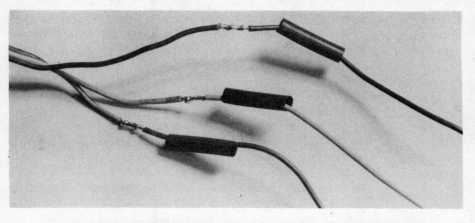

*Keep the heat shrink tubing away from the heat while soldering*

**Caution:** *Never use acid core solder or acid flux on electrical connections.*

If you intend to insulate the joint(s) with heat shrink tubing, slip one piece over each wire and push it back far enough to avoid any heat from soldering. Twist the ends of the wires you intend to join together.

Practice on wire scraps before attempting actual repairs. Hold the soldering gun or iron against the wiring joint (underneath it).

**Note:** *Use a thick piece of wood as a work surface – don't use metal; it will conduct heat away.*

Once the wires are heated sufficiently, touch the solder to the wiring (not the soldering gun/iron tip) and allow the solder to flow into the wiring joint. If the solder balls up around the gun/iron tip and doesn't flow into the joint, the joint isn't hot enough; continue heating the joint. Remove the gun/iron and allow the solder to cool without disturbing the joint. When the solder cools, inspect the joint. The solder should have penetrated throughout the entire joint. Resolder if necessary. Slip the heat shrink tubing into place (if used) and heat it as described under *Insulating connections.* If heat shrink tubing isn't available, apply tape to the joint for insulation.

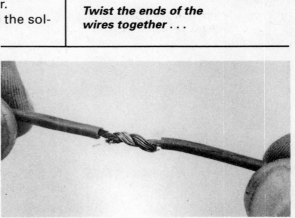

*Twist the ends of the wires together . . .*

*. . . until the splice looks like this*

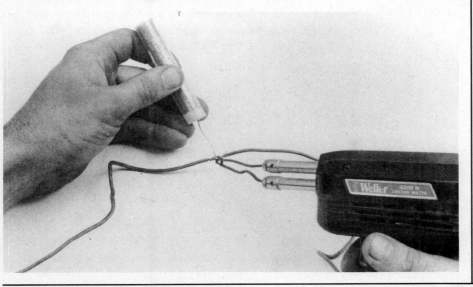

*Heat the wire first, then add the solder*

# Haynes electrical manual

## Insulating connections

Soldered and non-insulated crimp connections made on the positive side of the circuit must be insulated. Heat shrink tubing is the best way to insulate, since it does not unwind and come off over time like tape. Tape, however, is an effective insulation and can be used when shrink tubing is not available.

### Heat shrink tubing

Heat shrink tubing is available from electronics and auto parts stores. The tubing comes in various lengths and diameters. Select a diameter and length that will slip over the thickest part of the area to be insulated, overlapping the ends by about 1/4-inch. To install heat shrink tubing, cut a piece to the appropriate length for each connection and slip it over each of the wires before the connection is made. After the connection is made, slide the tubing into position and heat it with a match or lighter until it shrinks around the wire.

**Caution**: *Don't hold the match too close or you will melt the tubing!*

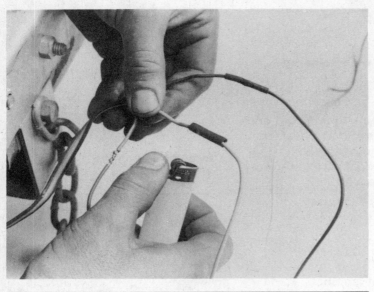

*After the connections are made, place the heat shrink tubing over the joints and heat it with a lighter or match*

### Tape

Electrical tape is available in a variety of materials and widths. For most purposes, quality 3/4-inch wide PVC tape with adhesive designed to remain sticky at low temperatures is best.

Center and roll the tape over the entire splice. Roll on enough tape to duplicate the thickness of the original insulation. Don't flag the end of the tape.

If the wire isn't protected by a conduit or other harness covering, tape the wire again. Use a winding motion to cover and overlap the first piece of tape.

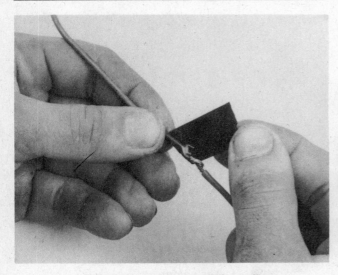

*Wind the tape around the splice, . . .*

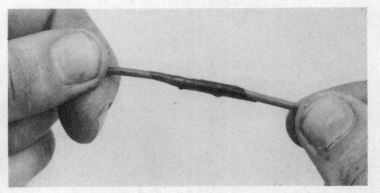

*. . . overlapping both ends of the wire insulation*

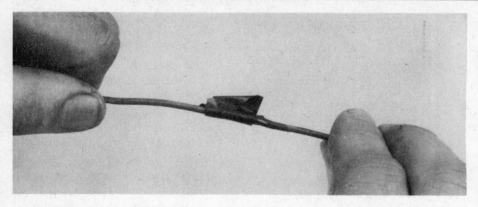

## Replacing fusible links

Fusible links are replaced in much the same manner as an ordinary section of wire. Using wire cutters, clip the old fusible link out of the harness and install a new piece of fusible link wire using crimp-type butt connectors as described above.

For more information on fusible links, see Chapter 1.

**Caution:** *Fusible links longer than nine inches may not provide sufficient overload protection.*

*Fusible links (arrow) are usually located near the battery*

## Repairing aluminum wire

The repair of aluminum wiring requires exceptional care to ensure satisfactory operation. Aluminum becomes brittle from vibration more readily than copper and should only be used to repair existing aluminum wiring, not for new installations.

Nuts, bolts, terminals and washers used with aluminum wiring must be compatible with aluminum to prevent electrolytic corrosion between dissimilar metals. Hardware should be made from aluminum or plated with aluminum or cadmium.

A special repair kit is available from General Motors (part no. 1684873, Group 2.530 – or equivalent) to facilitate aluminum wire repairs. This kit contains materials and instructions that can be used either to splice wire or crimp on new terminals. Use of the materials in this kit will prevent electrolytic corrosion.

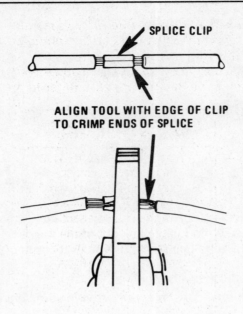

SPLICE CLIP

ALIGN TOOL WITH EDGE OF CLIP
TO CRIMP ENDS OF SPLICE

*To repair aluminum wiring, crimp
a special aluminum splice clip
onto the wire ends*

To make a splice, cut and strip the end of the wire as described previously. Apply a generous coat of petroleum jelly to the splice area. Select the proper-sized splice clip and place one wire end in each end of the clip. Crimp the clip firmly with a crimping tool or large slip joint pliers.

**Note:** *If more than one adjacent wire is being spliced, stagger (or offset) the splices by about 1-1/2 inches to avoid a thick lump in the harness.*

**Caution:** *Don't attempt to solder aluminum.*

## Choosing Wire

Sometimes, repairing the electrical system will involve replacing a section of wire. Since wire is by far the most common part of any electrical system, it's essential that you know a few things about selecting the right wire for the job.

Nearly all wiring in automobiles is constructed from stranded copper.

**Caution:** *A few vehicles have some aluminum wiring; do not splice aluminum wires to copper – the dissimilar metals will corrode, causing electrical failure.*

Wire is specified by gage, number of strands and type of insulation. Refer to the following information before you select wire.

### Wire gage

The amount of current that a circuit can carry is dependent on the cross-sectional area, or "gage," of the wire. Gage represents the cross-sectional area of the wire itself (the conductor), NOT including the insulation.

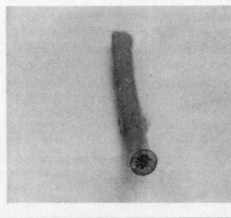

*About 60 percent of the total cross sectional area of this wire is insulation – gage refers to the cross–sectional area of the conductor*

In most automotive wire, over 60 percent of the total cross sectional area is insulation. If you don't want an electrical fire (from excessive resistance caused by a conductor that's too small), make sure you select wire based on the gage of the conductor.

Manufacturers may refer to wire sizes on schematics in either American Wire Gauge (AWG) or Metric sizes. See the accompanying AWG Conversion Table for equivalency comparisons.

# Diagnosing and correcting circuit faults

American Wire Gauge (AWG) sizes may be determined by measuring the diameter of the conductor (the bare wire) with the insulation removed. Refer to the Wire Gage Diameter Table for dimensions.

When choosing wire gage, the distance the wire must run and the amperage it will be expected to carry must be determined first. Refer to the Wire Gage Selection Table. Note that you can always use thicker wire (lower gage number) than is recommended.

| Metric Size mm² | AWG Size |
|---|---|
| 0.5 | 20 |
| 0.8 | 18 |
| 1.0 | 16 |
| 2.0 | 14 |
| 3.0 | 12 |
| 5.0 | 10 |
| 8.0 | 8 |
| 13.0 | 6 |
| 19.0 | 4 |
| 32.0 | 2 |
| 52.0 | 0 |

*Metric-to-AWG Conversion table*

| American Wire Gage | Wire Diameter in inches |
|---|---|
| 20 | 0.03196118 |
| 18 | 0.040303 |
| 16 | 0.0508214 |
| 14 | 0.064084 |
| 12 | 0.08080810 |
| 10 | 0.10189 |
| 8 | 0.128496 |
| 6 | 0.16202 |
| 5 | 0.18194 |
| 4 | 0.20431 |
| 3 | 0.22942 |
| 2 | 0.25763 |
| 1 | 0.2893 |
| 0 | 0.32486 |
| 00 | 0.3648 |

*Wire gage Diameter table*

| Circuit Amperes | | Circuit Watts | | Wire Gage (for length in feet) | | | | | | |
|---|---|---|---|---|---|---|---|---|---|---|
| 6V | 12V | 6V | 12V | 3' | 5' | 7' | 10' | 15' | 20' | 25' |
| 0 to 2.5 | 0 to 5 | 12 | 24 | 18 | 18 | 18 | 18 | 18 | 18 | 18 |
| 3.0 | 6 | 18 | 36 | 18 | 18 | 18 | 18 | 18 | 18 | 16 |
| 3.5 | 7 | | | 18 | 18 | 18 | 18 | 18 | 18 | 16 |
| 4.0 | 8 | 24 | 48 | 18 | 18 | 18 | 18 | 18 | 16 | 16 |
| 5.0 | 10 | 30 | 60 | 18 | 18 | 18 | 18 | 16 | 16 | 16 |
| 5.5 | 11 | | | 18 | 18 | 18 | 18 | 16 | 16 | 14 |
| 6.0 | 12 | 36 | 72 | 18 | 18 | 18 | 18 | 16 | 16 | 14 |
| 7.5 | 15 | | | 18 | 18 | 18 | 18 | 14 | 14 | 12 |
| 9.0 | 18 | 54 | 108 | 18 | 18 | 16 | 16 | 14 | 14 | 12 |
| 10 | 20 | 60 | 120 | 18 | 18 | 16 | 16 | 14 | 12 | 10 |
| 11 | 22 | 66 | 132 | 18 | 18 | 16 | 16 | 12 | 12 | 10 |
| 12 | 24 | 72 | 144 | 18 | 18 | 16 | 16 | 12 | 12 | 10 |
| 15 | 30 | | | 18 | 16 | 16 | 14 | 10 | 10 | 10 |
| 20 | 40 | | | 18 | 16 | 14 | 12 | 10 | 10 | 8 |
| 25 | 50 | | | 16 | 14 | 12 | 12 | 10 | 10 | 8 |
| 50 | 100 | | | 12 | 12 | 10 | 10 | 6 | 6 | 4 |
| 75 | 150 | | | 10 | 10 | 8 | 8 | 4 | 4 | 2 |
| 100 | 200 | | | 10 | 8 | 8 | 6 | 4 | 4 | 2 |

*Wire gage selection table*
*Find the amperes or watts the circuit is expected to carry on the left and the distance the wiring must run at the top – follow the columns until they intersect – for example, a 12 volt circuit which is 15 feet long and carries 10 amperes should use at least 16 gage wire*

# Haynes electrical manual

## Number of strands

The term "stranded" refers to the practice of using a number of smaller diameter wires instead of one larger one. Automotive electrical wire is stranded because of its flexibility and resistance to fracture. Stranded wire is 25 to 1200 times less likely to fracture than single-core wiring when exposed to vibration.

When referring to the number of strands, stranding is generally categorized as coarse, medium and fine. A battery cable is a typical example of coarse stranding. Under-the-dash wiring is medium strand. And constantly flexed wires, like those between the door and the body, or between the trunk and the body, are finely stranded.

Sometimes, the identifying number for a piece of wire will include the number of strands in the wire. Don't confuse this number with the wire gage number!

## Wire insulation

As long as you buy quality name-brand wire, you don't have to worry too much about insulation. Most quality automotive wiring is insulated with corrosion and temperature-resistant synthetic materials such as polyvinyl chloride (PVC). However, you should know that PVC has its limits: It will soften when exposed to temperatures over 200-degrees F and change shape under its own weight. Eventually, it may distort enough to expose the conductor. In underhood applications, where temperatures can exceed 300-degrees F, ordinary PVC isn't satisfactory. Instead, you want the new high-temperature PVC. It costs more, but it can handle higher under-hood temperatures. If you're doing wiring anywhere besides the engine compartment, regular PVC is fine.

# 4 Starting systems

The starting system rotates the engine's crankshaft at a speed fast enough to start the engine. Through a circuit of heavy cables, connectors and switches, current from the battery travels to the starter motor, which rotates the crankshaft and, when everything is working properly, starts the engine.

In this Chapter, we will look at the starting system and its individual components, discussing operation, troubleshooting and repair.

## Starting system components

The typical starting system includes the following components:
*Starter motor*
*Battery*
*Cables and wires*
*Ignition switch*
*Starter solenoid (either on the starter or remotely mounted)*
*Neutral start switch (most vehicles with automatic transmissions)*
*Clutch interlock switch (many vehicles with manual transmissions)*

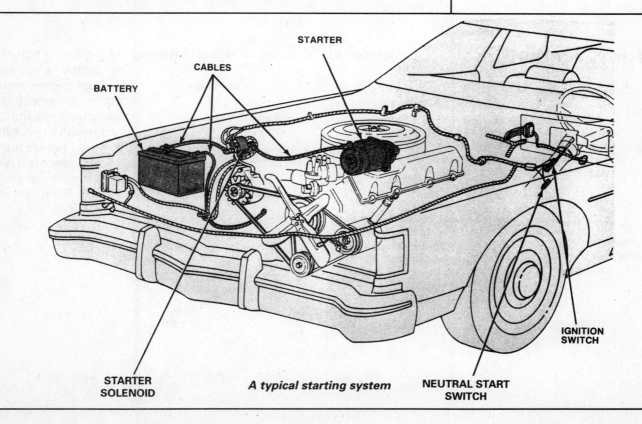

STARTER

CABLES

BATTERY

IGNITION SWITCH

STARTER SOLENOID

*A typical starting system*

NEUTRAL START SWITCH

## Starter motor

The starter motor is a powerful electric motor which rotates the engine's crankshaft quickly enough (about 200 rpm) to start it. When the starter is energized, the starter's pinion gear meshes with the teeth on the flywheel (or driveplate) ring gear. The pinion rotates, which spins the flywheel (and thus the crankshaft) and starts the engine.

*When the starter is energized, the pinion gear rotates, which spins the flywheel and starts the engine*

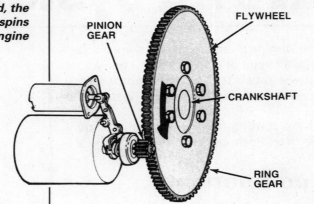

PINION GEAR

FLYWHEEL

CRANKSHAFT

RING GEAR

The starter motor has no method of cooling. It's intended to be operated for only short periods of time. If the starter isn't allowed to rest every 15 seconds or so – and given at least two minutes to cool off – the high current running through it can damage it in as little as 60 seconds.

## Battery

The battery supplies the electrical current that the starter needs to start the engine. The starter places a heavy load on the battery during starting, so the battery must have a strong charge.

## Cables and wires

Because the starter motor draws high current, heavy cable is used between the battery and the starter motor. Lighter gage wires are used to control the solenoid.

## Ignition switch

The ignition switch closes the circuit that energizes the starter solenoid. The switch is normally mounted on the steering column and actuated remotely from the ignition key through a rod. When the ignition key is turned to Start, electrical voltage is sent to the starter solenoid from the battery.

*This ignition switch is mounted on the steering column and operated remotely from the ignition key through an actuating rod*

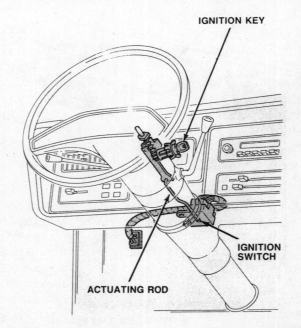

IGNITION KEY

IGNITION SWITCH

ACTUATING ROD

Most vehicles use a solenoid mounted on the starter. This type of solenoid serves two purposes: 1) to connect the battery to the starter and 2) to bring the starter drive pinion into contact with the flywheel ring gear during starter operation. The solenoid consists of two windings mounted around a cylinder containing a moveable plunger. A shift fork is connected to the plunger, and a pushrod and contact disk are assembled in line with the plunger. When the windings are energized (by turning the ignition key to Start), the plunger moves, pulling the shift fork and moving the drive pinion into mesh with the flywheel ring gear. The contact disk is pushed into firm contact with the two high-current terminals on the solenoid, connecting the battery to the motor.

## On-starter solenoid

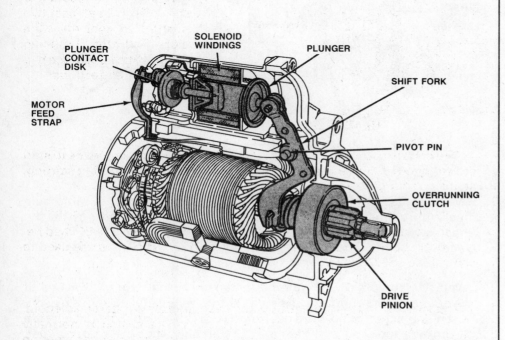

*A cutaway of a starter with the solenoid mounted on the starter*

The two windings in the solenoid are called the hold-in winding and the pull-in winding. The hold-in winding has fine wire windings and the pull-in winding has windings with a larger diameter wire. The pull-in winding and hold-in windings are used to pull the solenoid into position. Once the solenoid is in position, the magnetism from the hold-in winding is sufficient to hold the solenoid in position. The pull-in winding is shut off, permitting greater current flow through the starter motor. The pull-in winding is shut off when the contact disc contacts the high-current terminals.

Some vehicles (most Fords, for example) use a remotely mounted starter solenoid to connect the battery to the starter motor. The solenoid is located in the circuit between the battery and the starter motor, usually close to the battery. It operates much like a relay, except it has a moveable plunger (so "solenoid" is the correct terminology). When attracted by the solenoid windings, the plunger moves and closes electrical contacts that connect the battery to the starter. The windings are energized when the ignition key is turned to Start.

## Remote-type starter solenoid

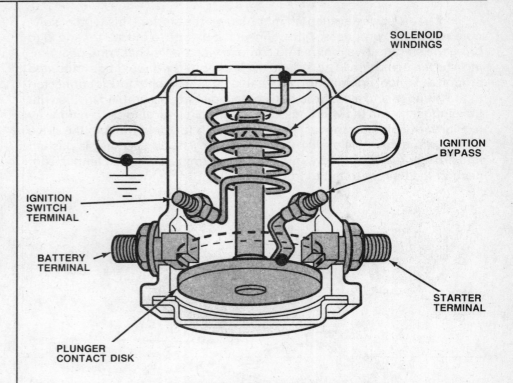

*A cutaway of a remote-mounted starter solenoid – the ignition bypass portion of the solenoid is used to bypass a resistor in the ignition system for full ignition voltage during starting*

Vehicles using this type of solenoid normally have a moveable pole shoe in the starter to engage the pinion gear with the ring gear on the flywheel.

## Neutral start switch

Vehicles equipped with automatic transmissions require a means of preventing the the engine from being started while in gear. For this reason, most manufacturers include a neutral start switch which is operated by the shift linkage and ensures the engine will start only when in Park or Neutral.

## Clutch interlock switch

On many vehicles with manual transmissions, a starter/clutch interlock switch assures the vehicle will not start unless the clutch pedal is pressed all the way to the floor. This switch is mounted on the clutch pedal.

## Starter motor design

To understand the design and operation of the starter motor, you need to recall some of the principles of electromagnets:

- A magnetic field is generated when current flows through a conductor.

- This field surrounds the conductor and extends over its entire length.

- The strength of this field is directly proportional to the amount of current flowing through the conductor.

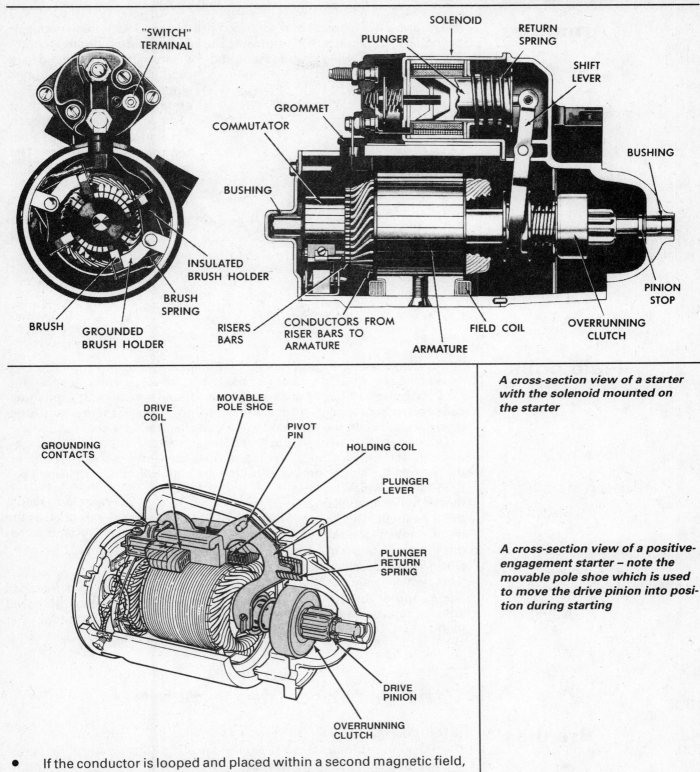

"SWITCH" TERMINAL

COMMUTATOR

GROMMET

BUSHING

INSULATED BRUSH HOLDER

BRUSH SPRING

BRUSH

GROUNDED BRUSH HOLDER

RISERS BARS

CONDUCTORS FROM RISER BARS TO ARMATURE

ARMATURE

FIELD COIL

OVERRUNNING CLUTCH

SOLENOID

PLUNGER

RETURN SPRING

SHIFT LEVER

BUSHING

PINION STOP

GROUNDING CONTACTS

DRIVE COIL

MOVABLE POLE SHOE

PIVOT PIN

HOLDING COIL

PLUNGER LEVER

PLUNGER RETURN SPRING

DRIVE PINION

OVERRUNNING CLUTCH

*A cross-section view of a starter with the solenoid mounted on the starter*

*A cross-section view of a positive-engagement starter – note the movable pole shoe which is used to move the drive pinion into position during starting*

- If the conductor is looped and placed within a second magnetic field, the two fields will interact. On one side of the loop, the fields will reinforce each other; on the other side, they will oppose each other.

The operation of all starter motors is based on these principles. Keep them in mind as you look at the following starter motor components.

## Armature

*A typical armature*

The armature is made of a soft iron core wrapped with many loops or "windings" of insulated copper wire. The windings are mounted lengthwise on the core, which strengthens and concentrates the magnetic field produced by the windings when they're energized. The armature is mounted on a shaft and the ends of each winding are connected to the commutator segments. The commutator conducts current to the windings through the brushes.

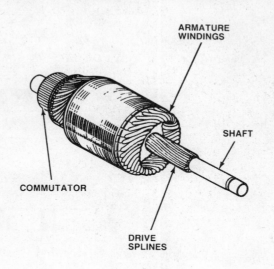

ARMATURE WINDINGS

SHAFT

COMMUTATOR

DRIVE SPLINES

## Field coils

The field coils create a magnetic field that surrounds the armature and causes the armature to rotate. The field coils are very strong electromagnets composed of heavy copper ribbons wound around soft iron cores called pole shoes. Each field coil is formed into an arc, so there is very little clearance between the coils and the armature rotating inside the coils.

On starters that use remote solenoids (often called positive-engagement starters), one of the pole shoes is moveable and attached to the lever that moves the starter drive. Current to the starter first flows through a holding coil which moves the pole shoe into its operating position. This movement moves the starter drive into position and also closes two grounding contacts which connect the starter motor to ground. The starter then begins rotating.

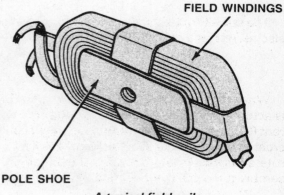

FIELD WINDINGS

POLE SHOE

*A typical field coil*

## Brushes

The brushes supply electricity to the armature through the commutator. The brushes are mounted on the commutator end housing and lightly held against the commutator by springs.

## Drive assembly

The drive assembly is installed on the end of the armature shaft. When the starter is operating, the pinion gear rotates with the armature to crank the engine.

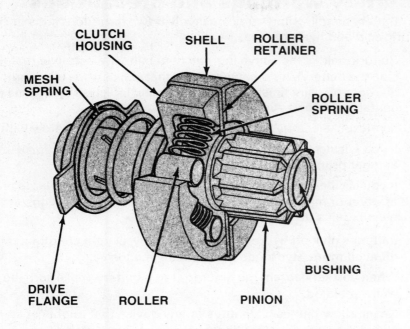

CLUTCH HOUSING  SHELL  ROLLER RETAINER

MESH SPRING

ROLLER SPRING

DRIVE FLANGE  ROLLER  PINION

BUSHING

*A typical overrunning clutch assembly*

To prevent damage to the pinion gear when the engine starts and the flywheel is rotating faster than the starter, most modern vehicles use a roller-type overrunning clutch. This device transmits torque in only one direction, turning freely in the other. Thus, the pinion can be driven by the flywheel for the brief period so you have time to turn the key away from the Start position.

## Frame

The starter frame supports the armature, field coils and end housings. It also serves as a convenient ground.

## Starter motor operation

When the ignition key is turned to the Start position, the starter solenoid is actuated. The solenoid allows current to flow to the starter motor. Current flows through the armature and field coils. The electromagnetic force created between the armature and the field coils causes the armature to rotate. As the armature rotates, the pinion gear on the end of the drive assembly turns the flywheel ring gear. This causes the crankshaft to rotate.

## Batteries

The battery is a central component in the starting system. Its primary function is to supply the necessary current to operate the starter motor. When cared for properly, a battery can provide many years of satisfactory service. If neglected or abused, a battery can fail very quickly.

## Battery warnings and precautions

Battery handling and servicing involves two hazardous substances: sulfuric acid and hydrogen gas.

**Sulfuric acid warnings**

- Sulfuric acid is the active ingredient in battery electrolyte (the fluid inside the battery). It's a powerful acid that will corrode all common metals, destroy paint finishes and clothing and inflict serious burns when it contacts skin and eyes.

- If you spill electrolyte on your skin, rinse it off immediately with water.

- If you get electrolyte in your eyes, flush them with water for 15 minutes and get prompt medical attention.

- If you accidentally ingest electrolyte, immediately drink large amounts of water or milk. Follow with milk of magnesia, beaten eggs or vegetable oil. Call a doctor immediately.

**Hydrogen gas warnings**

- Batteries give off hydrogen gas constantly. During charging, they give off even more. Hydrogen gas is highly explosive.

- When you service, charge or jump start a battery, make sure the area is well ventilated.

- Never allow flames, cigarettes or any device that might cause a spark anywhere near a battery being charged or jump started.

- When inspecting or servicing the battery, always turn the engine and all accessories off.

- Never break a live circuit at the battery terminals. An arc could occur when the battery, charger or jumper cables are disconnected, igniting the hydrogen gas.

**Miscellaneous warnings and precautions**

- Always wear safety goggles when performing any work on the battery.

- When loosening cables or working near a battery, keep metallic tools away from the battery terminals. The resulting short circuit or spark could damage the battery or ignite the hydrogen gas around the battery.

- Always disconnect the battery negative cable first and hook it up last.

- Never move a battery with the vent caps removed. Electrolyte can easily splash out.

- Always use a battery carrier when lifting a battery with a plastic case or place your hands at the bottom and end of the battery. If you're not careful, too much pressure on the ends can cause acid to spew through the vent caps.

- Use fender covers to protect the vehicle from acid spillage.

- Keep sharp objects out of the battery tray to avoid puncturing the case, and don't overtighten the battery hold-down.

## Maintaining the battery

**Note:** *Several tools are required for battery maintenance. Refer to the accompanying illustration before undertaking the following recommended service procedures.*

If you give a battery reasonable attention and care, its service life will be significantly longer than it will be if you don't. Proper maintenance also reduces the possibility of being stranded somewhere because of a dead battery.

**Tools and materials required for battery maintenance**

1 *Face shield/safety goggles* – When removing corrosion with a brush, the acidic particles can easily fly up into your eyes
2 *Baking soda* – A solution of baking soda and water can be used to neutralize corrosion
3 *Petroleum jelly* – A layer of this on the battery posts will help prevent corrosion
4 *Battery post/cable cleaner* – This wire brush cleaning tool will remove all traces of corrosion from the battery posts and cable clamps. If you have a side-terminal battery, you'll need one that is designed differently than this
5 *Treated felt washers* – Placing one of these on each post, directly under the cable clamps, will help prevent corrosion
6 *Puller* – Sometimes the cable clamps are very difficult to pull off the posts, even after the nut/bolt has been completely loosened. This tool pulls the clamp straight up and off the post without damage.
7 *Battery post/cable cleaner* – Here is another cleaning tool which is a slightly different version of number 4 above, but it does the same thing
8 *Rubber gloves* – Another safety item to consider when servicing the battery; remember that's acid inside the battery!

Check the battery electrolyte weekly. Perform the other maintenance items listed below every three months or 3000 miles.

**Note:** *This procedure is only possible on batteries with removable caps. Many modern batteries have sealed tops that do not allow you to check the electrolyte level or add water; however, there's often an indicator in the top of the battery that gives an indication of its electrolyte level, as well as its state of charge. If you have a maintenance free battery with removable caps, it's a good idea to occasionally check the electrolyte level, regardless of the manufacturer's recommendations.*

**1** Remove the vent caps on the battery. Look at the electrolyte solution and smell it. If it's in good shape, it should be clear. Discoloration and/or the presence of an odor similar to rotten eggs could indicate an excessively high charging rate (see Chapter 5) or an aged battery approaching the end of its service life

**2** Check the electrolyte level in each battery cell. It must be above the plates. There's usually a split-ring indicator in each cell to indicate the correct level. If the level is low, add distilled water only, then reinstall the caps.

**Caution:** *Overfilling the cells may cause electrolyte to spill over during periods of heavy charging, causing corrosion and damage to nearby components.*

**3** If you must add water frequently to the battery, inspect the case for cracks. If you can't find any cracks, the battery is probably being overcharged – check the charging system (see Chapter 5).

## Check the electrolyte

### Clean the battery

Clean the top and sides of the battery with a clean shop towel. Remove all dirt and moisture. Keeping the battery clean inhibits corrosion and also exposes cracks in the case, buckling and similar damage that might otherwise be hidden under the dirt.

Corrosion on the carrier, battery case and surrounding areas can be removed with a solution of water and baking soda. Apply the mixture with a small brush, let it work, then rinse it off with plenty of clean water.

### Inspect the case and cover

1   Inspect the case for cracks or buckling. The presence of either of these symptoms could indicate any of the following conditions:
   a) overly tightened hold-down fasteners
   b) loose hold-down fasteners
   c) An excessively high charging rate causing the battery temperature to be too high (see Chapter 5)
   d) The battery has sat for a long time in an under-charged condition (buckled plates)
   e) frozen electrolyte

*Battery terminal corrosion usually appears as light, fluffy powder*

*Regardless of the type of tool used on the battery posts, a clean, shiny surface should be the result*

*When cleaning the cable clamps, all corrosion must be removed (the inside of the clamp is tapered to match the taper on the post, so don't remove too much material)*

**2** Look for acid deposits on the battery cover. These normally indicate overfilling or gassing and spewing from an excessively high charging rate (see Chapter 5)

**3** Inspect the battery terminals for distortion, missing mounting bolts and corrosion. If corrosion is evident, disconnect the cables from the terminals, clean them with a battery brush and reinstall them. To minimize further corrosion, apply a layer of petroleum jelly to the terminals after you've reinstalled the cables.

**4** Make sure the battery tray is in good condition and the hold-down clamp is tight. If you remove the battery, make sure that nothing is in the bottom of the tray when you reinstall the battery. Don't overtighten the hold-down clamp fasteners.

Poor battery cable connections can cause starting problems and poor operation of the electrical system. The high current requirement of the starting system means that voltage loss through the cables must be minimized. Inspect the entire length of each battery cable for damage.

### Check the battery cables

**1** Look for cracked or burned insulation, frayed wire strands and corrosion. If you find any damage other than light corrosion, replace the cables – don't attempt to repair them.

**2** If light corrosion is evident on either cable, detach it from the terminal and clean it with a wire brush. If the corrosion can't be completely removed, it's too far advanced. Replace the cable.

*A Typical engine-to-body groundstrap*

**3** Don't forget to check the (often overlooked) engine-to-body groundstrap. If allowed to corrode or loosen, it can cause components grounding at the engine to malfunction.

### Replace any damaged or corroded cables

**Note:** *It's a good idea to replace battery cables in pairs, even if only one is visibly damaged.*

**1** Detach the old cable from the battery.

**2** After you have disconnected the old cable from the battery, trace it to its opposite end and detach it from the starter solenoid or ground location. Note the routing of each cable to ensure correct installation.

**3** Take the old cables with you when buying new ones. It is vitally important that you replace the cables with identical parts. Just because a cable has the same length and post type does not mean it's a good replacement. Make sure you get a cable that has the same (or larger) wire gage diameter as the original.

**4** Clean the threads of the solenoid or ground connection with a wire brush to remove rust and corrosion. Apply a light coat of petroleum jelly to the threads to prevent future corrosion.

**5** Attach the cable to the solenoid or ground connection and tighten the mounting nut/bolt securely, then reattach the cable(s) to the battery.

## Testing the battery

Before you begin testing the battery, perform all the checks listed under *Maintaining the battery* above. Often, you can identify the problem from these checks.

*The battery date code has information concerning the battery's manufacture date*

Nearly all battery manufacturers affix a battery date code to their batteries. Always refer to the battery's date of manufacture before proceeding with any tests. This information may help you decide if a battery is at the end of its service life.

The following tests will allow you to determine the battery's condition and also will help you find problems with the vehicle's electrical system that cause a constant drain on the battery.

## State-of-charge test

A battery cannot be accurately tested until it is at or near its fully charged state. Before proceeding to any other tests, check the state of charge using one of the methods described below. If the battery is not at the minimum charge level stated in the procedure below you're following, charge it. If the battery still won't reach the minimum level, replace it.

There are two common methods of checking the battery's state of charge: the hydrometer test and the open circuit voltage test. The hydrometer test has the added advantage of also revealing some types of internal battery damage. However, the hydrometer test can only be performed on batteries with removable caps.

## Hydrometer test
### (batteries with removable caps only)

This test allows you to check the state of charge of each of the battery's cells. It requires a hydrometer: a tool commonly available from auto parts stores for less than five dollars.

The hydrometer is a bulb-type syringe which, when squeezed and released, draws electrolyte from a battery cell. A float with a graduated specific gravity scale is housed inside the barrel of the hydrometer. When electrolyte is drawn in, the float rises and the specific gravity is read where the float scale intersects the level of the electrolyte in the hydrometer.

Specific gravity varies with temperature. As temperature rises, specific gravity decreases and vice versa. If the battery temperature is not 80-degrees F, the reading must be adjusted.

**Note**: *If the vehicle has not been driven for several hours, the battery temperature should be the same as the outside air temperature.*

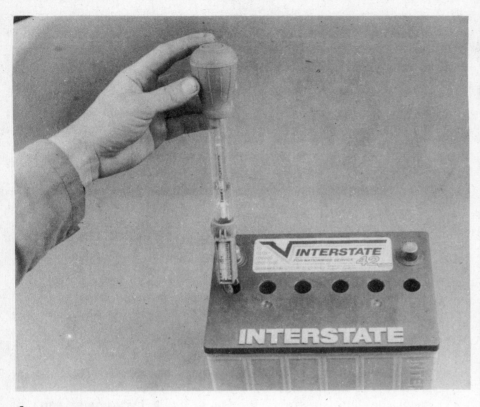

*Here's a battery hydrometer being used to draw electrolyte from a battery cell – this hydrometer has a thermometer on it (arrow) so it's easier to make temperature corrections*

**1** Remove all vent caps.

**2** Make sure the electrolyte level is high enough to withdraw the proper amount of electrolyte into the hydrometer barrel. If it isn't, top up each cell with distilled water.

**3** If the electrolyte level is high enough, you may proceed. If it isn't – and you have to add water – you'll have to wait a few hours before going on. Never take a reading immediately after you have added water. The water must mix thoroughly with the electrolyte for the hydrometer reading to be accurate.

**4** Holding the hydrometer upright, squeeze the bulb tightly with your thumb and index finger and insert the hydrometer pick-up tube into the first cell.

**5** Slowly release thumb pressure until the bulb is fully expanded and the float is suspended freely in the barrel (but not enough to force the float against the upper end of the hydrometer). Always hold the barrel vertically to prevent the float from binding or sticking to the sides.

**6** With the hydrometer at eye level, read the float scale at the electrolyte level.

**7** Squirt the electrolyte solution back into the cell.

**8** Record the specific gravity reading. If the battery temperature is not 80-degrees F, correct the reading. For every ten degrees above 80-degrees F, add 0.04 to the specific gravity. For every ten degrees below, subtract 0.04.

**9** To determine the approximate battery charge indicated by the hydrometer reading, refer to the accompanying table. If the reading is below 1.235, the battery must be recharged before proceeding to any other tests.

**10** Repeat steps 4 through 9 for each cell in the battery. If the readings among the cells vary more than 0.050, the battery is internally damaged. Replace it.

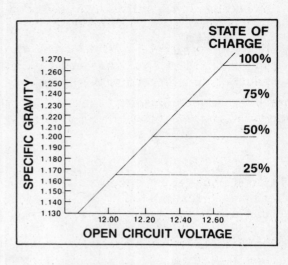

*Battery state of charge chart*

**11** When you're finished, disassemble the hydrometer in accordance with the manufacturer's instructions and rinse the barrel and float assembly with clean water. While the hydrometer is disassembled, inspect the float assembly for leaks. If the hydrometer can't be disassembled, suck clean water into it and expel it several times.

## Open circuit voltage test

This test requires a digital voltmeter.

**1** The battery's surface charge must be removed before accurate voltage measurements can be made. Turn on the high beams for ten seconds, turn them off, then let the vehicle stand for two minutes.

*To test the open circuit voltage of the battery, simply touch the black probe of a voltmeter to the negative terminal and the red probe to the positive terminal – a fully charged battery should read 12.6 volts or higher*

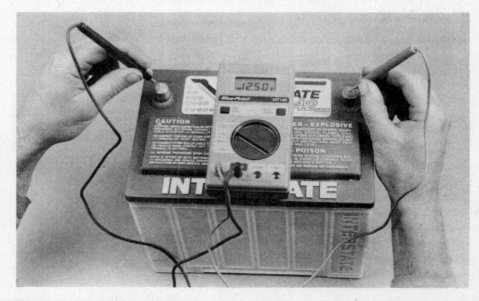

**2** With the engine and all accessories off, disconnect the battery's negative cable. Touch the negative probe of a voltmeter to the negative battery terminal and the positive probe to the positive terminal.

**3** Read the voltage. A 12-volt battery at or near full charge for this test should read 12.6 volts or above. If it's less than 12.4 volts, charge the battery before proceeding with any other tests.

**Note:** *If the voltmeter reading is negative, you have connected the meter backwards. Swap the probes to the opposite terminals.*

## Battery load test

This test evaluates the battery's ability to operate the starter and other heavy electrical loads. It requires a special load tester. These testers are available in different designs from automotive tool and equipment suppliers.

All load testers draw current from the battery while measuring its voltage level. The voltage level of a good battery will remain relatively steady under load, but a defective battery will show a rapid loss in voltage. Battery cold cranking amperage and temperature will affect the test results, so follow the instructions carefully.

**Note:** *The following instructions should apply to most batteries and most testers, but always follow the instructions included with your tester if they differ from the following.*

**1** Turn off the engine, vehicle accessories and the tester.

**2** Attach the tester's positive clamp (usually red) to the positive battery terminal and the negative clamp (usually black) to the negative battery terminal.

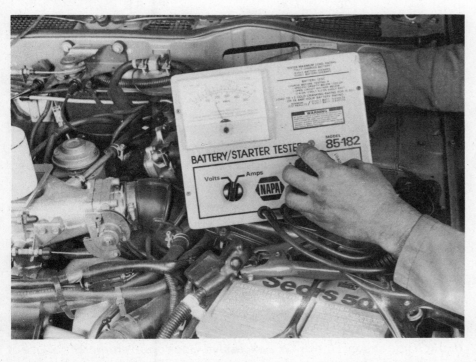

*Here's a load tester in use – note that this one has an ammeter so the battery load can be precisely dialed in, as shown – less expensive testers have a load switch and a voltmeter only*

**3**  With the clamps connected, the tester's voltmeter will indicate the battery's state of charge. If the state of charge is less than 12.4 volts for a 12-volt battery, the battery must be recharged before load testing. If recharging doesn't bring the voltage up to 12.4 volts or more, the battery is defective. Replace it

**4**  If the tester does not have an ammeter and has a load switch (not a dial), turn on the load switch.

**5**  If the tester is equipped with an ammeter, turn on the ammeter and rotate the load control knob to increase the load until the amperage reading is one-half of the battery's cold cranking amp (CCA) rating (listed on the battery). If the CCA rating is not listed on the battery, use the following guidelines to estimate battery size: Small (four-cylinder) engine – 300 CCA; medium (six-cylinder engine) – 400 CCA; large (8-cylinder engine) – 500 CCA. After the load is dialed in, switch the tester back to the voltmeter reading.

**6**  Maintain the load for 15 seconds. On 12-volt systems, the voltage reading should remain above 9.6 volts. The reading may be slightly lower if the outside air temperature is less than 70-degrees F. Compensate meter readings in accordance with the following chart:

| Approximate temperature (degrees Fahrenheit) | Minimum voltage |
|---|---|
| 70 | 9.6 |
| 60 | 9.5 |
| 50 | 9.4 |
| 40 | 9.3 |
| 30 | 9.1 |
| 20 | 8.9 |
| 10 | 8.7 |
| 0 | 8.5 |

**7**  If the voltage is below the minimum, replace the battery.

## Battery drain test

This test will indicate whether there's a constant drain in the vehicle's electrical system that can cause the battery to discharge.

**1**  Make sure no accessories are turned on. If the vehicle has an underhood light, verify it's working properly, then disconnect it.

**2**  Detach the cable from the negative battery terminal and attach one lead of a test light to the cable end. Touch the other lead to the negative battery terminal. The test light should not glow.

**3**  If the light glows, it indicates a constant drain which could cause a discharged battery.

**Note:** *On vehicles equipped with on-board computers, digital clocks, digital radios, power seats with memory and/or other components which normally cause a key-off battery drain, it's normal for the test light to glow dimly. If you suspect the drain is excessive, hook up an ammeter in place of the test light. The reading should not exceed 0.5 amps.*

**4** The prime suspects for current drain problems are lights (under-hood, glove box, trunk, etc.) that don't shut off properly. If the drain isn't caused by a light, remove the fuses one at a time until the cause of the drain is located. When you pull the fuse for the circuit that is draining the battery, the test light will go out.

**5** If the drain is still undetermined, the problem is likely a shorted start-er solenoid or a short in the wiring to the solenoid. Inspect the wiring and connections. If no short is found, disconnect the wires from the solenoid until the light goes out.

*To find out whether there's a drain on the battery, simply de-tach the negative cable and hook up a test light between the cable clamp and the negative battery post – if the light comes on with all accessories off, there's a drain*

## Booster battery (jump) starting

**Warning:** *Never attempt to jump start a frozen battery. It may explode.*

**Note:** *The cable connections for jump starting often allow only limited cur-rent flow. Depending on how much the battery's discharged, jumper con-nections may or may not start a vehicle with a weak battery.*

To avoid damage to the vehicle, the battery and yourself, observe the following precautions when using a booster battery to start a vehicle:

**1** Position the vehicles so that the jumper cables will reach. But, MAKE SURE THE VEHICLES DON'T TOUCH EACH OTHER!

**2** Make sure the transmission is in Neutral (manual) or Park (auto-matic).

**3** Make sure the ignition switch is in the Off position.

**4** Turn off the lights and other electrical loads.

# Haynes electrical manual

**Note:** *If the vehicle you want to start is equipped with a computer, it's a good idea to turn on the heater blower motor. This will prevent damage to the computer in case of an excessive electrical surge.*

**5** Make sure the booster battery is the same voltage as the dead one in the vehicle.

**6** Your eyes must be shielded. It's a good idea to wear safety goggles.

**7** If the booster battery has removable vent caps, remove the caps and lay a cloth over the vent holes.

**8** Make the jumper cable connections EXACTLY as follows:

a) Connect one end of the red jumper cable to the positive terminal of the discharged battery and the opposite end to the positive terminal of the booster battery.

b) Connect the black jumper cable to the negative terminal of the booster battery and then to a bolt or bracket on the engine block – NOT to the negative battery terminal – of the vehicle being jump started. This is an important precaution to prevent sparks which may cause an explosion.

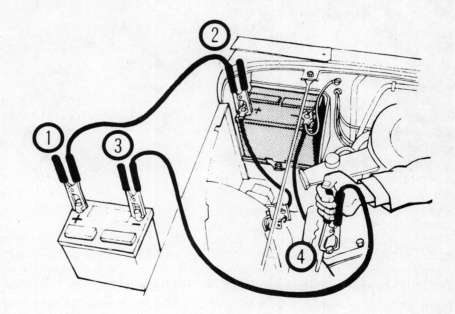

*Make the booster battery cable connections in the numerical order shown (note that the negative cable of the booster battery is NOT attached to the negative terminal of the dead battery)*

**9** Check the cables – make sure that they're not going to be in the way of the fan, drivebelts or any other moving parts when the vehicles are started.

**10** Start the engine of the vehicle with the good battery and run it at a moderate speed.

**11** Start the engine of the vehicle with the discharged battery.

**12** Reduce the engine speed to idle on both vehicles and leave all switches off to prevent damage to the vehicle electrical systems.

**13** Remove the cables in the reverse order they were attached.

| RESERVE CAPACITY RATING | | 80 or LESS | | | 81 - 125 | | | 126 - 180 | | | 181 - 250 | | | ABOVE 250 | | |
|---|---|---|---|---|---|---|---|---|---|---|---|---|---|---|---|---|
| Charging Rate (Amperes) | | 5 | 10 | 20 | 5 | 10 | 20 | 5 | 10 | 20 | 5 | 10 | 20 | 5 | 10 | 20 |
| **Open Circuit Voltage*** | **Specific Gravity** | **Charging Time in Hours** | | | | | | | | | | | | | | |
| 12.25-12.40 | 1.200-1.225 | 4 | 2 | 1 | 6 | 3 | 1½ | 8 | 4 | 2 | 10 | 5 | 2½ | 14 | 7 | 3 |
| 12.05-12.24 | 1.170-1.200 | 6 | 3 | 1½ | 8 | 4 | 2 | 12 | 6 | 3 | 16 | 8 | 4 | 22 | 11 | 5 |
| 11.90-12.04 | 1.145-1.170 | 8 | 4 | 2 | 12 | 6 | 3 | 16 | 8 | 4 | 22 | 11 | 5½ | 30 | 15 | 7 |
| Less than 11.90 | Less than 1.145 | 10 | 5 | 2½ | 14 | 7 | 3½ | 20 | 10 | 5 | 28 | 14 | 7 | 38 | 19 | 9 |

*Here's a chart that gives you approximate charging times for particular charging rates, battery ratings and battery states of charge*

# Charging a battery

**Warning:** *Charging batteries produce hydrogen gas, which is explosive. Charge batteries only in well ventilated areas and don't smoke or allow open flames or sparks anywhere near the battery. Always turn off the battery charger before connecting it or disconnecting it from the battery. Never attempt to charge a frozen battery. It might explode. Allow it to warm to 60-degrees F before hooking up the charger.*

**Caution:** *If the vehicle is equipped with a computer, always disconnect the battery when charging to ensure the computer is not damaged.*

When the battery's state of charge has been depleted, it must be recharged. Charging is simply passing a current through the battery from positive to negative, instead of from negative to positive as in discharging. The charging process reverses the chemical action and restores the electrolyte to its original state before discharge.

Charging methods and types of chargers vary widely. Regardless of the method and equipment you use, charging must be done carefully to achieve proper results and avoid damage to batteries and possible personal injury. Chargers includes their own instructions. Always follow these instructions to the letter. Never disregard the safeguards and procedures provided by the manufacturer.

There are three basic charging methods – slow charging, fast charging and constant potential charging. Slow charging is a low current (about 2 to 5 amps) applied over a long period of time. Fast charging is a high current (about 15 to 35 amps) applied over a relatively short period of time. Constant potential charging uses a type of charger that varies the amperage based on the battery's state of charge (a high amperage at the beginning of the charge cycle that tapers off as the battery approaches full charge).

Generally, slow charging is best, since there is little chance of damaging the battery by overcharging (one of the major causes of battery failure). If you care about your battery, don't fast charge unless you're in an emergency situation and must have the battery charged right away. If you choose to fast charge, monitor the battery carefully to avoid overcharging. Don't let the temperature get over 125-degrees F and watch for spewing of electrolyte.

A cold battery (below 40-degrees F) won't readily accept a charge. When a fast charger is connected to a cold battery, the charging rate will be low at first, then increase as the battery temperature increases.

# Haynes electrical manual

## Some miscellaneous battery facts

- When left standing and unused, a battery loses about one percent of its charge per day.
- In winter, when heavy demand is placed upon the battery, it's a good idea to charge it occasionally. Discharged batteries freeze more easily than fully charged ones.
- A fully charged battery freezes at -85-degrees F, half-charged at -15-degrees F and one-quarter charged at +15-degrees F.
- A fully charged battery at zero degrees F has only 40 percent of the cranking power it has at 80-degrees F.
- A battery left in a state of discharge will lose capacity.

## Troubleshooting the starting system

Most of the time, starting system problems aren't caused by the starter motor. They're caused by malfunctions elsewhere in the starting system, such as a discharged or defective battery, a bad battery cable connection or a weak or non-functional starter solenoid.

Listed below are the four most common starting system malfunctions, followed by procedures to help you identify the cause(s).

### The starter rotates, but the engine doesn't

1   Remove the starter, check the overrunning clutch and bench test the starter to make sure the drive mechanism extends fully for proper engagement with the flywheel ring gear (see *Overhauling starter motors* below). If it doesn't, disassemble the starter to locate the problem.

2   Check the flywheel ring gear for bent areas, missing teeth and other damage. With the ignition turned off, rotate the flywheel so you can check the entire ring gear.

### The starter is noisy

1   If the solenoid is making a chattering noise, first check the battery (see *Battery testing* above). If the battery's OK, check the cables and connections and perform the voltage drop and current draw tests described in the procedures below. If you have not located the problem, check the solenoid (see the procedure below).

2   If you hear a grinding, crashing metallic sound when you turn the key to Start, check for loose starter mounting bolts. If they're tight, remove the starter and inspect the teeth on the starter pinion gear and flywheel ring gear. Look for missing or damaged teeth.

3   If the starter sounds fine when you first turn the key to Start, but then stops rotating the engine and emits a zinging sound, the problem is probably a defective starter drive that's not staying engaged with the ring gear. Replace or overhaul the starter.

**4**   If the starter makes a high-pitched whine or clanging sound while it's rotating the engine, the clearance between the pinion gear and flywheel ring gear is probably incorrect. To check it:

a) Disconnect the negative battery terminal, then remove the flywheel cover and pull the starter drive out to mesh it with the ring gear.

b) Check the clearance between the gears. Generally, the pinion teeth should engage the flywheel teeth about 3/4 of the way down from the top of each tooth. GM recommends a clearance of about 0.020-inch between the teeth, which can be checked with a wire-type gauge. Check the clearance at several locations around the circumference of the flywheel. This will help you identify if the flywheel is bent or has runout.

c) On most GM starters, the clearance can be adjusted by removing the starter and adding or removing shims between the starter and engine. These shims are available at most auto parts stores. On most other vehicles, the clearance is not adjustable. You must replace the component causing the problem (usually the starter drive).

**5**   If the starter makes a high-pitched whine after the engine starts, as the key is being released, the return spring in the starter is weak or the pinion gear-to-ring gear clearance is too small. Check the clearance as described above. If it's OK, replace the return spring. On GM starters, the spring is located inside the solenoid. On many other starters, it's located within the starter.

## The starter rotates slowly

**1**   Check the battery (see *Battery testing* above).

**2**   If the battery is okay, verify all connections (at the battery, the starter solenoid and motor) are clean, corrosion-free and tight. Make sure the cables aren't frayed or damaged.

**3**   Check to see if the battery cables are the same gage as original equipment. Many inexpensive aftermarket cables use a smaller gage wire encased in thick insulation. They look as big in diameter as the original equipment cable, but their smaller diameter wire can't handle the amperage load. During the summer, when cranking loads are lighter, these cables may work OK. But when winter arrives, they often can't carry enough current and the starter rotates slowly. If you doubt any of the cables, check for a voltage drop (see the procedure below).

**4**   Check the voltage drops at the battery terminals, starter solenoid and starter connections (see the procedure below).

**5**   Check that the starter is bolted securely to the engine so it grounds properly. Also check the pinion gear and flywheel ring gear for evidence of a mechanical bind (galling, deformed gear teeth or other damage).

**6**   Check for a short to ground.

## Troubleshooting
### (continued)

**7**   Perform a current draw test.

**8**   If the current draw is excessive, and there are no excessive voltage drops in the starter circuit, either the starter is defective or there is a mechanical bind in the engine. With the ignition turned to OFF, rotate the engine through two revolutions by hand. If it rotates smoothly and easily, replace the starter.

### The starter does not rotate at all

**1**   Turn on the headlights and turn the key to Start. Have an assistant observe the headlights. If the headlights do not dim when you turn the key, check for an open in the starting system, as described in the procedure following this one. If the headlights dim, continue with this procedure.

**2**   Check the battery (see *Battery testing* above).

**3**   If the battery is okay, verify all connections (at the battery, the starter solenoid and motor) are clean, corrosion-free and tight. Make sure the cables aren't frayed or damaged.

**4**   Check the starter solenoid (see the procedure below).

**5**   Check to see if the battery cables are the same gage as original equipment. If you doubt any of the cables, check for a voltage drop as described in the procedure below.

**6**   Check for a voltage drop at the battery terminals, starter solenoid and starter connections (see the procedure below).

**7**   Check that the starter is bolted securely to the engine so it grounds properly. Also check the pinion gear and flywheel ring gear for evidence of a mechanical bind (galling, deformed gear teeth or other damage).

**8**   Check for a short to ground.

**9**   Test the starter current draw, as described below. If the current draw is excessive, and there are no excessive voltage drops in the starter circuit, the starter is defective or there is a mechanical bind in the engine. With the ignition turned to OFF, rotate the engine through two revolutions by hand. If it rotates smoothly and easily, replace the starter.

### Testing for an open in the starter circuit

**Warning:** *The starter may operate during the following tests, so make sure the vehicle is not in gear and stay away from components that move during engine operation.*

**Note:** *The battery must be in good condition and fully charged for the following tests (see Battery testing above).*

**1**   Check the starter solenoid (see below).

**2** If the solenoid check reveals no voltage at the control circuit wire, check the neutral start switch or the clutch interlock switch – if equipped (see below). If the switch tests good, the open is in the ignition switch or in the wiring between the fuse panel and the control circuit terminal on the solenoid.

**Note:** *Some vehicles are also equipped with interlock switches which will not allow the starter to operate if the oil level is low (mostly on vehicles with rotary engines) or the driver's seatbelt is not fastened (mostly early 1970's vehicles). If the vehicle is equipped with either of these types of switches, it will also need to be checked.*

**3** If the solenoid check reveals the solenoid is operating normally, have an assistant hold the ignition key in the Start position. Check for voltage along the cable running to the starter, beginning at the battery. When you reach a point where you find no voltage, the open lies between that point and your last test point.

## Checking for voltage drops

**Warning:** *The starter may operate during the following test, so make sure the vehicle is not in gear and stay away from components that move during engine operation.*

**Note:** *Chapter 3 contains additional information on checking for voltage drops.*

**1** Disable the ignition system. On most vehicles, you can simply pull the coil high tension lead from the distributor cap and connect a jumper wire between the terminal on the end of the wire and ground.

**2** In the starting system, the most common places for voltage drops to occur are at the cable connections at the battery, solenoid and starter, and along the cables.

**3** Have an assistant turn the key to Start while you check for a drop at each of these locations. There should be no more than a 0.1 volt drop at any connection or along any one-foot length of cable. There should be no more than a 0.5 volt drop between the battery and the starter.

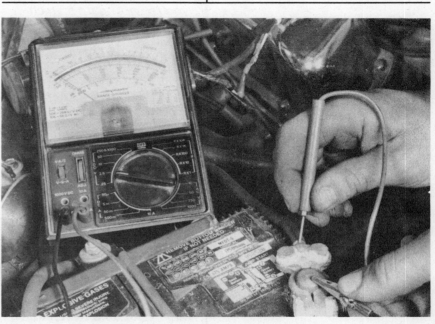

*Here a battery cable connection at the battery is being checked for a voltage drop*

## Troubleshooting
### (continued)

### *Testing the starter solenoid*

**Warning:** *The starter may operate during the following tests, so make sure the vehicle is not in gear and stay away from components that move during engine operation.*

**Note:** *The battery must be fully charged and in good condition for the following tests (see Battery testing above).*

**1** Disable the ignition system. On most vehicles, you can simply pull the coil high tension lead from the distributor cap and connect a jumper wire between the terminal on the end of the wire and ground.

**2** Have an assistant turn the ignition key to Start while you listen for a click at the solenoid. If there's a solid click, proceed to Step 6 or 7, as appropriate. If the click is weak or the solenoid chatters, proceed to Step 4.

**3** If there's no click, remove the control circuit wire (the small wire) from the solenoid terminal. Check for corrosion, looseness or other causes of a bad connection.

**Note:** *Some solenoids have two small-wire connections. One is for the solenoid's control circuit; the other bypasses an ignition resistor during starting. The one for the solenoid control circuit is often marked "S." If you're not sure which connection is which, check the wiring diagram for the vehicle.*

*Here are the terminals on a typical on-starter solenoid*

1 Battery cable terminal
2 Control circuit terminal
3 Starter motor strap

*Here are the terminals on a typical remote-mounted solenoid*

1 Cable connection (battery side)
2 Cable connection (starter side)
3 Control circuit terminal
4 Ignition bypass terminal

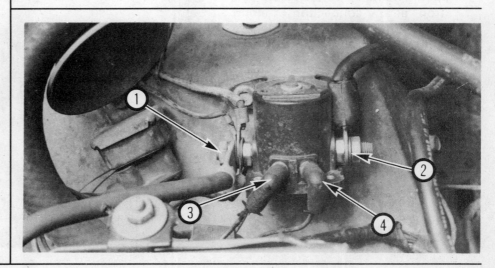

**4** Connect a jumper wire between the battery positive terminal and the solenoid's control circuit connection. A solid click indicates normal solenoid operation. If there's no click, or if the click is weak or the solenoid chatters, check for a loose solenoid, corrosion at the solenoid base or other causes of a bad solenoid ground. If the solenoid is tight and grounded properly, and it still doesn't click, replace the solenoid.

**5** While an assistant turns the key to Start, check for voltage at the control circuit wire with a voltmeter. If there's no voltage at the wire, there's an open in the in the circuit to the solenoid (see *Testing for an open in the starting circuit* above). Re-connect the control circuit wire.

**6** On vehicles with on-starter solenoids, have an assistant turn the key to Start while you check for a voltage drop between the battery cable terminal and the starter motor strap. The voltage drop should not exceed 0.2 volts. If it does, replace the solenoid.

**7** On vehicles with remote solenoids, have an assistant turn the key to Start while you check for a voltage drop across the two cable connections on the solenoid (connect the positive voltmeter probe on the battery side). The voltage drop should not exceed 0.2 volts. If it does, remove the cables, clean the connections and re-test. If it's still over 0.2 volts, replace the solenoid.

**8** On vehicles with remote solenoids, remove the control circuit wire and connect an ohmmeter between the solenoid's control circuit terminal and ground bracket. The ohmmeter reading should not exceed 5 ohms. If the resistance is higher, replace the solenoid.

**9** Restore the ignition system functions.

## Testing the neutral start switch

**1** A quick check for the neutral start switch is to place your foot firmly on the brake and hold the ignition key to Start while you move the gear selector through all its positions. If the starter operates in positions other than Park and Neutral, the neutral start switch is damaged or out of adjustment.

**2** To more completely check the switch, remove its electrical connector and hook up a jumper wire between the terminal of the connector that receives battery voltage and the terminal that leads to the starter solenoid. If the starter now operates normally, adjust or replace the switch.

**Note:** *Neutral start switch designs vary, and many incorporate back-up light switches. To properly check the switch, you may need to obtain the wiring diagrams for the vehicle. Also, check any specific procedures in the Haynes Automotive Repair Manual written for your vehicle.*

*This Ford neutral start switch is mounted on the transmission, at the shift lever connection – another common location for the switch is at the base of the steering column inside the vehicle*

## Troubleshooting
### (continued)

### Testing the clutch interlock switch

The clutch interlock switch is normally located under the dash, near the top of the clutch pedal arm. If the switch has two wires connected to it, remove its electrical connector and attach a jumper wire between the two terminals of the connector. If the switch has one wire, remove the connector and attach a jumper wire between the connector terminal and ground. If the starter now works normally, adjust or replace the switch.

*Here's a typical clutch interlock switch – it's mounted under the dash, at the top of the clutch pedal arm*

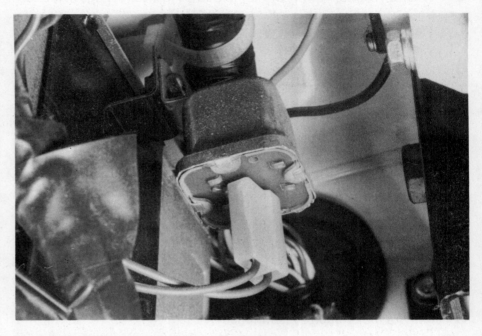

### Testing starter current draw

This test will tell you how much current is being drawn by the starter motor, cables and solenoid. It requires use of an inductive pick-up ammeter. This tool is available inexpensively from auto parts stores.

**Caution:** *Never operate the starter motor for more than 15 seconds at a time without pausing to allow it to cool down for at least two minutes. Overheating caused by excessive operation will seriously damage the starter motor.*

**1** Check that the battery is fully charged and in good condition (see *Battery testing* above). If it's not, this test will not be accurate.

**2** Disable the ignition system. On most vehicles, you can simply pull the coil high tension lead from the distributor cap, connect a jumper wire to it and connect the other end of the jumper to a good ground on the engine.

*Simple inductive ammeters like this are available from auto parts stores at reasonable prices*

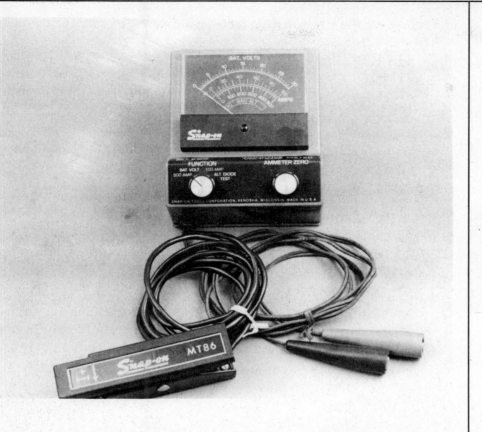

*Inductive ammeters like this one are more expensive, but they can also perform a variety of DC voltage and resistance tests on the alternator (or generator), voltage regulator, diodes, ballast resistors, etc.*

**3** In accordance with the manufacturer's instructions, hook up an inductive pick-up ammeter to the positive or negative battery cable.

**4** Have an assistant in the vehicle operate the starter for about ten seconds. Observe the ammeter scale. The reading shouldn't exceed 110 amps for a four-cylinder engine, 200 amps for a six-cylinder or small V-8 and 250 amps for a large V-8.

*Here's another simple inductive ammeter in use – to use it, simply hold it over the positive or negative battery cable (whichever cable has better clearance)*

## Starter motor removal and installation

**Note:** *Before removing the starter motor for repairs, be sure you have checked the other components in the starting system, as described earlier in this Chapter. Remember, most starting system problems are caused by* *the battery, cables and bad connections. The starter motor is seldom the culprit. This procedure is applicable to most vehicles. However, check the Haynes Automotive Repair Manual for your vehicle. It contains specific procedures which might vary from these.*

**1** Detach the cable from the negative battery terminal.

**2** Raise the vehicle and place it securely on jackstands.

**3** Remove any crossmembers or exhaust pipe sections that might interfere with starter removal.

**4** Remove any starter braces or shields, if equipped.

**5** Detach the wires from the solenoid (vehicles with an on-starter solenoid) or starter. Note which wires are connected to which terminals. If this does not appear self-evident by wire color and size, label the wires to prevent confusion during reassembly.

**6** Remove the nuts and/or bolts which attach the starter to the engine and/or transmission bellhousing. If any of the nuts or bolts are shimmed, note the location and number of shims for each fastener.

**7** Remove the starter from the engine. If there are shims beneath the starter, note how many so you can replace the same number on installation.

**8** Installation is the reverse of removal.

## Overhauling starter motors

Once the starter is off the vehicle, wipe it clean with a shop rag and solvent and place it on a work bench.

Check the pinion for damage and rotate it. It should only rotate easily in one direction. If it rotates easily in both directions, and the armature does not move, the overrunning clutch is faulty.

*Check the starter pinion for freedom of operation by rotating it in both directions with your fingers – it should only rotate freely in one direction*

Check the armature for freedom of rotation by rotating the pinion with a screwdriver in the overrunning clutch's locked position. Tight bearings or a bent armature shaft will prevent the armature from turning freely. If the armature can't turn freely, disassemble the motor immediately. If the armature does turn freely, perform a no-load test before you disassemble the motor.

The no-load test can point to specific defects which you can verify with further inspection when you disassemble the motor. You should also do a no-load test on a freshly overhauled motor prior to reinstallation, to verify that it operates properly.

To no-load test the starter, simply hook up a 12-volt battery as shown and jump the solenoid terminals with a screwdriver (vehicles with an on–starter solenoid). Don't run the starter for more than a few seconds at a time and make sure the battery is in good condition.

**Warning**: *Keep your fingers away from the rotating pinion gear!*

Follow the disassembly procedure photos for the type of starter you have. Inspection and testing procedures for the starter motor components follow the disassembly procedures.

*Check the armature for freedom of rotation by prying the pinion with a screwdriver – the armature should rotate freely*

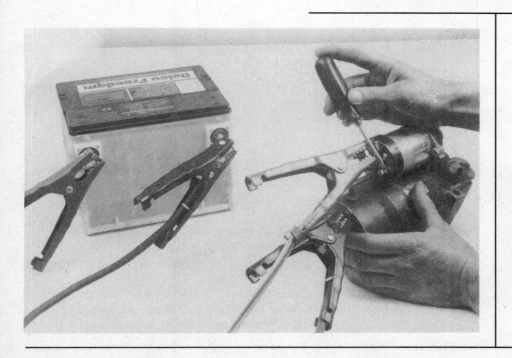

*To do a no-load bench test of the starter, hook up a 12-volt battery – positive to the battery terminal on the starter and negative to the starter case – if it has an on-starter solenoid, connect a jumper wire or an old screwdriver (as shown here) between the battery terminal and the solenoid control circuit terminal*

## Typical GM starter motor disassembly

**Note:** *Disassembly of other starter motor brands with on-starter solenoids is highly similar*

*Disconnect the field strap from the terminal on the solenoid*

*Remove the bolts which attach the solenoid to the starter drive housing*

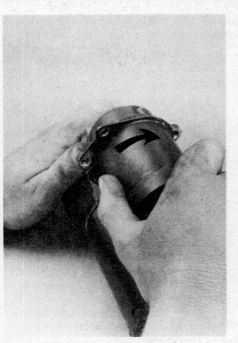

*Twist the solenoid clockwise . . .*

*. . . and separate it from the starter drive housing – remove the return spring and set it aside*

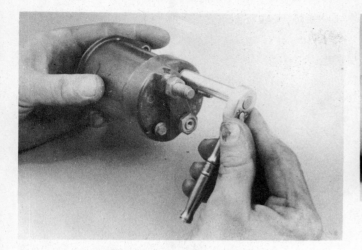

**Remove the two solenoid cover screws**

**Remove the nuts from the motor terminal (usually marked "B") and the switch terminal – terminal studs have welded leads, so avoid twisting the terminal when loosening the nut**

**Remove the solenoid cover and inspect the contacts – if they're dirty, clean them with contact cleaner; if they're burned or damaged, replace the solenoid**

**Remove the two through bolts from the starter and remove the drive end housing**

# Haynes electrical manual

## Typical GM starter motor disassembly
### (continued)

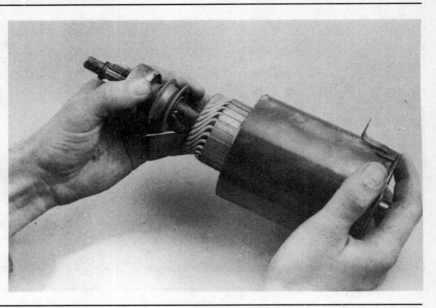

*Pull the armature and overrunning clutch assembly out of the field frame*

*Remove the commutator end frame*

*This is what the brushes, brush holders and springs look like when assembled properly*

*To remove the brushes, remove the small screw attaching the lead to each brush*

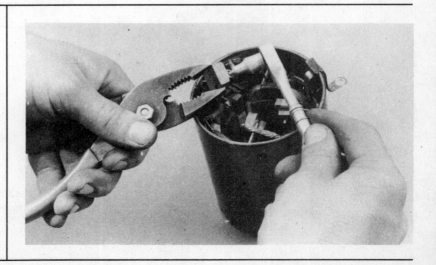

Inspect the brushes for wear – replace the set if any are worn to one-half their original length. Judging from this brush, the brushes in this starter should be replaced

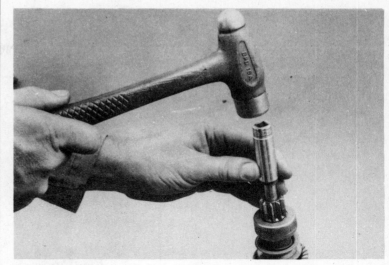

To remove the overrunning clutch from the armature shaft, remove the thrust collar from the shaft, slide an old socket onto the shaft so that it butts against the edge of the retainer, then tap the socket with a hammer and drive the retainer towards the armature and off the snap-ring

Remove the snap-ring from its groove in the shaft with a pair of pliers or a screwdriver – if the snap-ring is badly distorted, use a new one during reassembly

Slide the retainer off the armature shaft

Slide the drive assembly off the shaft – reassembly of the starter is the reverse of disassembly

# Haynes electrical manual

## Typical Ford (positive engagement)
## starter motor disassembly

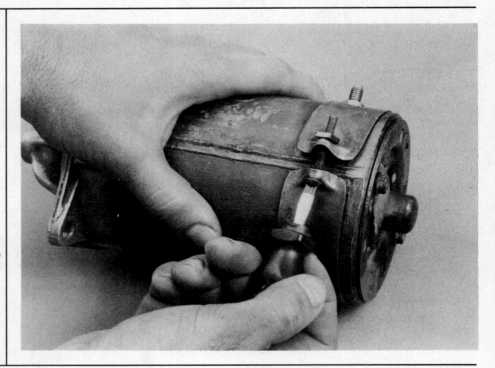

*Loosen the screw on the brush cover band*

*Remove the cover and the plunger lever return spring (not shown) – don't lose the spring*

*Loosen the through bolts*

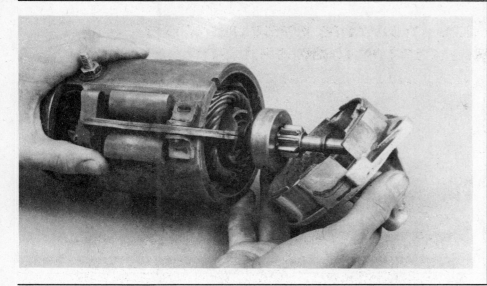

*Remove the drive end housing*

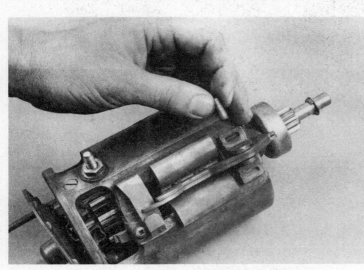

*Remove the pivot pin*

*Remove the starter drive lever*

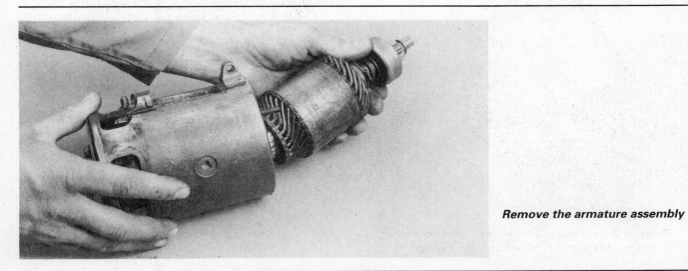

*Remove the armature assembly*

# Haynes electrical manual

## Typical Ford starter motor disassembly
### (continued)

*Remove the through bolts*

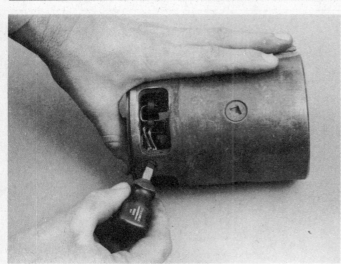

*Remove the two screws attaching the ground brushes to the frame*

*Tilt the brush end plate open as far as it will go – one of the brush leads is soldered to the inside of the starter frame and the lead has no slack – remove the spring for this brush . . .*

*. . . and remove the brush*

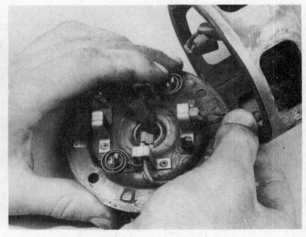

*Then flip the brush end plate open all the way*

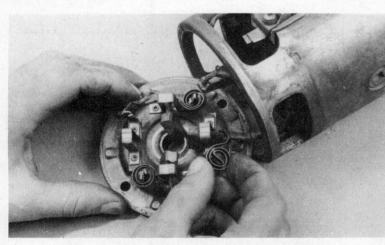

*Remove the spring for the other soldered brush*

*Remove the other soldered brush*

*Desolder the brushes from the field coil – reassembly of the starter is the reverse of disassembly*

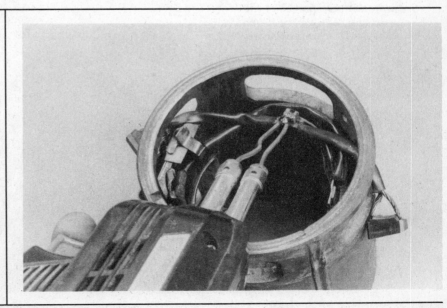

# Haynes electrical manual

Unscrew the two through bolts

## Typical Chrysler (gear reduction) starter motor disassembly

Remove the end plate

Separate the two halves of the starter and remove the brush terminal screw

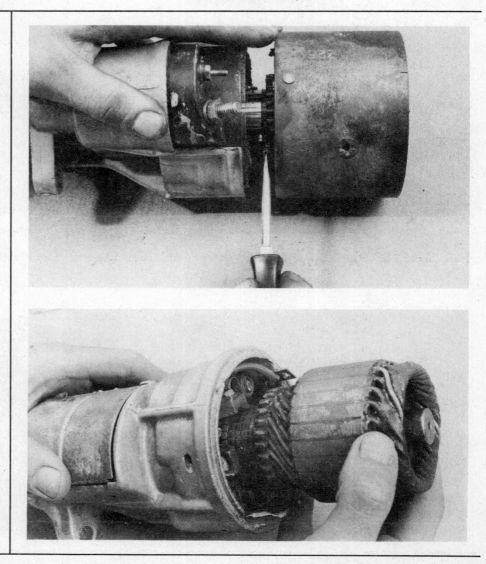

Pull out the armature assembly

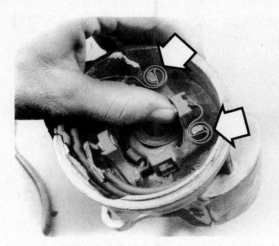

*Remove the brush springs (arrows)*

*Pull the brushes out with a pair of needle nose pliers*

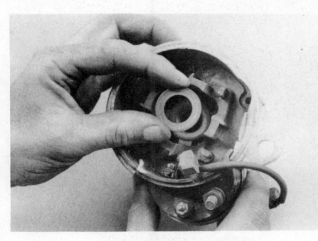

*Remove the washer*

*Remove the thrust washer*

*Remove the brush holder screw (arrow)*

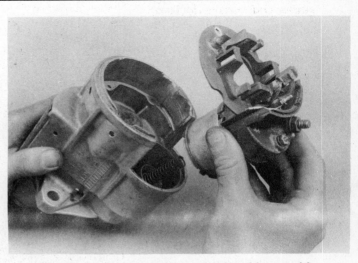

*Remove the brush holder and solenoid assembly*

# Haynes electrical manual

## Typical Chrysler starter motor disassembly
### (continued)

Remove the spring from the plunger

Remove the nut

Remove the insulator washer

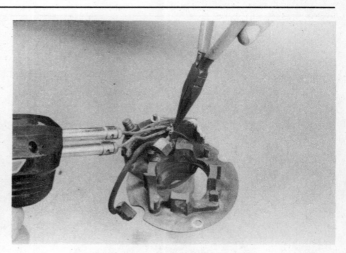

De-solder the shunt coil lead

Separate the solenoid from the brush holder assembly

Remove the plunger assembly

*Remove the clip (arrow) from the plunger*

*Remove the small washer from the plunger*

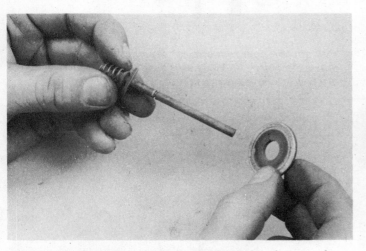

*Remove the contact (big) washer from the plunger – inspect it for wear and, if worn, flip it over on reassembly; if it's worn on both sides, replace it*

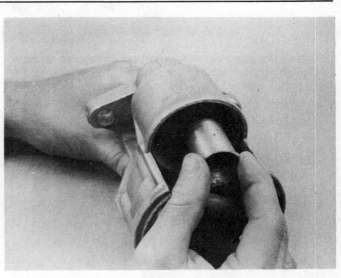

*Remove the solenoid core from the housing*

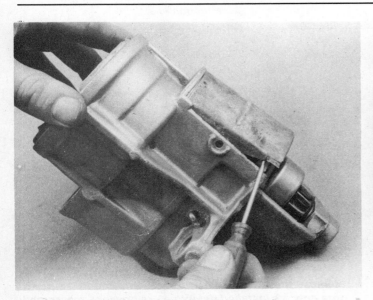

*Pry the cover from the housing*

*Remove the retainer from the gear reduction shaft*

# Haynes electrical manual

## Typical Chrysler starter motor disassembly (continued)

Pull out the gear reduction shaft far enough to remove this washer-clip-washer trio (arrows) – don't forget the order in which they're installed

Pull out the gear reduction shaft a little farther and re- move the clutch and actuator assemblies (arrows) – be sure to note how they're installed before removing them

Pull the gear reduction shaft out a little further and remove the gear

Remove the ring (arrow) and remove the gear reduction shaft

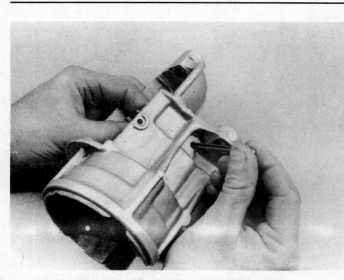

Remove the cotter pin from the housing

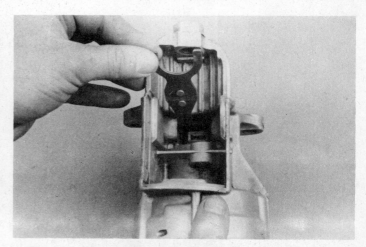

Remove the actuator fork from the housing – be sure to note how it's installed before you remove it – reassembly of the starter is the reverse of disassembly

## Starter motor inspection and testing

**1** Clean the overrunning clutch with a clean cloth. Clean the armature and field coils with electrical contact cleaner and a brush. Do not clean the clutch, armature or field coils in a solvent tank or with grease cutting solvents – they'll dissolve the lubricants in the clutch and damage the insulation in the armature and field coils. If the commutator is dirty, clean it with 00 sandpaper. Never use emery cloth to clean a commutator.

**2** Test the operation of the overrunning clutch. The pinion should turn freely in the overrunning direction only. Check the pinion teeth for chips, cracks and excessive wear. Replace the clutch assembly if damage or wear is evident. Badly chipped pinion teeth may indicate chipped teeth on the flywheel ring gear. If this is the case, be sure to check the ring gear and, if necessary, replace it.

**3** Inspect the brushes for wear. Replace them as a set if any are worn to one-half their original length. The brush holders must hold the brushes against the commutator. Make sure they're not bent or deformed.

**4** Check the fit of the armature shaft in the bushings at each end of the motor housing. The shaft should fit snugly in the bushings. If the bushings are worn, replace them or obtain a rebuilt starter motor.

**Inspection**

**Testing**
*Armature*

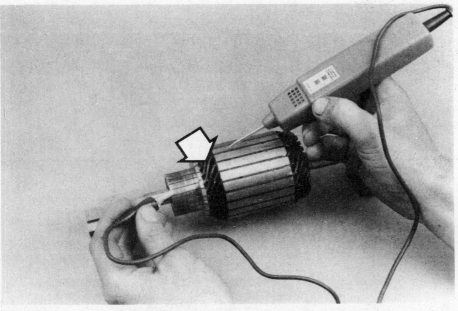

*Checking for a short between a commutator segment and the armature – note how each commutator segment and associated armature winding are joined by a conductor (arrow)*

**1** Check the commutator for wear. If it's heavily worn, out-of-round or the insulation strips between each segment are high, the armature should be turned on a lathe and the insulation strips should be undercut. This operation is best performed by a properly equipped automotive machine shop that's familiar with the procedure. It may be quicker and easier to obtain a rebuilt starter.

**2** Using an ohmmeter or a continuity tester, check for shorts between each commutator segment and the armature. Replace the armature if there are any shorts.

**3** Using an ohmmeter or a continuity tester, check for continuity between each commutator segment and the segment to its immediate right and left. There should be continuity. If there's no continuity, there's an open in the winding. The most likely places for opens to occur are at the points where the armature conductors join the commutator segments. Inspect these points for loose connections. Poor connections cause arcing and burning of the commutator segments as the starter motor is used. If the segments aren't too badly burned, the damage can often be repaired by resoldering the conductors to the segments and cleaning up the burned material on the commutator with 00 sandpaper.

**4** Shorts are sometimes produced by carbon or copper dust (from the brushes) between the segments. They can usually be eliminated by cleaning out the slots between the segments. If a short persists, you'll need to take the armature to a properly equipped shop to be tested on a growler. Often, it's easier to simply obtain a rebuilt starter.

**5** Check for grounds. These often occur as a result of insulation failure brought about by overheating the starter motor by operating it for extended periods. They can also be caused by an accumulation of brush dust between the commutator segments and the steel commutator ring. Grounds in the armature and commutator can be detected with an ohmmeter or a continuity checker. Touch one probe of the test instrument to the armature shaft and touch the other probe to each of the commutator segments. If the instrument indicates continuity at any of the segments, the armature is grounded. If cleaning won't correct the ground problem, replace the armature (often it's easier to simply obtain a rebuilt starter).

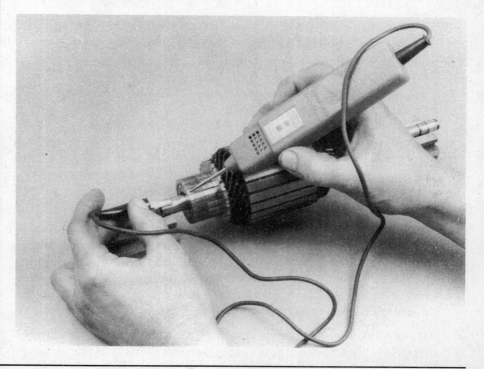

*Checking the armature and commutator for a ground*

**1** Using an ohmmeter or a continuity tester, place one probe on each field coil connector. The instrument should indicate continuity. If there's not continuity, there's an open in one of the field coils. It's best to obtain a rebuilt starter, since field coil replacement normally requires special tools.

**2** Place one probe of an ohmmeter or continuity tester on one of the field coil connectors. Place the other probe on the starter frame. Disconnect the shunt coil ground, if applicable, before you do this check. If the instrument indicates continuity, the field coils are grounded; obtain a rebuilt starter.

*Field coils*

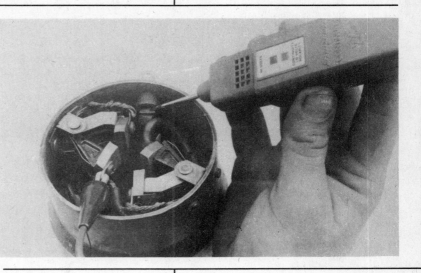

*Checking for an open in the field coils*

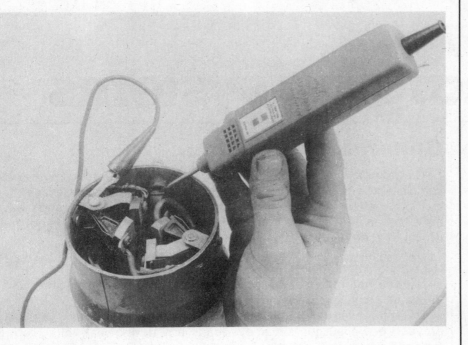

*Checking for a grounded field coil*

# 5 Charging systems

## General information

The charging system includes an alternator (or generator on some older vehicles), a voltage regulator, a charge indicator light or gauge (see chapter 7), the battery (see Chapter 4), a fusible link (see Chapter 1) and the wiring between all the components. The alternator or generator is normally driven by a drivebelt at the front of the engine.

This Chapter focuses on alternator-type charging systems since they are used on all modern vehicles.

The alternator produces current used to charge the battery and operate the vehicle's electrical system during engine operation.

The voltage regulator limits the alternator voltage to a preset value. This prevents power surges, circuit overloads, etc., during peak voltage output from the alternator. The voltage regulator is either a separate unit or integral with the alternator.

If the vehicle is equipped with a charge indicator light, it should come on when the ignition key is turned to ON, then immediately go out after the engine is started. If the vehicle is equipped with a voltmeter, it should normally indicate between 13 and 15 volts (12-volt system) when the engine is operating. If the vehicle is equipped with an ammeter, it should normally remain at or near the neutral position (not showing a significant charge or discharge) when the engine is operating. If the indicator light or gauge is not operating as described, there's probably a problem in the charging system.

Be very careful when making electrical circuit connections to a vehicle equipped with an alternator and note the following:

a) When reconnecting wires to the alternator from the battery, be sure to note the polarity.

b) Before using arc welding equipment to repair any part of the vehicle, disconnect the wires from the alternator and the battery terminals.

c) Never start the engine with a battery charger connected.

d) Always disconnect both battery cables before using a battery charger.

e) The alternator is driven by an engine drivebelt which could cause serious injury if your hand or clothes become entangled in it with the engine running.

f) Because the alternator is connected directly to the battery, it could arc or cause a fire if overloaded or shorted out.

g) Wrap a plastic bag over the alternator and secure it with rubber bands before steam cleaning the engine.

## Alternators and generators – basic theory of operation

The alternator or generator is a device that converts mechanical energy into electrical energy, providing current to charge the battery and power other electrical components on the vehicle.

*A typical alternator, disassembled*

1 *End Frame*
2 *Stator and diode plate*
3 *Rotor*
4 *End frame*
5 *Fan Pulley*
6 *Bearing*
7 *Brushes*
8 *Brush holder*
9 *Bearing retainer*
10 *Bearing*

# Haynes electrical manual

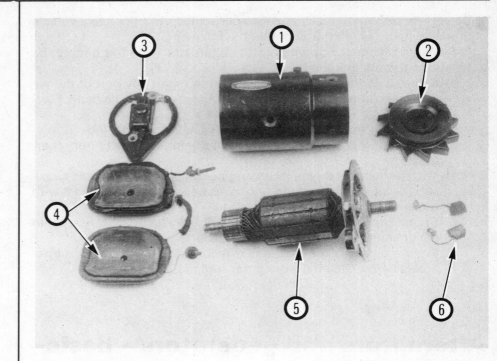

**A typical generator, disassembled**

1 Field Frame
2 Fan Pulley
3 Commutator end frame
4 Field windings
5 Armature
6 Brushes

Many older (mostly pre-1970's) vehicles use generators. Modern vehicles are equipped with alternators to handle the higher current demands of today's electrical systems. Alternators are lighter in weight, have a higher peak current capacity and produce more current at lower rotational speeds than generators.

Both alternators and generators produce current by creating motion between a conductor and a magnetic field. The principles of electromagnetism (discussed in Chapters 1 and 4) control how this current is produced.

In a generator, the armature (the conductor) spins inside the field windings (which create the magnetic field). Current is induced in the armature and flows through the brushes to be used in the electrical system.

In an alternator, the rotor (which creates the magnetic field) spins inside the stator (the conductor). Alternating current (AC) is induced in the stator, then changed to direct current (DC) by a diode bridge so it can be used in the vehicle's electrical system. The process of converting AC to DC is know as *rectification*.

## Maintenance

**Note:** *The following maintenance procedures apply to both alternator and generator-type systems*

**1**   The alternator drivebelt, wiring, connections and mounting bolts should be checked every six months or 6000 miles, as discussed below. Battery maintenance should be performed every three months or 3000 miles (see Chapter 4).

## Drivebelt check, adjustment and replacement

**2** Various types of drivebelts are used to drive the alternator. The drivebelt is normally located at the front of the engine. The condition and tension of the drivebelt are critical to the operation of the alternator. Excessive tension causes bearing wear, while insufficient tension produces slippage, noise, alternator vibration and belt failure. A slipping belt is a common cause of a malfunctioning charging system (undercharging). Because of their composition and the high stresses to which they are subjected, drivebelts stretch and deteriorate as they get older. As a result, the alternator drivebelt (as well as other engine drivebelts) must be periodically checked and adjusted.

**3** Sometimes alternators are driven by a V-ribbed belt. V-ribbed belts are often referred to as serpentine belts because of the winding path they follow between various drive, accessory and idler pulleys.

**4** With the engine off, open the hood and locate the alternator drivebelt at the front of the engine. Using your fingers (and a flashlight, if necessary), move along the belt, checking for cracks and separation of the belt plies. Also check for fraying and glazing, which gives the belt a shiny appearance. On V-ribbed belts, also check for separation of the ribs from the rubber, torn or worn ribs and cracks in the ridges of the ribs. Both sides of the belt should be inspected, which means you'll have to twist the belt to check the underside. Use your fingers to feel a belt where you can not see it. If any of the above conditions are evident, replace the belt.

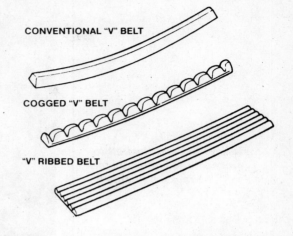

*Different types of drivebelts are used to drive alternators*

**Check**

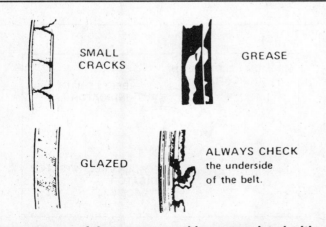

*Here are some of the common problems associated with drivebelts (check the belts very carefully to prevent an untimely breakdown)*

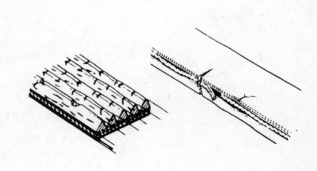

*Check a V-ribbed belt for signs of wear like these – if the belt looks worn, replace it*

# Haynes electrical manual

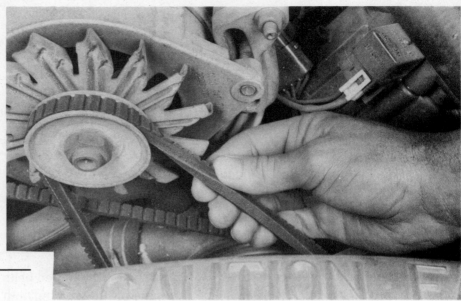

*Be sure to twist the belt to inspect the underside for cracks, fraying, etc*

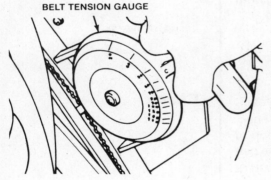

BELT TENSION GAUGE

*A drivebelt tension gauge is often recommended for checking the belts (the unit illustrated is a Burroughs model – follow the manufacturer's instructions)*

**5** The most accurate way to check drivebelt tension is to use a special drivebelt tension gauge. Many manufacturers recommend using a special gauge to check tension on their vehicles (particularly vehicles using V-ribbed belts). For specifications and special procedures, check the Haynes Automotive Repair Manual written for your particular vehicle.

**Note:** *Some vehicles are equipped with an automatic tensioner which can be checked visually to make sure the indicator is in the proper range. Replace the belt with a new one when the indicator is out of the range specified by the manufacturer.*

**6** If you do not have a special gauge, and cannot borrow one, the following method is recommended as an alternative. Lay a straight-

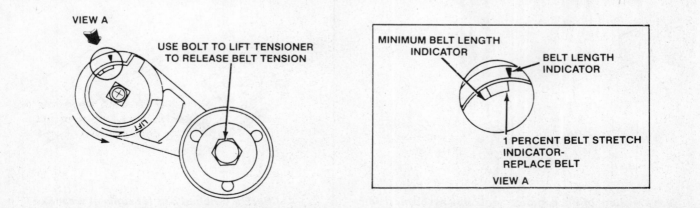

*On some models the drivebelt is automatically tensioned and requires no service as long as it is in good condition and the indicator is in the proper range*

edge across the longest free span (the distance between two pulleys) of the belt. Push down firmly on the belt at a point half-way between the pulleys and see how much the belt moves (deflects). Measure the deflection with a ruler. The belt should deflect 1/4-inch if the distance from pulley center-to-pulley center is between 7 and 11 inches; it should deflect 1/2-inch if the distance from the pulley center-to-pulley center is 12 to 16 inches.

7   If the drivebelt tension or deflection is not correct, adjust it, as described below. If it's correct, check the alternator mounting bolts to be sure they're tight.

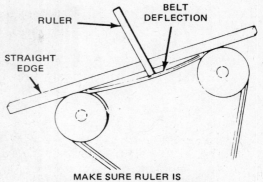

*Measuring drivebelt deflection with a straightedge and ruler*

## Adjustment

**Note:** *The following procedure is general in nature. For more specific procedures, check the Haynes Automotive Repair Manual written for your particular vehicle. On some vehicles, the drivebelt is automatically tensioned and requires no service as long as it is in good condition and the indicator is in the proper range.*

8   On many vehicles, the alternator is mounted by a locking bolt and a pivot bolt or nut. Both must be loosened slightly to enable you to move the alternator to adjust the belt. After the two bolts have been loosened, move the alternator away from the engine (to tighten the belt) or towards the engine (to loosen the belt). On some vehicles,

*On many vehicles, the alternator is held in place with pivot and locking bolts (arrows)*

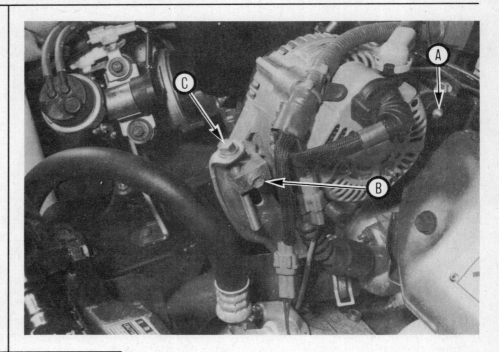

*On some vehicles, after loosening the pivot bolt (A) and locking bolt (B), an adjustment bolt (C) can be used to adjust the drivebelt tension*

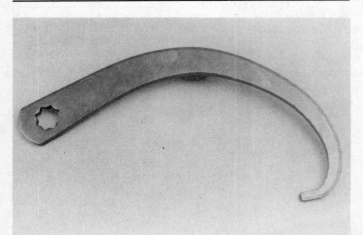

*Sometimes a special tool is needed to adjust the belt tension – these tools may be purchased at automotive supply stores*

*To move a typical idler pulley, loosen the locking bolts (A), then turn the adjustment bolt (B)*

you can loosen or tighten an adjustment bolt or nut to move the alternator. If there's no adjustment bolt or nut, move the alternator by hand; it may be necessary to use a special tool or some sort of a prybar. If this must be done, be very careful not to damage the alternator housing. When the tension is correct, retighten all bolts and nuts, starting with the locking bolt.

9    On some vehicles (particularly vehicles with serpentine belts), the belt is adjusted by moving a separate idler pulley, as shown in the accompanying illustration.

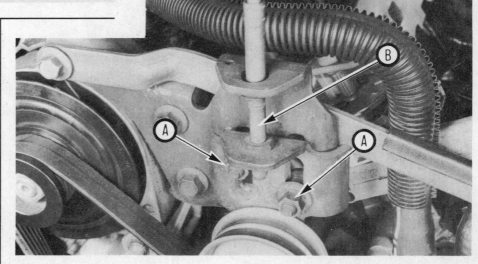

**10** To replace the drivebelt, follow the procedures for drivebelt adjustment, but slip the belt off the pulleys and remove it. Since belts tend to wear out more or less at the same time, it's a good idea to replace the other drivebelts at the same time. Mark each belt and the corresponding pulley grooves so the replacement belts can be installed properly.

**11** Take the old belts with you when purchasing new ones in order to make a direct comparison for length, width and design.

**12** Adjust the belts as described above.

**13** When replacing a serpentine belt, make sure the new belt is routed correctly or the water pump could turn backwards, causing overheating. A label showing the drivebelt type and routing is normally located in the engine compartment or in the vehicle's owner's manual. Also, serpentine belts must completely engage the grooves in the pulleys.

## Replacement

*Most vehicles with serpentine belts have a label showing drivebelt routing located in the engine compartment*

**14** Next inspect the alternator wiring for cracking, deterioration, chafing or any other signs of wear. Replace any wires as necessary (see Chapter 3).

**15** Disconnect the negative battery cable and check the tightness of all electrical connections on the alternator.

## Wiring check

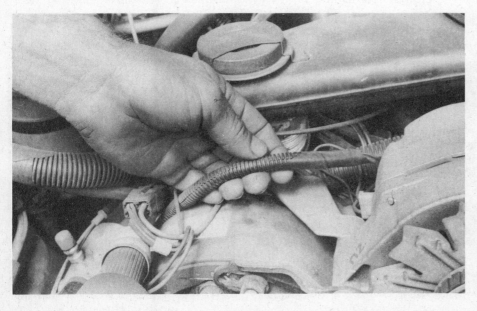

*Inspect the wiring going to the alternator – if the vehicle has a split conduit like this, open it to expose the wires inside*

## Troubleshooting (alternator-type systems)

**With your hand, try turning the pulley to see if the belt slips**

**Note:** *Steps 1 through 4 of this procedure also apply to generator-type systems.*

**1**    If a malfunction occurs in the charging system, do not automatically assume the alternator is causing the problem. First check the following items:

a) Check the drivebelt tension and condition, as described in the previous Section. Replace it if it's worn or deteriorated. If the drivebelt tension is correct, try turning the alternator pulley with your hand to see if the belt is slipping. If it slips, replace the belt.

b) Make sure the alternator mounting bolts are tight (see the previous Section).

c) Inspect the alternator wiring harness and the connectors at the alternator and voltage regulator. They must be in good condition, tight and have no corrosion.

d) Check the fusible link (if equipped) or main fuse located between the starter solenoid and alternator. If it is burned, determine the cause, repair the circuit and replace the link or fuse (The vehicle will not start and/or the accessories will not work if the fusible link or main fuse is blown). Sometimes a fusible link or main fuse may look good, but still be bad. If in doubt, remove it and check for continuity.

*Most vehicles have a fusible link or main fuse (arrow)*

e) Start the engine and check the alternator for abnormal noises (a shrieking or squealing sound indicates a bad bearing).

f) Check the battery (see Chapter 4). Make sure it's fully charged and in good condition (one bad cell in a battery can cause overcharging by the alternator).

g) Disconnect the battery cables (negative first, then positive). Inspect the battery posts and the cable clamps for corrosion. Clean them thoroughly if necessary (See Chapter 4). Reconnect the cables (positive first, then negative).

h) With the key off, connect a test light between the negative battery post and the disconnected negative cable clamp.

   1) If the test light does not come on, reattach the clamp and proceed to Step 2.

   2) If the test light comes on, there is a short (drain) in the electrical system of the vehicle. The short must be repaired before the charging system can be checked.

   3) Disconnect the alternator wiring harness.

     (a) If the light goes out, there's a problem in the alternator. Replace it.

     (b) If the light stays on, pull each fuse until the light goes out (this will tell you which component is shorted).

**2** Using a voltmeter, check the battery voltage with the engine off. It should be approximately 12.5 volts (12-volt system).

**3** Start the engine, increase engine speed to approximately 2000 RPM and check the battery voltage again. It should now be approximately 14 – 15 volts.

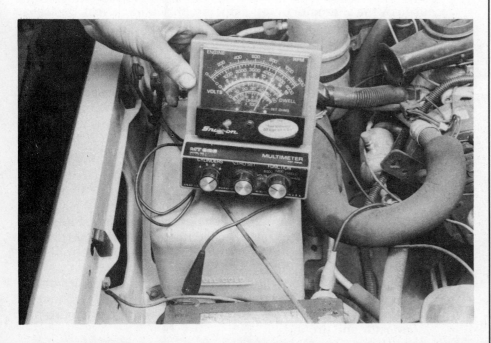

*Connect a test light between the negative battery post and negative battery cable*

*Connect a voltmeter to the battery – the black lead to the negative post and the red lead to the positive post*

**4** Turn on the headlights. The voltage should drop, and then come back up, if the charging system is working properly.

**5** If the voltage reading is more than approximately 15 volts, check the regulator ground connection (vehicles with remotely mounted regulators). If the ground is OK, the problem lies in the regulator, the alternator or the wiring between them. If the vehicle has an internal regulator, replace the alternator. If the vehicle has a remotely mounted regulator, remove the electrical connector from the regulator and repeat Step 3. If the voltage drops with the regulator disconnected, replace the regulator. If the voltage is still high, there's a short in the wiring between the alternator and regulator or there's a short in the rotor or stator within the alternator. Check the wiring. If the wiring is OK, replace the alternator.

**6** If the voltage is less than 13 volts, an undercharging condition is present. If the vehicle is equipped with an indicator light, turn the ignition key to ON and see if the light illuminates. If it does, proceed to the next Step. If it doesn't, check the indicator light circuit (see Chapter 7). In some vehicles, a faulty circuit could cause the alternator to malfunction.

**7** If the indicator light circuit is OK, check for a bad ground at the voltage regulator. If the ground is OK, the problem lies in the alternator, regulator or the wiring between them. If the vehicle has an internal regulator, replace the alternator. If the vehicle has a remotely mounted regulator, check the wiring. If necessary, disconnect the negative battery terminal and check for continuity, using the vehicle's wiring diagram for reference. If the wiring is OK, you'll have to determine whether the problem lies in the alternator or regulator.

**8** A good way to determine whether an undercharging problem is caused by the alternator or regulator is with a full-field test. Basically, the full-field test bypasses the regulator to send full battery voltage to the alternator's field (the rotor). If the charging voltage is normal when the alternator is "full-fielded," you know the alternator is OK. If the voltage is still low, the problem is in the alternator. It's best to obtain wiring diagrams for the vehicle to determine the best way to send battery voltage to the field. However, the following gives some general guidelines which may help you in determining how to full-field the alternator:

a) On older Delco (GM) alternators with remotely mounted regulators ("B"-circuit type), disconnect the electrical connector from the regulator and connect a jumper wire between the BATT and F terminals of the connector.

b) On Ford Motorcraft alternators with remotely mounted regulators ("B"-circuit type), disconnect the electrical connector from the regulator and connect a jumper wire between the A and F terminals of the connector.

c) On Chrysler alternators with remotely mounted electronic voltage regulators ("A"-circuit type), disconnect the regulator connector and connect a jumper wire between the green wire terminal of the connector and ground.

Make the connections with the ignition turned OFF, then repeat Step 3, above. The voltage reading should be high (about 15 to 16 volts). If it's not, the alternator is faulty. If it is, the regulator is probably bad.

**Caution:** *Full-fielding sends high voltage through the vehicle's electrical system, which can damage components, particularly electronic components. Carefully monitor the charging system voltage during full-fielding to be sure it doesn't exceed 16 volts. Also, do not operate a full-fielded alternator for an extended period of time. Operate it only long enough to take the voltage reading.*

## Alternator – removal and installation

**Note:** *If you're replacing the alternator on a vehicle with an external regulator, it's a good idea to also replace the regulator (see the next Section).*

**1** Disconnect the negative battery cable.

**2** Remove the drivebelt (see *Maintenance* above).

**3** Detach all electrical connectors, taking note how they come off.

**4** Remove the alternator mounting bolts and lift it from the engine compartment (see *Maintenance* above).

*The electrical connectors on an internal regulator type alternator (GM)*

*The electrical connectors on an integral regulator type alternator (Ford)*

*On some types of alternators the identification numbers are stamped in the housing*

**5** If you are replacing the alternator, take the old alternator with you when purchasing a replacement unit. Make sure the new/rebuilt unit is identical to the old alternator. Look at the terminals – they should be the same in number, size and locations as the terminals on the old alternator. Finally, look at the identification markings – they will be stamped in the housing or printed on a tag or plaque affixed to the housing. Make sure these numbers are the same on both alternators.

**6** Many new/rebuilt alternators do not have a pulley installed, so you may have to switch the pulley from the old unit to the new/rebuilt one. When buying an alternator, find out the shop's policy regarding installation of pulleys – some shops will perform this service free of charge. For further information on pulley removal see *Alternator Overhaul* (below).

**7** Installation is the reverse of removal.

**8** After the alternator is installed, adjust the drivebelt tension (See *Maintenance* above).

**9** Check the charging voltage to verify proper operation of the alternator (See *Troubleshooting* above).

*Another type of stamped identification number*

## Voltage regulator – replacement (generator and alternator-type systems)

**Note:** *This procedure applies only to vehicles with remotely mounted regulators. Many alternator-type systems have regulators integral with the alternator. For information on these, see* Alternator overhaul *below.*

**1** Detach the cable from the negative terminal of the battery.

**2** Locate the regulator in the engine compartment.

**3** If the vehicle has an alternator, unplug the electrical connector from the voltage regulator.

**4** If the vehicle has a generator, label the wires then detach the wires from the regulator.

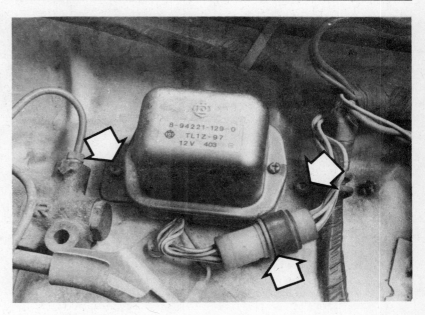

*Here's a typical mechanical voltage regulator for an alternator – to remove it, unplug the connector and remove the mounting bolts (arrows)*

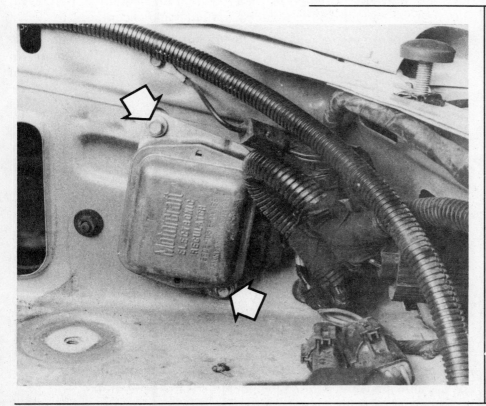

*Here are the mounting bolts on a typical electronic regulator*

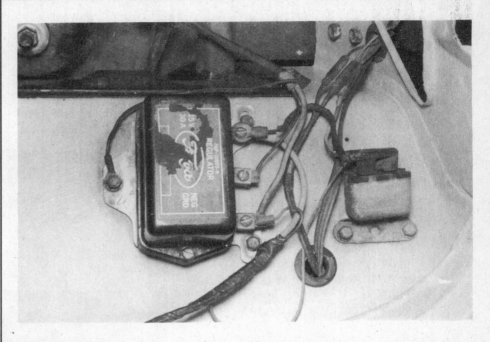

*Here's a typical generator voltage regulator with three connections for wires and three mounting bolts*

**5** Remove the regulator mounting bolts and lift the regulator from the engine compartment.

**6** Installation is the reverse of removal.

**7** If the vehicle has a generator, it will be necessary to polarize the regulator before the engine is started, as discussed in Steps 8 and 9 below. Caution: Never try to polarize a regulator on an alternator-type system or damage to the electrical system could occur.

**8** To polarize the regulator on a generator-type system with an externally grounded field circuit (Delco-Remy), momentarily connect a jumper wire between the battery terminal and the armature terminal of the regulator.

**9** To polarize the regulator on a generator-type system with an internally grounded field circuit (Ford), disconnect the wire from the field terminal on the regulator and momentarily touch it to the battery terminal on the regulator.

## Generator – removal and installation

**Warning:** *Anytime a generator is removed or wires disconnected, the regulator must be polarized or damage will occur to the charging system (see Voltage regulator replacement above).*

**Note:** *Before replacing the generator, be sure you have eliminated other possible causes of a charging system malfunction (see Troubleshooting above).*

**1** Disconnect the negative terminal of the battery.

**2** Label the wires and remove them from the generator.

*Label all wires before removing them – most generators will have three wires (arrows)*

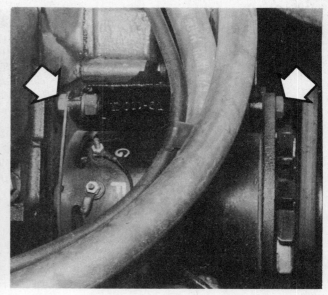

*Typical generator mounting bolts (arrows)*

*Typical generator identification tag*

**3** Loosen the mounting bolts and nuts, then loosen the locking bolt. Remove the drivebelt, remove the bolts and lift the generator from the vehicle.

**4** If the generator will be replaced, be sure to compare the identification tag with that of the new generator, to verify the units are the same.

**5** If the generator is equipped with an oiler cap, add a few drops of oil to the oiler caps to lubricate the bearings.

**6** Installation is the reverse of removal.

**7** Before starting the engine, polarize the regulator (see *Voltage regulator replacement* above).

**8** Hook-up a voltmeter to verify that the system is charging, as described in *Troubleshooting* (above).

*If the generator has a lubrication hole like this, add a few drops of oil to lubricate the bearings*

## Alternator overhaul

**Note:** *Special tools are needed to overhaul an alternator. These tools include an ohmmeter, soldering gun and special pullers and installers. Before disassembling the alternator, check the availability and prices overhaul kits and also the prices of new and rebuilt alternators. Often, you'll find it easier – and sometimes less expensive – to obtain a rebuilt unit.*

### Disassembly

**Note:** *Some late model alternators are not intended to be disassembled and rebuilt. These usually have through-bolts with special heads or rivets in place of the through-bolts.*

**1**   Scribe or paint a line across the alternator housing to ensure correct reassembly.

**2**   Remove the pulley. Some alternators require special pullers and installers. Do not try to pry off the pulley or you could damage the pulley or alternator housing. On other types of alternators, the pulley can be removed with common hand tools. After the pulley has been removed, some alternators will have a spacer. On some models, the brush holder and/or regulator should also be removed at this time.

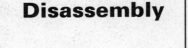

*Some late model alternators cannot be rebuilt – they can be identified by special bolts (arrows) or rivets*

*Paint or scribe a line across the length of the alternator housing to ensure correct reassembly*

TOOL C-4068
OR C-4333

VEE
BELT
PULLEY

DRIVE
END
SHIELD

BEARING
RETAINER
SCREW

*On some alternators, special pullers are needed to pull off the fan pulley – sometimes, a standard puller can be substituted*

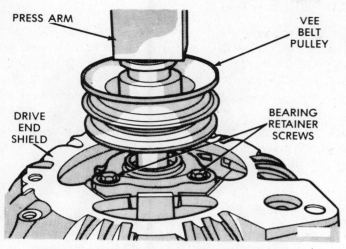

PRESS ARM

VEE BELT PULLEY

DRIVE END SHIELD

BEARING RETAINER SCREWS

**A press is needed to reinstall certain pulleys**

**Damage to the fan pulley can occur if the wrong tool is used to remove or install the pulley**

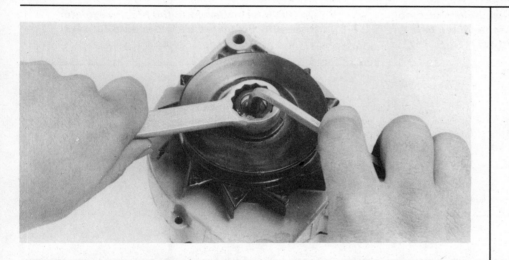

**Common hand tools can be used to remove some fan pulleys**

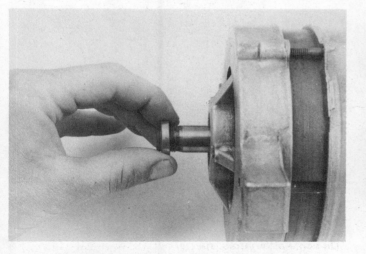

**After the fan pulley has been removed, some alternators will have a spacer**

**On some models the brushes can be removed without disassembling the alternator**

*To remove the regulator/brush holder assembly on this Ford alternator, remove the four screws (arrows)*

*On this Bosch alternator, the brush/regulator assembly is secured by two screws (arrows)*

*Remove the through bolts (arrows)*

**3**  Remove the housing through bolts.

**4**  Carefully separate the end frames. On some late-model alternators it is necessary to heat the rear end frame. This expands the end frame so it will separate from the rotor bearing.

*Carefully separate the end frames*

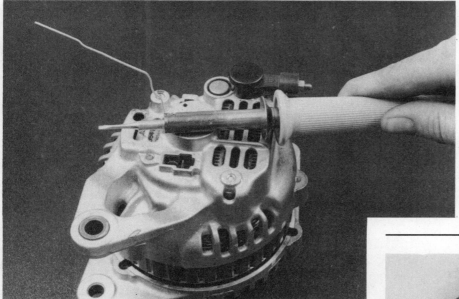

*On some late model alternators, like this Mazda unit, it is necessary to heat the rear end frame with a 200 watt soldering iron to expand the rotor shaft bearing bore enough to separate the housings*

*On some models, you can remove three nuts (arrows) and carefully separate the stator from the end frame*

**5** On some models, the stator can be removed by removing three nuts on the inside of the rear housing. On other models, the stator and the diode plate must be removed as an assembly. On other models, the stator must be desoldered for removal. If you remove the diode plate, take note of any spacers or insulators behind the plate.

*On some models, the stator and diode plate must be removed as a unit – remove the nuts (arrows) . . .*

*. . . and carefully separate the stator and diode plate from the end frame*

*On some models, the stator must be desoldered before removing it from the diode plate*

**6** Remove the brush holder and/or regulator.

**7** Special pullers and installers are recommended to remove and install the bearings. However, the alternative methods described in the illustration captions work on some alternators.

**Note:** *Be extremely cautious when using the alternative methods – the bearings and aluminum end frames are easily damaged.*

*After the stator/diode plate has been removed, take note of any spacers or insulators as to where they go*

*If the stator and diode plate were removed as an assembly, carefully unsolder the connections*

*If the brush holder has not already been removed, remove it now – this holder is secured by two screws (arrows)*

This brush holder and regulator assembly is secured by two screws (arrows)

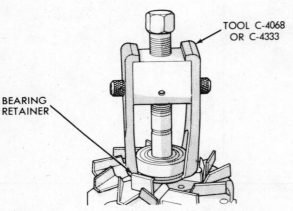

BEARING RETAINER

TOOL C-4068 OR C-4333

Special tools are needed to remove some alternator bearings, but . . .

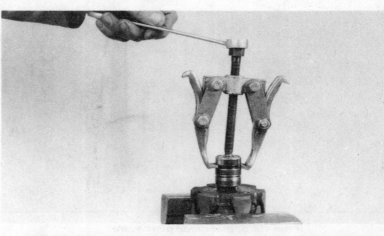

. . . sometimes a common two jaw puller can be used to remove the bearing – a hammer and socket the same diameter as the bearing inner race can be used to tap the new bearing into place

Here's still another method of removing and installing bearings. Place the end frame in a vise with one socket the same diameter as the bearing outer race and one larger than the outer race. When the vise is tightened, the bearing will be driven out. Use the same method to install the new bearing.

*A typical example of a burned out brush/regulator holder*

*A typical example of worn out brushes*

**8** After the alternator has been completely disassembled, clean all parts with electrical contact cleaner. Do not use de-greasing solvents; they can damage the electrical parts. Look for cracks in the case, burned spots and parts exhibiting signs of wear or other damage. Replace parts as necessary.

## Inspection

*A typical example of worn out slip rings*

**9** With an ohmmeter, check the rotor for opens and grounds. Replace the rotor or obtain a rebuilt alternator if either condition is present.

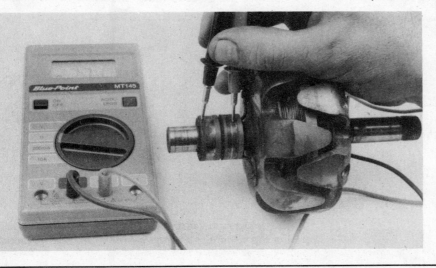

## Testing

*Check for continuity between the two slip rings – if there's no continuity, the rotor is open and should be replaced*

Check for continuity between each slip ring and the rotor shaft – if there's continuity, the rotor is grounded and should be replaced

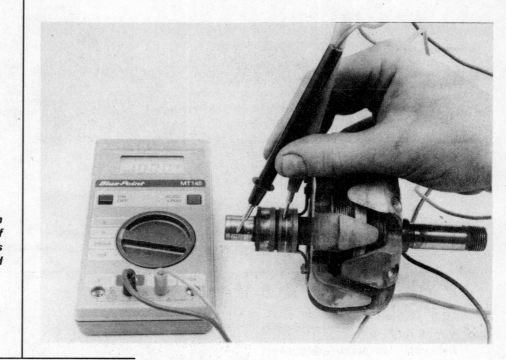

**10** If the rotor checks out OK, clean the slip rings with 400 grit or finer polishing cloth.

**11** Check the stator for opens and grounds. Replace the stator or obtain a rebuilt alternator if either condition is present.

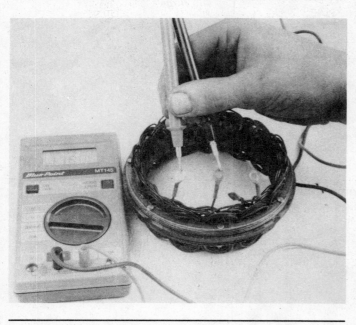

Check for continuity between these two stator terminals . . .

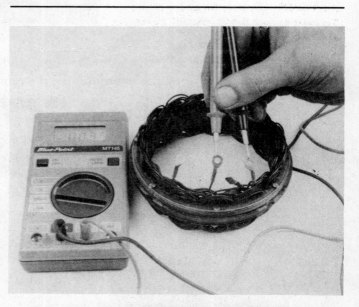

. . . and these two – if there's no continuity, there is an open in the windings and the stator should be replaced

*Check for continuity between each stator terminal and ground – if there's continuity, the stator is grounded and should be replaced*

**12** Check each diode or diode trio and rectifier bridge, as described in the accompanying illustrations. Replace any faulty parts.

*If the alternator has diodes, connect an ohmmeter between each diode terminal and the diode case, then reverse the ohmmeter leads – if there's one high and one low reading, the diode is OK – if the readings are about the same, the diode should be replaced*

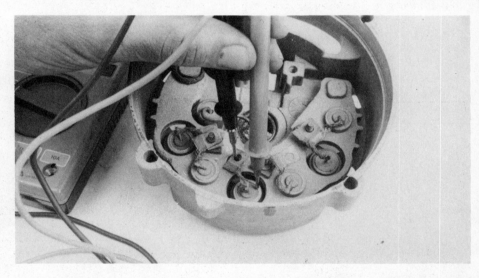

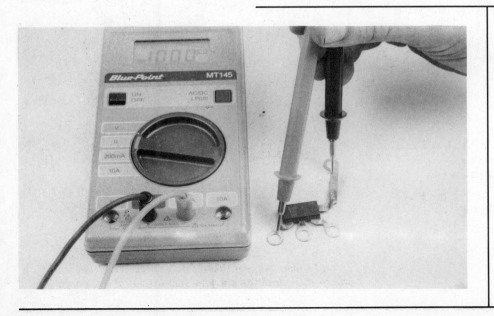

*If the alternator has a diode trio like this, connect an ohmmeter as shown, then reverse the ohmmeter leads – one high and one low reading indicates a good diode trio – if the readings are about the same, the diode trio should be replaced*

# Haynes electrical manual

*If the alternator has a rectifier bridge like this, connect an ohmmeter as shown – one lead to the insulated heat sink (1) and the other to the metal clip; take a reading, then reverse the ohmmeter leads and take another reading – you should get one high and one low reading – if the readings are about the same, replace the rectifier bridge. Next, repeat this test with the other two clips, then repeat the entire test between the three clips and the grounded heat sink (2)*

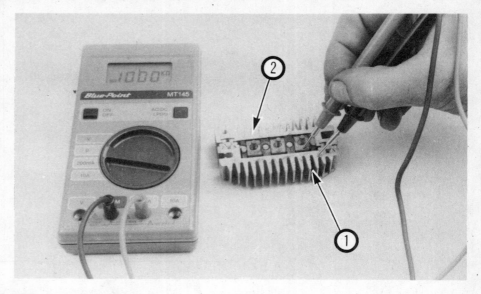

## Assembly

**13** Assembly is the reverse of disassembly.

**14** Before installing the brush holder, insert a paper clip to hold the brushes in place during assembly. Remove the clip after assembling the alternator.

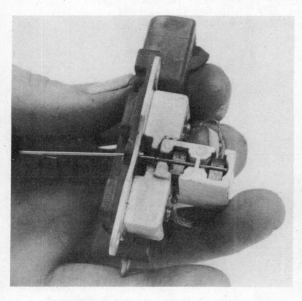

*Before installing the brushes, insert a paper clip as shown, to hold the brushes in place during installation*

*After reassembly, simply pull the paper clip out*

#  6 Lighting systems

## General Information

The lighting circuits are among the most important parts of your vehicle's electrical system. They make night driving possible and alert others when you slow down or change direction. A properly operating lighting system is essential to being safe – and legal – on the road.

Fortunately, troubleshooting and repairing lighting system circuits is relatively easy. Most lighting failures are caused by blown fuses, burned out bulbs, corrosion and loose connections. On most vehicles, you can access lighting system components (with the exception of the turn signal switch) quickly and easily, using normal hand tools.

## Light bulbs

There are dozens of light bulbs in use on a typical vehicle today, illuminating everything from the road in front to the license plate in the rear. Basically, a bulb is nothing more than two posts (connected to the positive and negative contacts) with a thin strand of tungsten wire (called a filament) between them. When current flows through the filament, it heats up (due to resistance) and emits light. The glass dome over the bulb is used to contain the oxygen-free atmosphere necessary to keep the filament from burning out when it heats up.

## General description

*From the left, the first four bulbs have what's called a bayonet base – the positive contact(s) are on the bottom of the base and the ground contact is the brass sleeve that forms the side of the base. Note that the second and fourth bulbs have two positive contacts – these are for the two filaments inside the bulb. The fifth bulb from the left is called a cartridge bulb – its contacts are on either end of its glass tube. The bulb on the right is a press-in type. It has no base; its filament wires extend through the glass and serve as contacts.*

*Here's an indication of a failed bulb – the dark-colored residue inside the glass is from the filament evaporating*

Normally, it's easy to tell when a bulb has failed; either the filament will be broken or there will be a black or gray film on the inside of the glass dome (this is residue from evaporation of the filament). However, the only way to be absolutely sure if a bulb's good is to remove the bulb and hook up its positive and negative contacts to the battery using jumper wires (polarity is not critical – it can be hooked up either way). Use a fused jumper wire on the positive side to protect against a short circuit. If the bulb lights, it's good.

Some bulbs have two filaments, so the bulb acts electrically like two separate bulbs. These types of bulbs are commonly used for turn signal/parking light applications – one filament is the turn signal light and the other is the parking light. Both circuits of a dual-filament bulb must be checked before it can be considered good.

*Here you can see the two filaments of a dual-filament bulb*

## Bulb replacement

### Brake, turn signal, parking and back-up light bulbs

**1** First, check to see if the bulb socket can be accessed from behind the lens. On rear-mounted bulbs, access is usually through the trunk (or cargo area). You may have to remove a cover to get at the bulb socket. On front-mounted bulbs, you can usually access the socket by reaching up from under the bumper. Once you've reached the bulb socket, rotate it counterclockwise about 1/4-turn and pull it out.

**2** If there's no access to the bulb socket from behind the lens, there are normally screws along the outside of the lens. Remove the screws and pull the lens off. It may stick a little since there's a weather-sealing gasket behind it. If necessary, pry gently with a small screwdriver.

*To remove a bulb socket, rotate it counterclockwise 1/4-turn, then carefully pull it out*

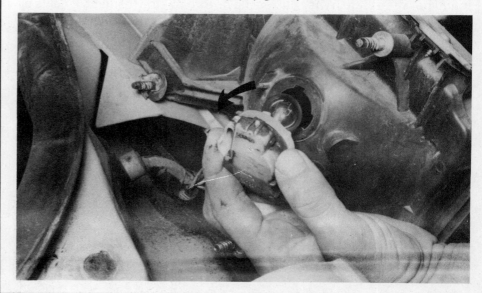

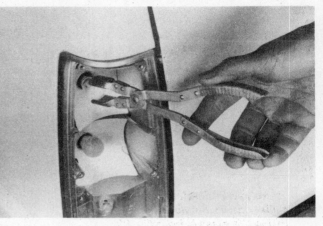

**To remove the bulb from the socket, push in firmly, then turn it 1/4-turn counterclockwise**

**Bulb removal tools like this make removing bulbs safer and prevent breakage**

**3** Once the bulb is exposed, push in and turn it about 1/4-turn counterclockwise. If you're having difficulty turning the bulb, use a special bulb removal tool or protect your hand with a leather glove or a thick rag.

**Caution:** *Don't force a stubborn bulb by turning it with your bare hand. The stress of removal often causes bulbs to break, and your fingers could be severely cut when this happens.*

If the bulb is broken, remove the base of the bulb from the socket with a pair of needle-nose pliers.

**4** Be sure to check the socket for corrosion, loose wires and worn or missing terminals. If the socket is corroded, clean it with a small wire brush.

**5** Place the new bulb in the socket, aligning the indexing lugs with the slots in the socket. Press in firmly and rotate the bulb about 1/4-turn clockwise

**If a bulb is broken, you can remove it with a pair of needle-nose pliers**

**A special wire brush like this will remove corrosion from the bulb socket**

**6** Double-filament bulbs normally have staggered indexing lugs, so, when installing the new bulb, be sure the indexing lugs match the socket. If the bulb does not rotate easily into place after pushing it firmly into the socket, do not force it; you've probably got the indexing lugs in the wrong slots. Remove the bulb, rotate it 180-degrees and try again.

**7** If the lens was removed, inspect the weather-sealing gasket to be sure it's not damaged. Replace it, if necessary.

*On dual-filament bulbs, the indexing lugs (arrows) are staggered*

## Side marker lights

**1** Much like the signal lights above, side marker lights are normally accessed in one of two ways: 1) by removing the lens or 2) by removing the bulb socket from inside the trunk or cargo area (rear) or inside the fender (front).

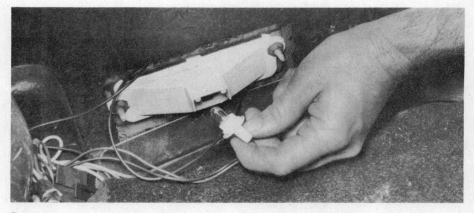

*This side marker bulb is accessible by removing the bulb socket*

**2** Press-in type side marker lights normally slide straight out of the socket, making replacement easy. Be sure to check for corrosion, loose wires and worn or missing terminals

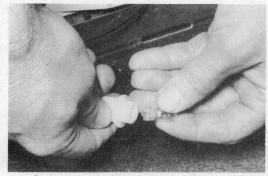

*Press-in bulbs like this simply slide out of the socket*

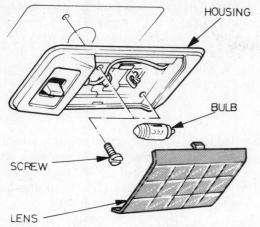

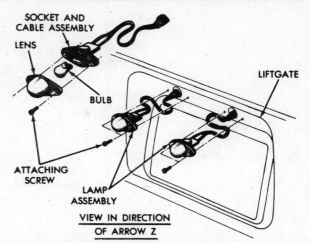

*Dome light bulbs, like this one on a Honda Accord, are often accessible after popping off the lens with a small screwdriver*

*The license plate light bulbs on this Chrysler station wagon are accessible after removing the lenses*

Replacement procedures for license plate, dome, map, ash tray and other bulbs vary greatly from vehicle to vehicle. Inspect the lens and housing carefully to find the easiest method of removal. Bayonet type bulbs are removed by pushing in firmly and rotating the bulb 1/4-turn counterclockwise. Cartridge and press-in type bulbs are removed by simply pulling them out.

## Headlights

Sealed beams are the traditional type of headlight, and many vehicles on the road today are still equipped with them. Depending on the design, a sealed beam uses either one or two tungsten filaments in a sealed glass case, which contains a non-oxygen atmosphere for the filament(s). Sealed beams containing one filament are used for the high beam. Sealed beams containing two filaments are used for both the high and low beams.

## Other light bulbs

## General information

### Sealed beams

*Headlights are marked to indicate their type and also to show which side goes up (the numbers are always at the top)*

Depending on the number of filaments, a sealed beam has two or three spade terminals extending through it's base. Dual-filament high/low beams have three terminals: one for high beam, one for low beam, and one for a ground. These lights have a number 2 formed into the lens to further aid in identifying them while they're on the vehicle. Single-filament high beams have only two terminals and have a number 1 formed into the lens.

## Halogen sealed beams

Since 1979, many vehicles have come originally equipped with halogen sealed beam headlights. Halogen (also know as quartz iodine or quartz halogen) sealed beams are also a popular lighting system upgrade for older vehicles, since they emit substantially more light than standard sealed beams. Upgrading is as easy as replacing lights, since halogen sealed beams are available in the same dimensions as standard sealed beams. Halogen lights are relatively inexpensive and draw about the same current as standard sealed beams, so it's usually not necessary to modify the vehicle's electrical system when upgrading. These lights are distinguished from standard sealed beams by the word "halogen" on their face.

*Halogen sealed beam headlights are marked on their face*

**Caution**: *Halogen lights get very hot. To avoid burning yourself, never touch a halogen light when it is on or shortly after it has been turned off. Also, do not install a standard sealed beam in a vehicle designed for a halogen light.*

## Aerodynamic headlights

In the early 1980's, some manufacturers began equipping vehicles with aerodynamic headlights. These lights are shaped so they offer less air resistance when the vehicle is moving down the road. Another feature of these lights is a small halogen inner bulb which can be replaced without removing or replacing the headlight assembly.

**Caution**: *The bulb in an aerodynamic headlight contains halogen gas under pressure. The bulb may shatter if it is scratched or dropped. Do not touch the glass. Handle the bulb by the base only.*

*An aerodynamic headlight*

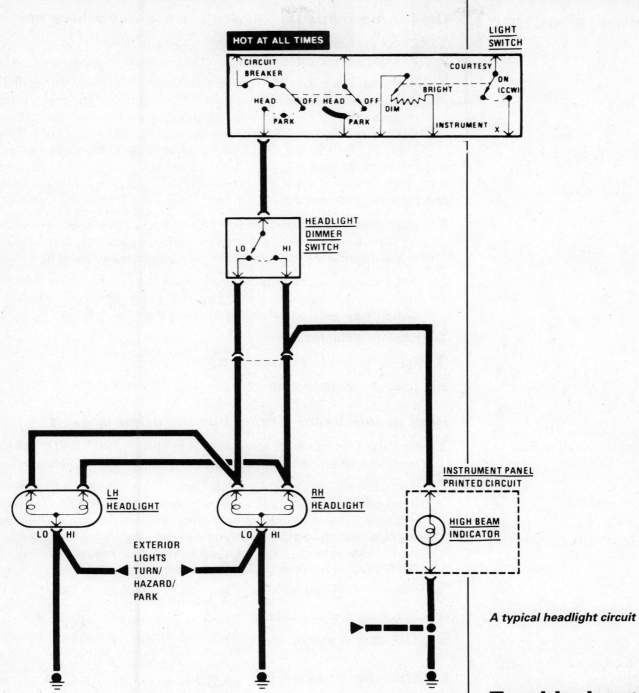

*A typical headlight circuit*

# Troubleshooting

When checking for a headlight failure, be sure to check the headlights on high and low beams. A two-filament light may have one of its filaments working, but the other may be burned out. Headlight circuits may have circuit breakers and/or fuses. Circuit breakers are normally located in the fuse panel or in the headlight switch. Some headlight systems have relays, either for the high beams only, or for both the high and low beams.

The most common failures are burned out or broken lights, blown fuses, corroded sockets and loose or dirty ground wires. The following is a list of common failures and diagnosis strategies.

# Haynes electrical manual

## One or more headlights don't work, but others do

**1** Check the fuse(s), look for corrosion at the fuse terminals and check for corrosion or a poor connection at the faulty light(s).

**2** If you haven't located the problem, connect a jumper wire between the ground terminal of the non-functioning headlight and a good chassis ground. Connect a fused jumper wire between the battery positive terminal and the positive terminal(s) of the headlight. If the headlight now works, check for a bad ground. If the headlight does not work, replace it.

## No headlights work

**1** Check the fuse or circuit breaker and look for corrosion at the fuse or circuit breaker terminals. If the fuse continues to blow or the circuit breaker continues to cycle, check for a short (see Chapter 3).

**2** If the vehicle has a headlight relay, check the relay. A quick (but not conclusive) check is to listen for a faint click when the headlight switch is turned on. To thoroughly check the relay, refer to Chapter 3.

**3** Check the dimmer switch.

**4** Check the headlight switch.

**5** Check for an open or short circuit (see Chapter 3).

## High or low beam works, but the other doesn't

**1** Check the fuse, look for corrosion at the fuse terminals and check for corrosion or a poor connection at the non-functioning light(s).

**2** If you haven't located the problem, connect a jumper wire between the ground terminal of each non-functioning light and a good chassis ground. Connect a fused jumper wire between the battery positive terminal and the positive terminals of each non-functioning light. If the lights now work, check for a bad ground, then proceed to Step 3. If the lights still don't work, replace them.

**3** Check the high-beam relay (if equipped) (see Chapter 3).

**4** Check the dimmer switch

**5** Check for an open or short circuit (see Chapter 3).

## Lights burn out quickly

An overcharging condition is indicated. Check the charging system (see Chapter 5).

## One headlight is dim, but others are normal

**1** Check for corrosion or a poor connection at the dim light.

**2** Check for a poor ground connection.

**3** Check for excessive voltage drop in the wiring to the light (see Chapter 3).

## All Lights go dim

**1** Check for a weak battery or a charging system malfunction (see Chapters 4 and 5).

**2** Check for corrosion at connections and other causes of high resistance in the headlight circuit.

## Lights flicker

**1** Check for loose or corroded connections at the headlights.

**2** Check for a loose or corroded ground connection.

**3** If the vehicle has a circuit breaker, check for a short circuit (which would cause the circuit breaker to cycle).

## Lights glare, blinding approaching drivers

**1** Check for a problem causing the rear of the vehicle to ride lower than normal (i.e., low tire pressure, incorrect tires or wheels, sagging rear springs).

**2** Adjust the headlights as described later in this Chapter.

---

**1** Remove the headlight bezel. In some cases, the bezel may be part of the vehicle's grille, so it may be necessary to remove the grille or part of the grille.

**2** Remove the three or four screws that secure the headlight retainer. DON'T disturb the (usually larger) headlight adjusting screws or the adjustment will be altered. Some vehicles have a spring attached to the retainer. Before removing the screws, use a hooked tool to detach it from the retainer. On some models with round headlights, you only need to loosen the retainer screws and rotate the retainer to disengage it from the screws.

# Headlight replacement

## Sealed beam headlights

*After removing the bezel, remove the headlight retainer screws – DON'T disturb the adjusting screws (arrows) or the headlight aim will be altered*

**3** Carefully remove the headlight retainer and pull the headlight out enough to unplug the connector behind it. Remove the headlight.

**4** Installation is the reverse of removal. Be sure the number on the lens is at the top. Check the headlights for proper operation and aiming before using them on the road. Normally, if the adjustment screws were not disturbed, the headlight will not need adjustment.

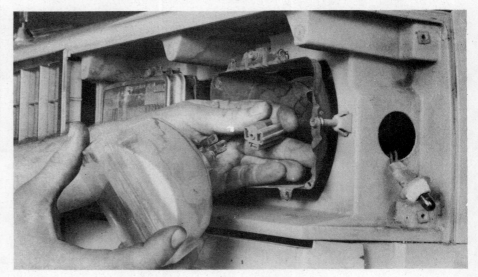

*Once the retainer is removed, unplug the headlight from its connector*

## Retractable headlights

**1** Expose the headlights by turning them on.

**2** Disconnect the negative cable from the battery.

**3** Allow the headlights to cool completely, then follow the procedure above for sealed beam headlights. Re-connect the battery's negative cable.

## Aerodynamic headlights

**Caution:** *The halogen inner bulb gets very hot in operation. Do not touch it while it's operating or shortly after it's been turned off. Don't remove the old bulb until a new bulb is ready to be installed. Leaving the bulb removed will allow dust and moisture to enter the headlight assembly and damage the reflector.*

**1** Open the hood and detach the electrical connector from the head-light bulb.

**2** Remove the bulb retaining ring by rotating it counterclockwise.

**3** Pull the bulb straight out of the socket. Do not touch the glass bulb. Hold it by the base.

**4** Install the bulb with the flat side of the base facing up. The bulb may need to be turned slightly left or right so the tabs align properly with the socket. Once the tabs are aligned, push the bulb into the socket. Slip the retaining ring over the base and turn it clockwise to lock it in place.

**5** Reinstall the electrical connector and check the lights for proper operation.

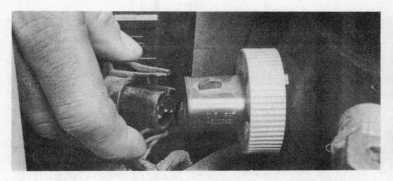

*To remove the bulb from an aerodynamic headlight, lift the tab on top of the connector and pull it out of the bulb, . . .*

*. . . remove the retaining ring by rotating it counterclockwise . . .*

*. . . then pull the bulb straight out*

Headlights must be aimed correctly. If adjusted incorrectly, they could blind the driver of an oncoming vehicle and cause a serious accident or seriously reduce your ability to see the road. The headlights should be checked for proper aim every 12 months and any time a new headlight is installed or front end body work is performed.

Headlights can be adjusted in a variety of ways. The following two procedures are within the abilities of most home mechanics

## Headlight aiming

*Here's where the adjusting screws are located on most rectangular headlights*

Before the headlights are adjusted, be sure there aren't any unusually heavy loads in the trunk, the gas tank is half-full and the tires are inflated to the proper pressure.

Headlights have two spring-loaded adjustment screws: one controlling vertical movement and one controlling horizontal movement. When adjusting, be sure to make the last turn of the adjustment screw clockwise.

*On this Toyota Camry with aerodynamic headlights, the upper adjusting screw (arrow) moves the beam horizontally and the lower screw (accessible under the housing with a Phillips head screwdriver) moves it vertically*

## Beam position aiming

This is the simplest method; however, it's only an interim step which will provide temporary adjustment until the headlights can be adjusted by a professional.

**1** Position the vehicle on a level surface, a few inches in front of a blank wall. The vehicle must be perpendicular to the wall.

**2** Attach masking tape vertically to the wall in reference to the vehicle centerline and the centerlines of the headlights.

**3** Now place a long piece of tape horizontally in reference to the center-lines of all the headlights.

**4** Move the vehicle straight back to a point 25 feet from the wall.

**5** Turn the headlights on and note the position of the high-intensity zone of the beams in relation to the tape marks.

**6** On low beam, the high intensity zones should be two inches below the horizontal line and two inches to the right of the headlight vertical lines. If you have a two-headlight system, you only need to adjust the headlights on low beam.

**7** In a four-light system, the high and low beams are adjusted separately. Adjust the low beams as described in the previous Step. To adjust the high beams, turn them on and note the position of the high intensity zones. They should be vertically centered, with the exact center just below the horizontal line.

**8** Adjustments are made by turning the adjustment screws as necessary to move the high intensity zones into their correct positions.

Mechanical aiming is more precise than beam position aiming. There are several methods, all requiring special aiming equipment. The method described below requires the use of two special aiming units: one for the left headlight and one for the right. They are normally available from automotive tool and equipment suppliers. With these, you can make horizontal and vertical adjustments with professional results.

## Mechanical aiming

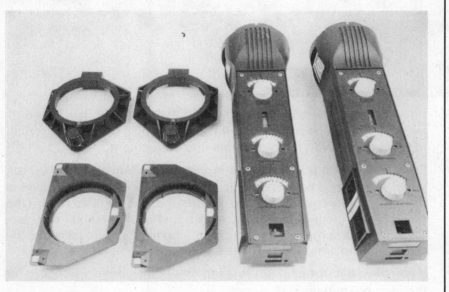

*Mechanical aiming devices like these can help you obtain professional results – on the left are adaptors for various types of headlights*

You can spend less by buying a single-unit aimer, but most of these can only be used to make vertical adjustments. Adjustments made with such aimers should be considered an interim step until the lights can be adjusted professionally.

**Note:** *The following procedure may not apply specifically to the type of aimers you have selected. Follow the instructions included with the aimers if they differ from these.*

**1**   Park the vehicle on a uniformly flat and smooth surface. A concrete driveway usually works well.

**2**   Lay each aimer unit on the floor in front of the vehicle and adjust its vertical level indicator until it's level with the floor. The indicator is usually a bubble in liquid, such as in a carpenter's level.

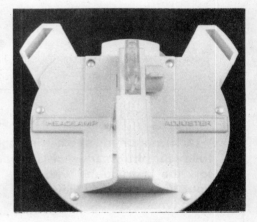

*An aiming device like this is quite inexpensive, but can only be used for vertical aiming*

**3**   Select the correct adaptor for the headlight type, then attach each unit to the correct headlight – the units are usually marked "right" and "left." If you have a four-headlight system, start with the low beams first.

*A suction cup holds the aimer in place on the headlight – be sure the small bumps on the surface of the headlight glass align with the notches in the aimer*

*Make the vertical adjustment before checking the horizontal aim*

**4** Check each unit's vertical level indicator. They should look the same as when they were on the floor. If necessary, turn the vertical adjusting screws to bring the headlights into adjustment.

**5** Next, look down the sight hole in each unit. Reflected in a mirror, you'll see the two horizontal adjusting marks, which should be lined up. If the marks are not lined up in both units, you'll need to turn the horizontal adjusting screw on one or both headlights until they are. This may take some trial and error, working from one headlight to the other, making small adjustments.

**6** If you have a four-headlight system, repeat the above procedure for the high beam lights.

## Installing auxiliary lights

Aftermarket fog and driving lights can greatly enhance visibility in difficult driving situations. The following photo sequence is intended to supplement the instructions that come with lighting kits. Follow the instructions with your kit when they differ from what's printed here.

We've chosen this set of KC fog lights to illustrate a typical installation – the set is relay-controlled and comes complete with a wiring harness, switch, relay and connectors. It can be ordered from KC HiLites, P.O. Box 155, Williams, AZ 86046

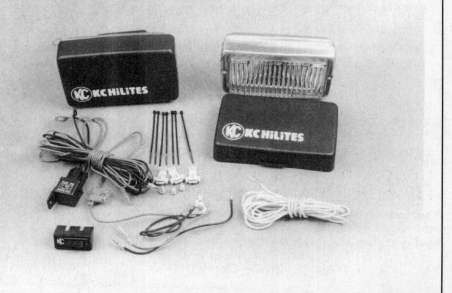

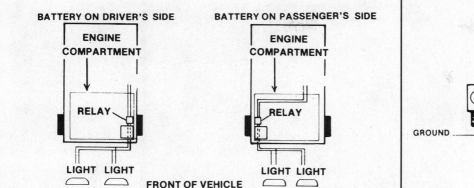

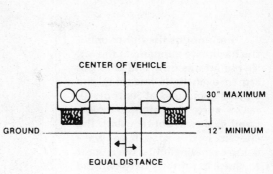

Before you begin installing the lights, lay out the wiring harness in the engine compartment to determine how you'll route the wires and where you'll mount the relay – to get the wires into the passenger compartment, you can usually take advantage of a hole that already exists in the firewall – make sure the hole has a grommet so the wires won't get chafed

First, decide where the lights will be mounted. Select a spot that's within 12 to 30 inches above the road and as close to the road as possible. Be sure the lights will not be in the way of the headlights and will not seriously disturb airflow through the radiator.

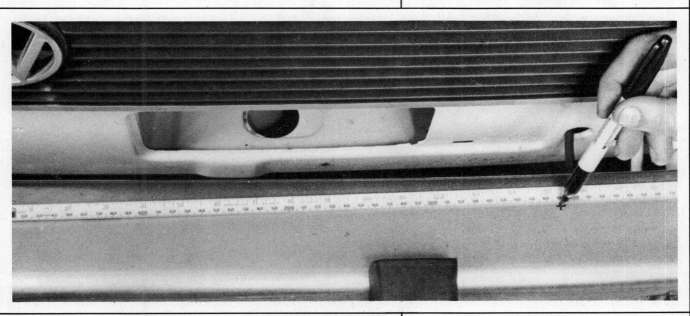

Carefully lay out the mounting locations of the lights – be sure they're an equal distance from the center of the vehicle. Before drilling any holes, make sure the lights will fit in the selected location with adequate clearance.

Drill holes at the mounting locations, . .

# Haynes electrical manual

. . . then mount the lights using the hardware supplied in the kit. If your kit has only one wire going to each light (meaning the light is grounded at its mount), make sure the mount makes good electrical contact with the chassis. In this case, if we were using one-wire lights, we'd want to check continuity between the bumper and the frame and add a ground strap, if necessary

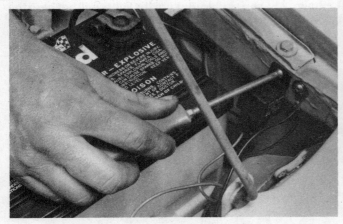

If your kit uses a relay and/or a separate ground connection for the lights, drill holes and attach them securely to the vehicle – make sure the ground connection makes good electrical contact with the chassis

You'll probably have to splice wires to hook up the lights. In accordance with the manufacturer's instructions, we've used snap-splice connectors here so we can tap into wires without cutting them – if the connections will be exposed to weather, it's a good idea to use solder (see Chapter 3)

Route the wires to the lights – try to run the wires along the vehicle's wiring harness or route them where they will not interfere with moving components and can be secured easily, away from sharp surfaces

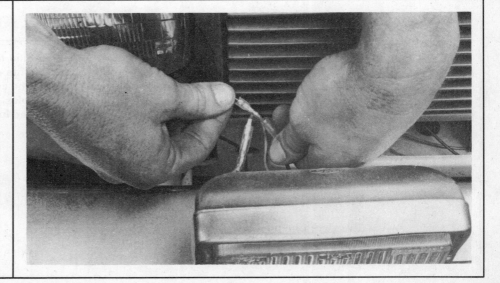

# Lighting systems

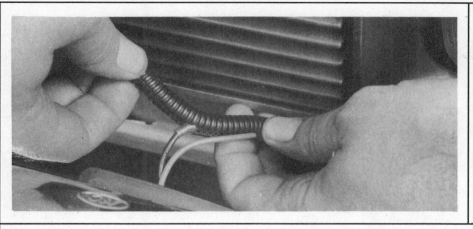

Our kit came with split vinyl conduit to fit over the wires – if yours doesn't, it's a good idea to get some for the areas of the wiring exposed to weather or abrasion.

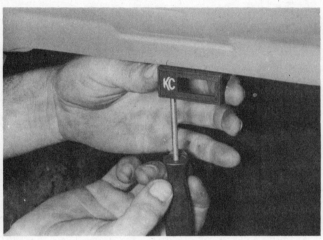

Working in the vehicle, locate the switch where it cannot be accidently turned on . . .

. . . then install it and hook up the electrical connections

Connect the positive wire to a positive power source – since our kit uses an in-line fuse, we're connecting directly to the battery – DO NOT hook up directly to the battery without a fuse!

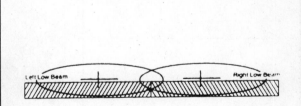

After the lights are installed, they'll have to be aimed. To aim fog lights, position the vehicle on a flat surface, 25 feet from a wall and turn on the headlight low beams. Mark the center of the beams with masking tape X's on the wall, then turn off the low beams and turn on the fog lights. Position the highest portion of the fog light beam so it's on or below the tape marks on the wall.

# Haynes electrical manual

## General information

## Turn signals and hazard warning lights

Generally, there are two types of turn signal systems. In one type, the wiring and bulbs for the rear turn signal lights are shared with the brake light circuit. To operate the turn signals in the rear, the turn signal flasher, when activated by the turn signal switch, connects and disconnects one of the brake/turn signal lights from the power source, bypassing the brake light switch. Separate circuits for the front turn signal lights are also operated through the turn signal switch and flasher.

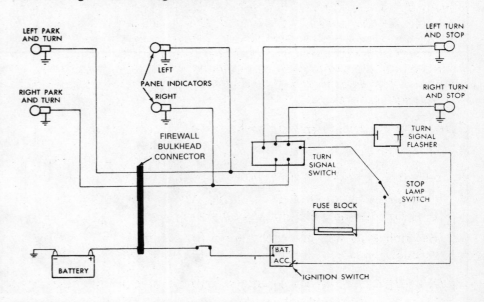

*Here's a typical example of a turn signal circuit that shares the rear portion of the wiring with the brake light circuit*

*A typical flasher unit*

In the other type of turn signal system, there are separate circuits for the turn signals and brake lights. When a rear turn signal light is blinking in this system, the brake lights, if applied, will remain on.

Hazard light circuits typically operate through the turn signal circuit. A separate flasher unit, when activated by the hazard light switch, connects and disconnects all turn signal lights from the power source.

There are several types of turn signal and hazard flashers, but their basic function is the same. Their location varies from manufacturer to manufacturer, but they are often located on or near the fuse panel. When replacing a faulty flasher unit you will find that most parts stores have "standard" and "heavy-duty" flashers. The heavy-duty type is primarily used in trucks and other vehicles which have many high wattage bulbs in the circuit. In most vehicles, a standard flasher is used. If you sometimes tow a trailer equipped with stop, turn and tail lights, you may need to use a heavy-duty flasher.

## Troubleshooting

The most common problems in the turn signal and hazard light circuits are burned out bulbs, blown fuses, defective flasher units and corroded or loose connections. The first step in diagnosing a failure is to visually check the lights. Operate the turn signal or hazard lights and walk around the vehicle, checking to see which lights are not working. Once you've identified the problem, check all the possible causes in the following list. If the symptom persists after checking all the possible causes, check the turn signal switch and wiring, as discussed in the procedure following the symptom list.

**Note:** *On some vehicles, the turn signal switch and hazard light switch (usually integrated into one unit) are wired separately, but the wiring between the switches and lights is shared. This makes checking the wiring between the switch and the signal lights simple. For example, if the turn signals do not work on one or both sides, but do work when the hazard lights are turned on, you know the wiring between the turn signal/hazard switch and the lights is good. The problem probably lies at the turn signal fuse, flasher or switch.*

### One turn signal light on one side doesn't work

**1** Check the bulb.

**2** Check for a corroded, worn or damaged bulb socket.

**3** Check for a bad ground. Use a jumper wire between the ground side of the turn signal bulb and a good chassis ground.

**4** Beginning at the non-functioning light and working backward through the circuit, check for a short or open (see Chapter 3).

### Hazard lights or turn signals light but don't flash

Replace the turn signal or hazard flasher

### Turn signals don't light in either direction

**1** Check for a blown fuse.

**2** Check the turn signal bulbs.

**3** Check for corroded, worn or damaged bulb sockets.

**4** Check for a bad ground. Use a jumper wire between the ground side of the turn signal bulbs and a good chassis ground.

**5** Replace the turn signal flasher.

**6** Check the turn signal switch (see below).

**7** Check for a short or open (see Chapter 3).

### Front and rear turn signal lights on one side don't work

**1** Check the bulbs.

**2** Check for corroded, worn or damaged bulb sockets.

**3** Check for bad grounds. Use jumper wires between the ground sides of the turn signal bulbs and a good chassis ground.

**4** Check the turn signal switch (see below).

### Flasher rate too fast or too slow

**1**   Make sure the correct flasher is installed.

**2**   Make sure the correct bulbs are installed.

**3**   If the rate is too fast, check for an overcharging condition (see Chapter 5). If the rate is too slow, check for a weak battery or an undercharging condition (see Chapters 4 and 5).

### Indicator light(s) on dash panel don't flash (glow steadily)

**1**   Check the signal lights with the circuit turned on.

**2**   If the signal lights are also glowing steadily, replace the flasher.

**3**   If the signal lights are not on, check the signal light bulb.

**4**   Check for a corroded, worn or damaged bulb socket.

**5**   Check for a bad ground. Use a jumper wire between the ground side of the non-functioning signal light(s) and a good chassis ground.

**6**   Beginning at the non-functioning light(s) and working backward through the circuit, check for an open.

### Indicator light(s) don't work, but signal lights do

Check for a burned out indicator light bulb, corroded socket or bad ground connection.

### Turn signals work but hazard lights don't

**1**   Replace the hazard flasher.

**2**   Check for a faulty hazard flasher switch (these are usually integral with the turn signal switch).

## Turn signal switch check and replacement

**Check**

Note: *The check and replacement of the turn signal switch varies from vehicle to vehicle. Be sure to check the appropriate Haynes Automotive Repair Manual for your particular vehicle. Before following this procedure, be sure you have checked all other possible causes of the failure (see above).*

**1**   Locate the correct wiring diagram for the vehicle. Determine which wire carries current from the turn signal flasher to the turn signal switch and which wires carry current from the switch to the turn signal lights.

**2**   Find the turn signal switch connector, located near the bottom of the steering column. You may have to remove a cover from below the column.

**3**   Find the terminals on the connector associated with wires you identified in Step 1.

*To access the turn signal switch connector, you may have to remove a cover below the steering column*

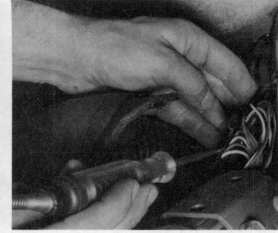

*Probing the back side of the switch connector with a test light*

**4**  Turn on the left turn signal.

**5**  Connect a test light to the back side of the terminals you identified in Step 1. Don't unplug the connector.

**6**  The test light should flash when you probe the terminal that supplies current to the switch. If it doesn't, there's an open in the circuit between the battery and the switch.

**7**  The light should also flash when you probe the terminals that carry current to the left turn signal lights. The light should not light when you probe the terminals that supply current to the right turn signal lights.

**8**  Turn on the right turn signal and repeat the previous Step.

**9**  If the switch fails any of the tests in Steps 7 and 8, replace it.

## Replacement

The replacement procedures for turn signal switches vary greatly from vehicle to vehicle. The following procedure applies to many General Motors vehicles; however, you should always check the Haynes Automotive Repair manual for your specific vehicle. **Warning:** *To avoid system damage and possible personal injury, do not perform this procedure on models equipped with airbags. Take the vehicle to a dealer service department.*

**10**  Remove the steering wheel cover to expose the securing nut. In some cases, a small cover in the center simply pulls off. In other cases, screws at the back of the steering wheel secure the cover. Disconnect any wires running from the cover to the steering wheel.

*On this steering wheel, screws at the back secure the cover*

*Removing the snap-ring from the steering shaft*

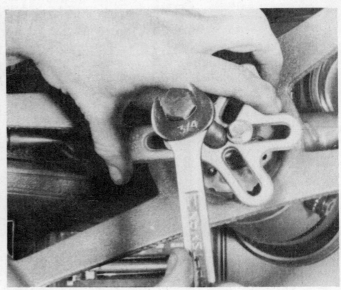

*Removing the steering wheel with a puller*

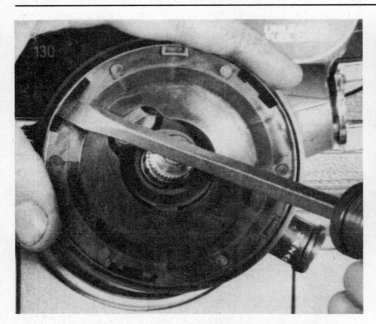

*Remove the plastic cover plate, if equipped*

*Remove the snap-ring and lock plate*

**11** If there's a snap-ring on the steering shaft, above the securing nut, remove it.

**12** Mark the relationship of the steering wheel to the steering shaft to ensure proper alignment on installation.

**13** Remove the steering wheel securing nut, then use a puller to detach the steering wheel from the shaft.

**14** Remove the plastic cover plate, if equipped.

*Remove the cancelling plate and spring*

*On some models, like this one, a screw in the center secures the hazard switch button; on others, it simply unscrews. Once you've removed the button, remove the three screws (arrows) – you may have to rotate the outer portion of the switch to expose all the screws*

**15** Remove the lock plate. It's held in place by a snap-ring that fits into a groove in the steering shaft. The lock plate must be depressed to relieve pressure on the snap-ring. A special U-shaped tool which fits on the shaft should be used to depress the lock plate as the snap-ring is removed from its groove.

**16** Lift off the cancelling plate and spring.

**17** Remove the screw that attaches the turn signal lever to the switch, then detach the lever from the side of the column.

**18** Remove the hazard flasher button, then remove the three screws that secure the turn signal switch.

**19** Disconnect the electrical connector located on the steering column, under the dash. It may be necessary to remove a panel for access.

**20** Tape the switch connector terminals to prevent damage, then feed the connector up through the column support bracket and pull the switch, wiring harness and connector out the top of the steering column.

**21** Installation is the reverse of removal, but note the following: Make sure the wiring harness is in the protector as it is pulled into position. Set the switch in the neutral position before sliding it over the shaft. When installing the steering wheel, be sure to align the marks you made when you removed it.

*Pull the switch, wiring harness and connector out the top of the steering column*

# Haynes electrical manual

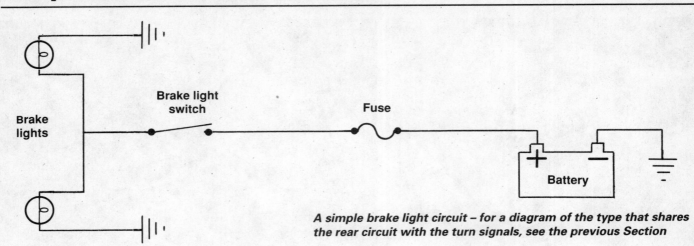

Brake light switch

Fuse

Brake lights

Battery

*A simple brake light circuit – for a diagram of the type that shares the rear circuit with the turn signals, see the previous Section*

## Brake lights

### General information

The brake light circuit has a switch mounted on the brake pedal or pedal support. On some vehicles, such as Volkswagens, the switch is mounted in the master cylinder and is hydraulically operated.

The brake lights on many vehicles use the same circuit as the rear turn signals. On these vehicles, current flows from the brake light switch, through the turn signal switch and then to the brake lights. For a diagram of this type of circuit, see the Section on turn signals in this Chapter.

Since 1986, vehicles sold in the U.S. have a third or high-level brake light mounted in the rear window or built into the rear of the vehicle. These lights are wired separately from the turn signal lights and work only when the brakes are applied.

### Troubleshooting

#### One brake light does not work, but others do

1  Check the bulb.

2  Check the bulb socket for corrosion, damage and worn terminals.

3  Check for a bad ground connection by hooking up a jumper wire between the negative terminal of the non-functioning light and a good chassis ground. If the light now works, repair the faulty ground connection.

4  Beginning at the non-functioning light and working backward through the circuit, check for an open or short (see Chapter 3).

#### No brake lights work

1  Check the fuse and check for corrosion at the fuse terminals.

2  Check the brake light switch (see below).

3  Check for a bad ground at the brake light bulbs (see above), burned out bulbs and corroded or loose connections.

**4** On vehicles where the brake light circuit is shared with the rear portion of the turn signal circuit, the *turn signal* switch may be faulty. Check it as discussed in the previous Section, but note the following:

   a) In Step 1, instead of locating the wire going from the turn signal flasher to the turn signal switch, locate the wire going from the brake light switch to the turn signal switch.

   b) In Step 4, instead of turning on the turn signal switch, activate the brake light switch or connect a jumper wire between the terminals of its connector.

   c) In Steps 6 and 7, the test light will glow steadily instead of flashing.

   d) In Step 7, the test light should light at all the switch-to-light terminals.

   e) Ignore Step 8.

### Brake light bulbs burn out quickly

Check for an overcharging condition (see Chapter 5).

---

**1** To find the brake light switch, check the Haynes Automotive Repair Manual for your vehicle. On most vehicles, it's located on the brake pedal arm, on a bracket above the pedal arm or on the master cylinder.

**2** If your vehicle has cruise control, there may be two switches or the brake light switch may have four terminals: two for the brake lights and two for the cruise control. If you're not sure which switch or terminals are for the brake light switch, check the wiring diagram for your vehicle.

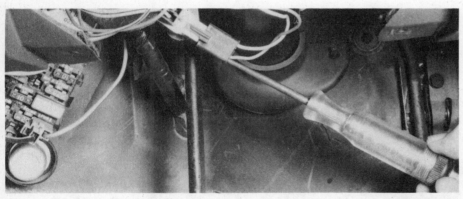

**3** After locating the brake light switch, probe the two terminals in the switch's electrical connector with a test light. The light should light when checking one of the terminals. It should not light when checking the other terminal. If it doesn't light at either terminal, there's an open or short between the battery and the switch.

**4** Use your hand to firmly depress the brake pedal and check the terminals again with the test light. This time, the light should light at both terminals. If it only lights at one terminal, the brake light switch must be adjusted or replaced. Check the Haynes Automotive Repair Manual for procedures specific to your vehicle.

## Brake light switch check

*Probing the terminals at the brake light switch with a test light*

## General information

## Back-up lights

Back-up light circuits are almost identical to simple brake light circuits. They are operated by a mechanical switch that turns the lights on when the transmission is in Reverse. Switch locations vary from vehicle to vehicle, but most are mounted somewhere on the gearshift linkage or the steering column. Some switches are mounted on the transmission and are operated by a cam within the transmission. On some vehicles with an automatic transmission, the back-up light switch is mounted on or near the neutral safety switch.

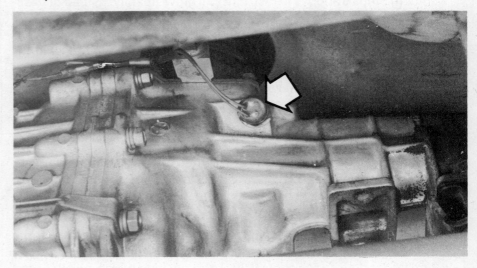

*This back-up light switch is mounted in the transmission case (arrow)*

## Troubleshooting

Since back-up light circuits are highly similar to simple brake light circuits, the same troubleshooting procedures apply. The primary difference between the two types of circuits is that back-up light circuits are usually wired through the ignition switch, and the ignition switch must be on for the back-up lights to work. If the troubleshooting procedures listed in the Section on brake lights do not solve your problems, suspect a faulty ignition switch.

*This Ford neutral safety switch has an integral back-up light switch – it's mounted on the transmission case where the shift linkage hooks up*

# Wiring a trailer

A trailer lighting system is generally simpler than the vehicle's lighting system. Usually, a trailer has brake lights, turn signal lights and side marker lights. Very few trailers are equipped with back-up lights. However, before you purchase any equipment, you should check your state vehicle code to see what equipment is required to be legal. Many auto parts stores stock trailer lighting equipment, including kits which contain lights, wiring and connectors.

The rear-facing bulbs on conventional trailer lights are dual-filament: one filament for the tail light and one for the brake and turn signal lights. This makes them easily compatible with vehicles that have combined brake light and rear turn signal circuits. If the tow vehicle has separate lights for the brake lights and rear turn signals, you'll need a special converter to tow trailers with conventional lights.

Side marker lights are not always legally required, but are highly recommended even if they're not required. They use single-filament bulbs with a red lens in the rear and an amber lens in front. Don't reverse this lens arrangement or install the same color lenses front and rear; this is a standard arrangement and it's usually illegal to deviate from it

If the trailer will be used to carry a boat, and you'll be launching the boat from the trailer, it's best to obtain special waterproof lights. These have watertight housings that keep the bulb and socket dry when the trailer is submerged.

**This rear side marker light is combined on the same mounting bracket with the main rear-facing light – be sure the marker light in the rear is red . . .**

## Obtaining the necessary equipment

**This converter permits vehicles with separate brake light and rear turn signal circuits to tow trailers with conventional lights (which have combined brake light and turn signal circuits)**

**. . . and the one in front is amber**

# Haynes electrical manual

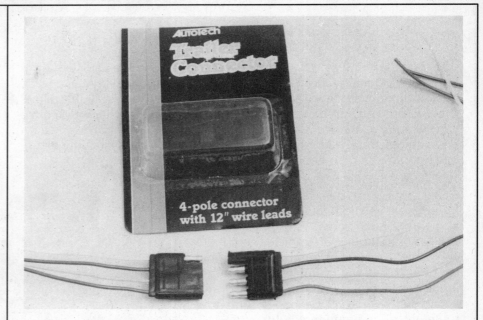

Here's a typical trailer connector with four wires – be sure the female end of the connector (on left) is connected to the tow vehicle – this prevents accidental shorts when the trailer is not connected and the connector end is stowed in the trunk or cargo area

Since the trailer won't be permanently attached to the tow vehicle, you'll need to install a connector between the tow vehicle and trailer, somewhere near the trailer tongue. Standard trailer connectors normally have four wires on each side (one for each brake light/turn signal, one for the tail lights and one for ground). Get one that can only be connected one way so you won't make any mistakes when you hook up the trailer. Also, when installing the connector, make sure the female half of the connector is installed on the tow vehicle. This prevents shorts when the trailer is not connected.

## Attaching the lights

Trailer lights are normally designed for universal installation. Usually, all you need to do is drill one or two holes at the mounting location (make sure the lights are at the legal height above the road and visible from a following vehicle). Since trailers tend to vibrate, be sure to use lockwashers when mounting the lights.

## Connecting and routing the trailer wires

Although most trailer lighting kits include snap-splice connectors, it's best not to use them when wiring the trailer itself. A good soldering job produces the most reliable and weatherproof connection. Use shrink-wrap to insulate soldered connections on the trailer (see Chapter 3).

Nylon clamps like this are the best way to secure the wiring to the trailer

**Don't wrap wire around metal objects like this – trailer vibration may cut the insulation, causing shorts**

When routing wires along the trailer, use nylon clamps or tie-straps. Do not wrap wires around metal parts (such as bolts or wire clips). Vibration will cause the insulation to wear through, and the wire will be shorted to ground.

When making ground connections, you have two choices. The best method is to run a separate ground wire from each light, which all join to a common ground wire, which is connected securely to a known good ground on the tow vehicle. If you want to save some wire and trust the trailer frame as a good ground, you can use an alternative method: connect the ground wire from each light to the trailer frame, then connect a wire between the front of the trailer frame and a known good ground on the tow vehicle.

If you use the trailer frame for a ground path, make sure your connections are secure and attached to bare metal – you may have to scrape away some paint

**Note:** *Be sure to use the female end of the trailer connector on the tow vehicle to prevent the possibility of shorts when the trailer is not connected.*

On vehicles where the rear turn signal and brake light circuits are shared, four connections need to be made: one for the left turn/brake light, one for the right turn/brake light, one for the tail light and one for ground. On vehicles with separate brake light and turn signal circuits, five connections are necessary: one for the brake lights, one for each turn signal, one for the tail lights and one for ground.

## Wiring the tow vehicle

# Haynes electrical manual

Once you've located the wiring to the tow vehicle's lights (usually it's inside the trunk), trace it toward the front of the vehicle, to a connector where you can hook up a test light. Turn on each turn signal and check the wiring with the test light. When the test light flashes, you know you've found the brake/turn signal wire (vehicles with combined circuits) or the turn signal wire (vehicles with separate circuits).

Next, turn off the turn signals and turn on the parking lights. Again check the wiring with the test light. When the test light glows, you've found the tail light wire.

If the vehicle has separate brake/turn signal circuits, you'll also next need to locate the brake light wire. Have an assistant depress the brake pedal while you again check the connector with a test light. When the test light glows, you've found the brake light wire. If you'll be using conventional trailer lights, be sure to use a converter between the vehicle's and trailer's wiring.

Before connecting the wiring to the vehicle's harness, be sure it's the right length. Hook up the trailer to get a good idea of the necessary length. Be sure to leave enough slack for extreme right and left turns.

Snap-splice connectors will allow you to tap into the tow vehicle's wires without disturbing them (see Chapter 3). This type of connector should be sufficient inside the vehicle, where the connections won't be exposed to weather. However, as discussed earlier, they're usually not the best bet on the trailer itself.

It's okay to route the wiring between the trunk weatherstrip and trunk lid. Just be sure the wiring is clamped lightly – clamped tightly enough so no strain is placed on the connections inside the trunk, but not so tight as to damage the wiring.

**Tap into the vehicle's wires where they're most accessible – it's a good idea to use a few nylon clamps so the connections won't be strained in use**

**If the wiring is coming from inside the trunk, it's ok to clamp the wiring between the trunk and weatherstrip – be sure there's enough slack in the wiring to allow for turns in both directions**

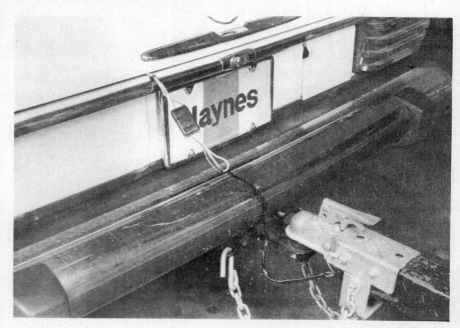

# 7

# Indicator lights and gauges

The dashboard indicator lights and gauges are your "eyes" into the vehicle's vital signs. They keep you informed of the operating conditions of the engine and electrical system. Instrument panels include various combinations of gauges and indicator lights. Most vehicles use an array of indicator lights in combination with a few gauges. Some instrument panels are equipped with gauges for every engine and electrical function, but they're usually found only on sportier or more expensive models. We'll look at gauges in a minute. First, let's look at some typical indicator light circuits.

## Indicator light circuits

An indicator light is usually nothing more than a small lens with a bulb behind it. Typically, it tells you the nature of the warning with a printed statement (Door Ajar, Tail Lamp Out, etc.), or a small International Standards Organization (ISO) symbol (a gas pump, a thermometer in water, etc.). This warning is printed on the dash immediately below each indicator light on older vehicles; on newer vehicles, it's usually printed right on the lens itself.

*A typical indicator light display uses a light behind a red lens with the type of problem or condition being indicated imprinted on the lens*

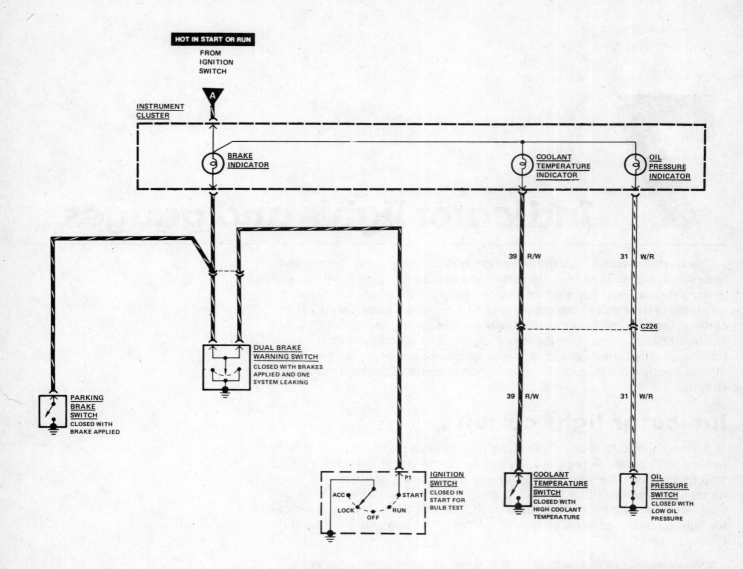

*A schematic of typical indicator light circuits*

The sending unit in an indicator light circuit is a switch connected to a device that senses changes in oil pressure, coolant temperature or whatever parameter the sending unit is designed to monitor. The switch is normally open, but, when the parameter being monitored goes out of an acceptable range, the sensing device closes the switch contacts, completing the circuit to ground and causing the indicator light to illuminate.

Most indicator lights also illuminate when you turn the ignition key to On or Start. This "self test" mode is designed to tell you the indicator light bulb and wiring are in good shape.

Indicator light circuits are normally very dependable, but when a problem does occur, the sending unit, wiring connections or light bulb is usually at fault.

# Indicator lights and gauges

Adequate oil pressure is critical to proper engine function, so most vehicles are equipped with some sort of oil pressure indicator light. The oil pressure indicator light on the dash is connected to an oil pressure sending unit on the engine. This sending unit contains a diaphragm which responds to changes in oil pressure. When oil pressure is below a pre-set value (usually about five psi), the switch is closed and the light on the dash is illuminated. When oil pressure rises above the pre-set value, the diaphragm opens the switch, interrupting the indicator light's path to ground and turning off the light.

## Oil pressure indicator light

*A typical oil pressure sending unit for an indicator light – this Volkswagen unit is mounted at the rear of the cylinder head . . .*

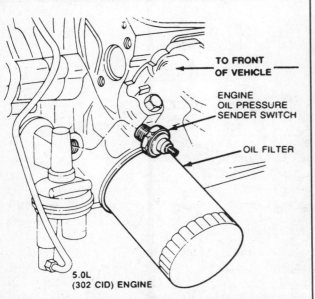

TO FRONT OF VEHICLE

ENGINE OIL PRESSURE SENDER SWITCH

OIL FILTER

5.0L (302 CID) ENGINE

*. . . this Ford unit is located next to the oil filter on the front of the engine . . .*

*. . . and this Hyundai unit is located on the side of the engine block, below the exhaust manifold*

The oil pressure sending unit is located on the engine, usually high on the cylinder head or at the rear of the engine block, as far from the oil pump as the manufacturer could put it. Why so far from the pump? Because the farther it is from the pump, the lower the pressure. If pressure is good at the sending unit, it's usually OK anywhere in the lubrication system.

If the oil pressure light circuit is operating properly, the light should be illuminated when the ignition key is turned to On (engine off), then go out within a few seconds after the engine is started. If the light comes on during engine operation, turn off the engine immediately and locate the problem before returning the vehicle to normal service.

## Engine temperature indicator light

A safe operating temperature is also critical to proper engine operation. When engine coolant temperature rises too high (usually about 250-degrees F), coolant boilover and major engine damage can occur. The engine temperature indicator light warns the driver when coolant temperature rises too high, allowing him to shut the vehicle down before major damage occurs.

Most engine temperature indicator circuits function the same as oil pressure indicator circuits. The primary difference is in the sending unit, which is immersed in engine coolant. A bimetallic strip in the sending unit is sensitive to temperature changes and bends to close the sending unit contacts (and thus connect the indicator light to ground) when coolant temperature reaches a predetermined level.

*A typical coolant temperature sending unit for an indicator light – this GM unit is located at the front of the engine . . .*

*. . . and this Dodge unit is located in the thermostat housing*

COOLANT SWITCH

THERMOSTAT HOUSING

# Indicator lights and gauges

Some engine temperature indicator circuits have two lights, one to indicate the "too hot" condition and another to indicate when the engine temperature is *below* the normal operating range. This system uses a coolant temperature sending unit with two terminals. The sending unit is connected to two light bulbs on the dash and to the battery through the ignition switch. When the ignition switch is first turned on to start the cold engine, a bimetallic strip inside the sending unit closes the circuit between the battery and the Cold light. The Cold light, which is usually blue, comes on and stays on until the engine approaches its normal operating temperature. As the coolant heats up, the bimetallic strip inside the sending unit starts to bend. By the time the coolant reaches its normal operating temperature, the bimetallic strip bends enough to cease contact with the terminal for the Cold light, opening that circuit and turning off the blue light. If the engine coolant overheats, the bimetallic strip bends even further and contacts the other terminal, closes the circuit and turns on the red Hot light.

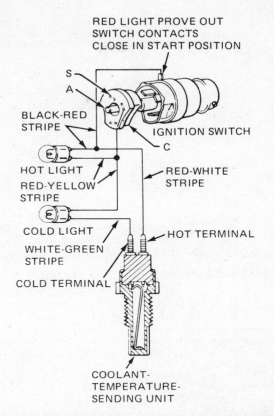

*This Ford temperature indicator system uses two lights to indicate both when the engine has overheated and when temperature is* below *the normal operating range*

## Low fuel level indicator light

All vehicles are equipped with a fuel level gauge (which we'll get to in a moment). Some vehicles also have a special indicator light which turns on when the fuel tank is nearly empty, giving the driver an additional warning that the fuel supply is getting low.

The low fuel level indicator light circuit includes the warning light, a relay and a thermistor assembly in the tank. A thermistor is a special type of resistor that *loses* resistance as its heats up (just the reverse of a typical wire resistor). As long as there's enough fuel in the tank, the thermistor is submerged in the fuel and stays cool. But when the fuel drops below a certain level, the thermistor is exposed to vapors and starts to heat up. This allows more current to flow from the battery through the warning relay winding. The increased current flow through the relay winding produces a stronger magnetic field. When the field becomes strong enough to pull the relay contact points together, it completes the circuit from the battery to the indicator light, warning the driver that the fuel supply is low.

Low fuel level indicator circuits usually have a self-testing circuit to verify the light bulb, relay and wires are OK. When the ignition switch is turned to Start, a pair of contacts in the ignition switch connect the relay directly to the battery to turn on the warning light. If the light is malfunctioning, but comes on when the key is turned to Start, the problem is likely in the wiring to the thermistor or in the thermistor itself. If the light doesn't come on when the key is turned to Start, the bulb is burned out, the relay is defective or the circuit is open or shorted.

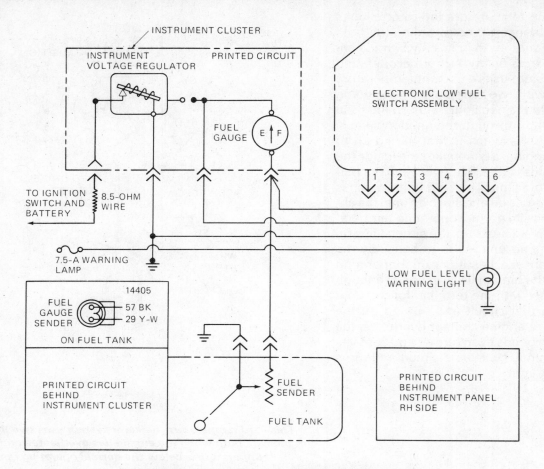

*A typical electronic low fuel level indicator circuit*

Some newer vehicles use an electronic low-fuel-level warning system. This system also has a fuel-level indicator light, but instead of using a thermistor in the tank, it monitors the voltage difference between the two terminals of the fuel gauge. As the needle moves toward E (empty), the voltage increases. When the tank is about one-eighth full, the voltage is great enough to turn on the low-fuel-level warning light.

## Charge indicator light

The charge indicator light is connected between the voltage regulator and the battery through the ignition switch. The indicator light is connected in parallel with a resistor. Current flows through the resistor and the indicator light on its way to the alternator field. The voltage drop through the resistor provides enough voltage to the indicator light to make the light glow. It glows until the engine starts and the alternator begins to charge the battery. When this happens, the voltage is the same on both sides of the resistor and the light. So the light goes off, indicating that the alternator is charging the battery. On some vehicles with an internal regulator type alternator, the light also comes on when charging voltage is too high. Note that – unlike temperature, pressure and low-fuel-level indicating circuits – the charge indicator light circuit has no sending unit.

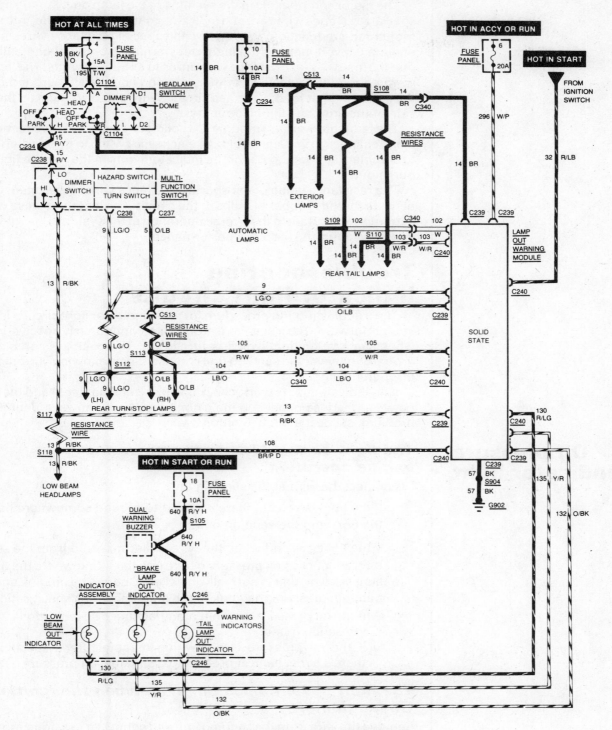

*A typical lamp out warning system*

Lamp out warning systems monitor the operation of low beam headlights, brake lights and tail lights. The arrangement of lamp out indicators varies from one vehicle to another, but the basic operation of most systems is the same.

## Lamp out warning system

The major components in the system are the lamp out warning module, special resistance wires and the indicator light(s). When all the lights being monitored are functioning properly, the special resistance wires provide about a 0.5 volt input to the lamp out warning module. If one bulb goes out, the input of the resistance wire drops to about 0.25 volts. The lamp out warning module detects this difference and completes a ground path to the indicator light for the affected circuit. With battery voltage on the other side of the light, the light illuminates.

The lamp out warning module is a solid-state unit designed to measure small changes in voltage levels. An electronic switch in the module closes to complete a ground path for the indicator lights in the event a light bulb burns out.

The resistance value of the special resistance wires is selected to compensate for the number of bulbs in the circuit. The length of these wires is extremely important to the overall operation of the system. Changing their length will hurt the system's performance.

# Troubleshooting indicator light circuits

The troubleshooting procedure for most indicator light circuits is pretty straightforward. Basically, indicator lights continuously receive voltage whenever the ignition switch is turned on. The circuit is completed to ground whenever the sending unit contacts close, allowing current to flow through the light.

If no indicator lights work, check the fuse (see Chapter 1) and the wiring between the fuse panel and indicator lights. If you haven't identified the problem, suspect a faulty ignition switch.

## Oil pressure indicator light

### *The light on the dash comes on during engine operation*

Disconnect the wire at the sending unit.

**1** If the light is still on, there's a short to ground somewhere between the light and the sending unit.

**2** If the light goes off when the wire is disconnected from the sending unit, connect an oil pressure gauge into the fitting where the oil pressure sending unit is normally installed. Operate the engine and compare the pressure readings to the manufacturer's specifications.

   a) If the oil pressure is within manufacturer's specifications, replace the sending unit.

   b) If the oil pressure is not within manufacturer's specifications, there's a mechanical problem causing low oil pressure.

### *The light never comes on, even when the ignition is On (engine off)*

Remove the wire from the sending unit and connect it to a good ground on the engine.

**1** If this causes the light to come on, check for a bad connection at the sending unit. If the connection is good, replace the sending unit.

**2** If the light still doesn't come on, check the indicator bulb, socket and the wiring between the bulb and sending unit. If they check out OK, the problem is in the ignition switch or the wiring between the fuse panel and the light.

### *The light comes on when the engine is operating*

**1** Check the strength of the antifreeze, the radiator cap and the cooling system for leaks (refer to the Haynes Automotive Repair Manual for your particular vehicle).

**2** If you know the cooling system is operating properly and the engine is not overheating, but the light still comes on when the engine is operating, check for a short to ground in the wiring between the indicator light bulb and sending unit. If the wiring is OK, replace the sending unit.

### *The light does not operate*

**1** The light should illuminate in the "self test" mode (usually when the ignition key is turned to Start). If it doesn't, leave the ignition on (engine off), remove the wire from the sending unit and ground it on the engine block. If the light now illuminates, check for a bad connection at the sending unit. If the connection is OK, replace the sending unit.

**2** If the light does not illuminate when the wire is grounded, check the bulb, bulb socket and wiring between the bulb and sending unit. If they check out OK, the problem is in the ignition switch or the wiring between the fuse panel and the light.

## Electric gauge circuits

There are two types of electrically operated fuel gauges – balancing-coil and thermostatic.

Balancing coil systems consist of a sending unit and a gauge on the dash. Both units are connected in series by a wire to the battery (through the ignition switch). When the ignition switch is turned on, current from the battery flows through both the sending unit and gauge. The sending unit consists of a variable resistor and a sliding contact that's connected to a float lever. As the fuel level in the tank rises and falls, the float lever moves up and down, which in turn alters the position of the sliding contact on the variable resistor.

As the fuel level goes down, the float moves down too, and the sliding contact moves to reduce the resistance. So most of the current passing through the left-hand coil in the gauge flows through the resistor to ground. Little current flows through the right-hand coil, so the left-hand coil is magnetically stronger than the right-hand coil. The armature – and the pointer – thus swing to the left, and indicate a low fuel level.

When the fuel level is high, the float is up, and the sliding contact adds more resistance to the circuit. Therefore, most of the current going through the left-hand coil continues on through the right-hand coil. Thus the right-hand coil is relatively stronger and this causes the armature and pointer to swing toward the right, indicating a high fuel level.

## Coolant temperature indicator light

## Fuel gauges

### Balancing-coil type fuel gauges

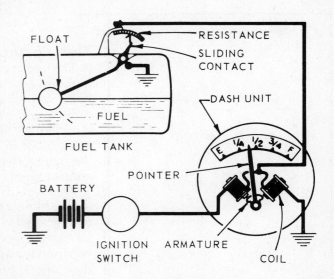

*A typical balancing coil type fuel gauge system*

# Haynes electrical manual

## Thermostatic type fuel gauges

There are two types of thermostatic fuel gauges. The older type has thermostatic blades (bimetallic strips) in both the tank unit and the dash unit. The newer type has a thermostatic blade in the dash but uses a variable resistor – similar to the unit for a balancing coil type described previously – in the fuel tank. Let's look at the older type first.

## Twin thermostatic blade type

The tank float actuates a cam that causes more or less warpage of the thermostat blade in the tank. The blade has a heating coil wrapped around it, and this coil is connected through a similar heating coil in the gauge unit to the battery (through the ignition switch). When the ignition is turned on, current flows through both coils and heats up the thermostat blades in both the gauge and the sending unit, bending both blades. In the dash unit, this bending movement is transferred by linkage to the dash pointer, causing it to move across the indicator face. In the tank unit, the bending blade eventually causes a set of contacts to open. If the fuel level is low, the original bending produced by the cam is slight. Only a small amount of bending (by the heating coil effect) will cause the contacts to open. As soon as they open, the heating effect ceases in both the instrument panel and the tank units. The thermostatic blades begin to straighten. In the tank unit, the contacts close again and the heating effect takes place once again. The contacts continue to open and close like this constantly. The amount of warpage produced in the tank thermostatic blade is, therefore, approximately reproduced in the dash unit. This causes the dash unit to indicate the fuel level in the tank.

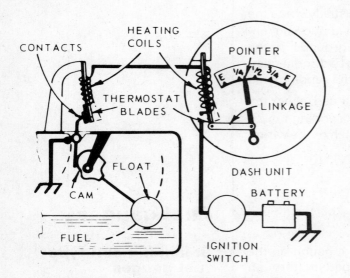

*A typical twin thermostatic blade type fuel gauge system*

## Thermostatic blade/variable resistor type

The newer type of thermostatic fuel gauge uses a variable resistor in the tank and a thermostatic blade in the gauge. The fuel sender unit in the tank has a resistor and a sliding contact that slides up and down as the float moves up and down. When it's up, indicating a full tank, the resistance is at a minimum, allowing maximum current to flow. This heats the thermostatic blade in the gauge to its maximum, causing it to warp and moving the needle to F (indicating a full tank). Note that this system doesn't use contact points that open and close.

This type of fuel gauge uses an instrument voltage regulator which is also thermostatic in operation. When the coil in the voltage regulator is connected to the battery, it heats up, causing the thermostatic blade to warp. As the blade warps, it opens the contact points, disconnecting the coil from the battery. The coil cools, the thermostatic blade straightens and the contact points close. The whole process is repeated. This action continues and keeps the voltage to the fuel-gauge system from increasing beyond the designed value.

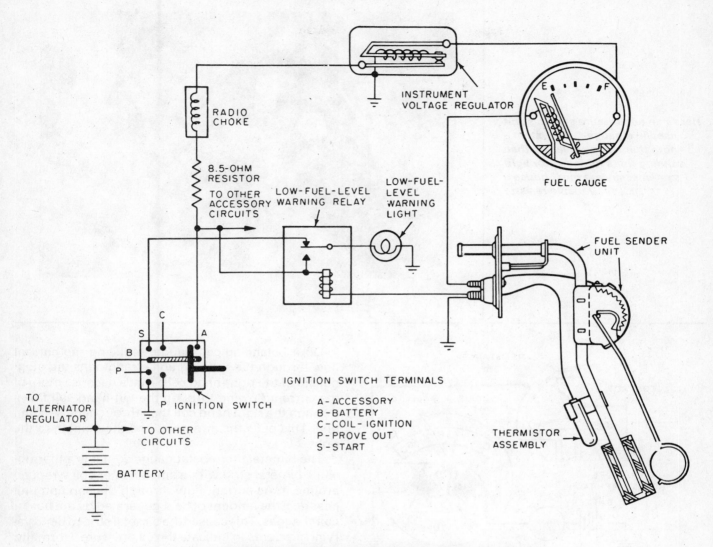

INSTRUMENT
VOLTAGE REGULATOR

RADIO
CHOKE

8.5-OHM
RESISTOR

TO OTHER
ACCESSORY
CIRCUITS

LOW-FUEL-LEVEL
WARNING RELAY

LOW-FUEL-
LEVEL
WARNING
LIGHT

FUEL GAUGE

FUEL SENDER
UNIT

IGNITION SWITCH TERMINALS

A - ACCESSORY
B - BATTERY
C - COIL - IGNITION
P - PROVE OUT
S - START

TO
ALTERNATOR
REGULATOR

TO OTHER
CIRCUITS

BATTERY

IGNITION SWITCH

THERMISTOR
ASSEMBLY

*A typical blade/variable resistor type fuel gauge system*

Note that the system also includes a radio choke and resistor. The voltage surges produced when the points open and close could cause radio interference. The choke coil and resistor smooth out the voltage surges and prevents this from happening.

## Oil pressure gauges

There are two types of electrically-operated oil pressure gauges: balancing-coil and bimetal thermostat type. Each type has two separate units. One is the sending unit on the engine; the other is the gauge on the dash.

On both types of gauges, the sending unit on the engine has a variable resistor and a moveable sliding contact. As pressure increases, a diaphragm moves up. This moves the contact along the resistor, which reduces the amount of current that can flow through the sending unit.

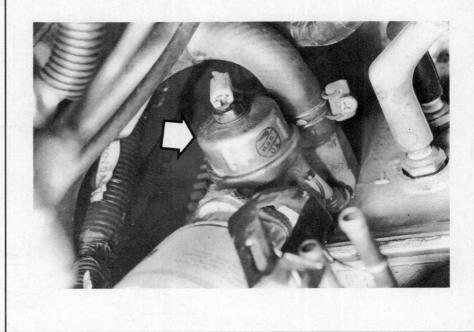

*Here's an oil pressure sending unit used in a gauge-type system – note that it's much larger than sending units for indicator light systems, since it must house a variable resistor*

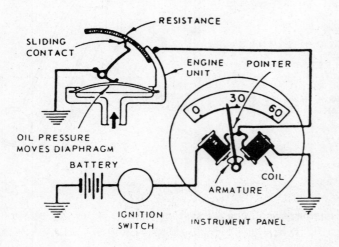

*A typical balancing coil type oil pressure gauge – bimetal thermostat type gauges use this same type of sending unit but operate similarly to the blade/variable resistor type fuel gauge*

On a balancing-coil gauge, reducing the current flow through the sending unit strengthens the magnetism of the right-hand coil. That's because more of the current flowing through the left-hand coil flows through the right hand coil than through the sending unit. This pulls the armature, and the pointer, to the right.

The bimetal thermostat gauge contains a thermostatic bimetal strip with a small heater coil wrapped around it. As current flow through the sending unit changes, the amount of heat generated by the heater coil changes. This causes the bimetal strip to bend varying amounts to indicate the oil pressure. Normally, the voltage to a thermostatic gauge is controlled by an instrument voltage regulator, as described for fuel gauges (above).

## Engine coolant temperature gauges

As with oil pressure gauges, there are two types of coolant temperature gauges: balancing-coil and bimetal thermostat. The circuits operate the same as their oil-pressure counterparts. Coolant temperature sending units for gauge circuits use a sensor that changes resistance as temperature changes. The sending unit is immersed in engine coolant; its appearance and location are the same as a sending unit for a coolant temperature indicator light (see *Indicator light circuits* above).

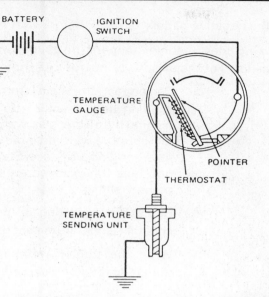

*A typical bimetal thermostatic type engine coolant temperature gauge*

An ammeter or voltmeter is used on some vehicles instead of, or in addition to, the charge warning light. Ammeters measure charging or discharging current in amperes, or "amps." Ammeters are wired between the alternator and the starter solenoid main power terminal.

Voltmeters indicate the voltage in the electrical system, which is usually a pretty good indication of the battery's state of charge. Voltmeters can be connected in parallel with any circuit that's switched off by the ignition switch.

## Ammeters and voltmeters

## Installing an accessory gauge kit

A typical set of accessory gauges, like the Equus kit shown in the accompanying illustrations, consists of an oil pressure gauge, a water temperature gauge and a voltmeter. The following general installation procedure applies to most typical gauge sets. Your kit will also include detailed information about the installation of each gauge, its sending unit and the wiring between the two. Follow the instructions included with your kit when they differ from the following.

**This gauge kit from Equus, a typical aftermarket accessory gauge set, includes the oil pressure and water temperature sending units, adapters, wires, illumination bulbs, mounting bracket and hardware and the gauges themselves. It can be ordered from Equus Products Inc., 17291 Mt. Hermann, Fountain Valley, CA 92708**

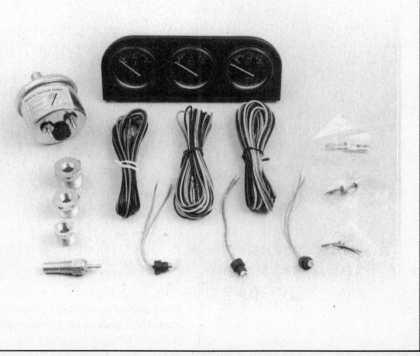

# Haynes electrical manual

## Sending units

**1** Detach the negative battery terminal before starting.

**2** If your kit includes a coolant temperature gauge, drain the coolant below the level of the existing temperature sending unit.

**3** Disconnect the lead from the existing sending unit. If you're planning on reattaching the oil pressure warning or coolant temperature warning indicator light to the new sending unit, see Step 16. If you're not, tape the exposed end of the wire to prevent shorts.

**4** Remove the existing oil pressure and/or coolant temperature sending units.

**5** Wrap the threads of the new sending unit(s) with teflon tape.

**Locate the original coolant temperature sending unit and remove it (it'll normally be screwed into the cylinder head, intake manifold or thermostat housing)**

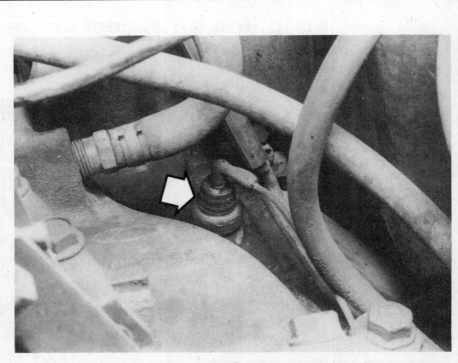

**Find the original oil pressure sending unit and remove it (it will be located somewhere on the cylinder head or the engine block)**

# Indicator lights and gauges

**Note:** *The senders provided with most kits are chassis ground, i.e. there's no external ground wire, because they're grounded through the engine. The instructions in some kits may warn against using teflon tape on the threads of such designs because it might prevent proper grounding. In our experience, an unsealed thread is an unacceptable tradeoff, because the fitting may leak oil or water, and over-tightening a brass fitting may result in stripped threads. Besides, we have found that when you screw in the sending unit, or adapter, the teflon tape shears along the crest of the thread of each screw, allowing current to flow to ground. Just be sure to verify there's continuity with a test light or meter.*

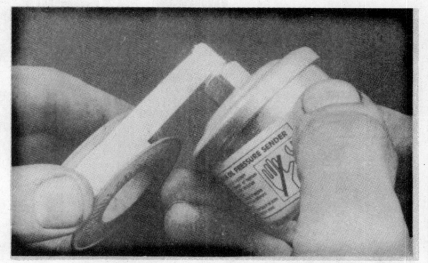

**Be sure to wrap the threads of each sending unit with teflon plumber's tape to prevent leaks**

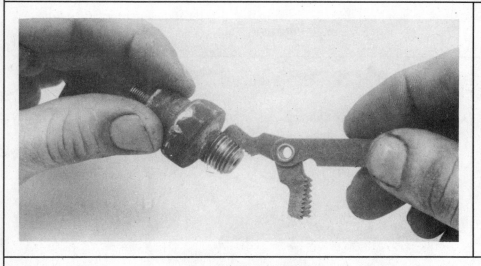

**Measure the thread pitch of the old sending unit and compare it to the thread pitch of the new sending unit – Murphy's Law states that the two won't match . . .**

**6** Install the sending unit.

**Note:** *You may need an adapter fitting to match the diameter and thread pitch of the new sending unit to the threaded bore for the old sending unit. Your kit will have a variety of adapters and one of them should fit. If none of them work, get the right fitting from a dealer or contact the manufacturer of the kit.*

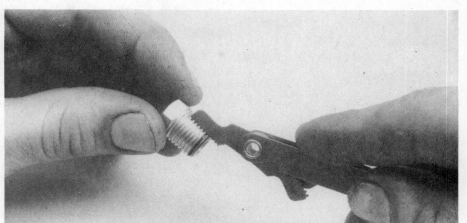

**. . . so compare the thread pitch of the old sending unit to each adapter until you find the right one . . .**

... install the adapter onto the new sending unit ...

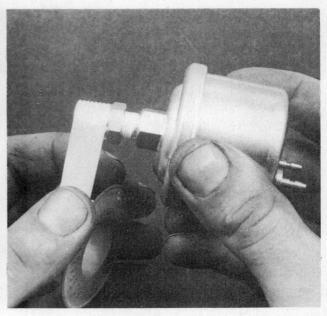

... wrap the threads of the adapter with a little teflon tape ...

... and, finally, install the sending unit and adapter

## Gauges

**7** Select a good mounting location and mount the gauge bracket in accordance with the manufacturer's instructions. We chose an under dash installation because it's easy to install the bracket to the underside of the dash and the wiring is hidden, but you can put the gauges just about anywhere. If you do decide to put them under the dash, make sure they clear your legs and you can see them easily. If you're drilling into the dashboard, be sure to use a drill bit slightly smaller than the diameter of the bracket mounting screws provided in the kit. And be sure to use screws with a fairly coarse thread pitch. Screws with a fine thread pitch will pull out more easily than screws with a coarser pitch.

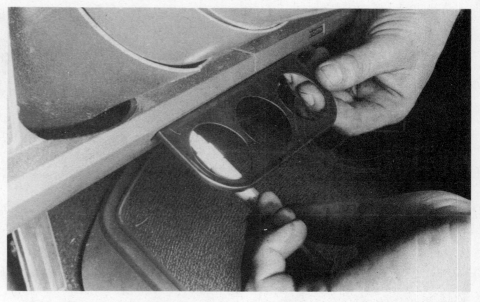

**Place the mounting bracket where you want it and, using the mounting holes in the bracket as a template, mark the holes you want to drill with a marking pen**

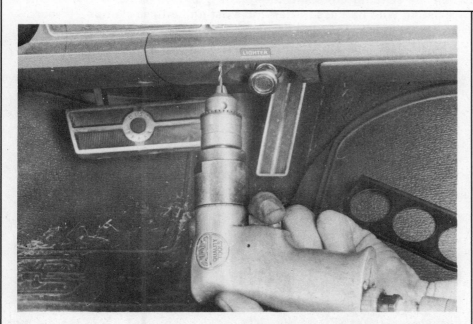

**Note:** *Most kits will include more than enough wire to hook up each gauge. Generally, three wires will be included for each gauge: a red wire for power, a black wire for ground and some other color (often yellow) for connecting the sending unit to the gauge (excepting the voltmeter, which doesn't have a sending unit). The kit manufacturer has no idea how much wire you will actually need for each section, so none of the wires are fitted with connectors. You'll have to measure the wire, cut off the excess and attach a connector (usually included in the kit) to each end of the wire. If you want to reattach a warning indicator light, you may have to cut off the old connector and replace it with one compatible with the terminal on the new sending unit.*

**Drill the holes for the mounting bracket screws**

## Wiring

# Haynes electrical manual

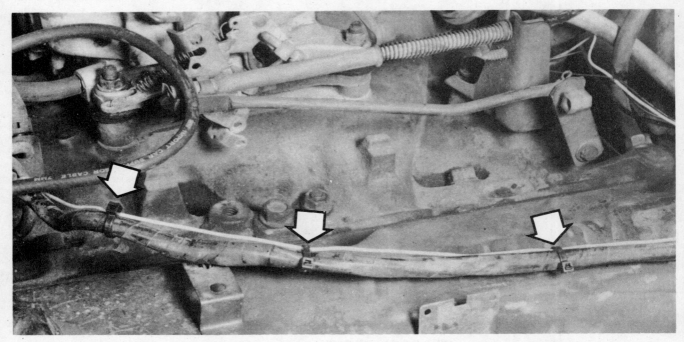

When laying out the wires between the sending units and the gauges, and the wires between the gauges and ground, try to follow existing wire harness routes and existing harness clamps – if there aren't any clamps, use cable ties to attach the wires to the harness

**8** Lay out the wires between the sending units and the gauges. If possible, try to follow an existing wire harness route. Thread the sending unit wires under existing cable ties, or fasten them to the harness with new ones. Be sure to keep the wires away from any sharp edges or hot engine components.

**9** Look for a grommet in the firewall and push the wires through just far enough so you can pull them through from under the dash.

Find a grommeted hole in the firewall and thread the wires through it (pick a hole high on the firewall to avoid air leaks into the passenger compartment)

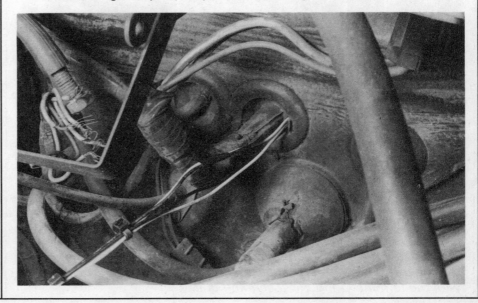

**10** Don't cut any wires until you have a pretty good idea of how long they need to be. When you cut off the excess, allow an extra foot to play with, just in case you need some slack.

**11** Most oil pressure and water temperature gauges have three terminals on the back: "S" for sending unit, "+" for the hot lead wire and "−" for the ground lead wire. The S designation is typical but not universal. Study the instructions in your kit carefully before attaching any wires.

**12** Attach the forward end of each wire to the designated terminal on its corresponding sending unit and the other end to the designated terminal on the gauge. For example, on our Equus kit, the terminals on the oil pressure sending unit and the oil pressure gauge are designated "S" (a typical designation). Our water temperature gauge also has an S terminal, but the water temperature sending unit only has one terminal, so it's pretty hard to goof it up!

Attach the forward end of each wire to its designated terminal (on this water temperature sending unit, that's not a problem – there's only one terminal – but on some oil pressure sending units, there may also be a terminal for the indicator light, so don't get them mixed up!)

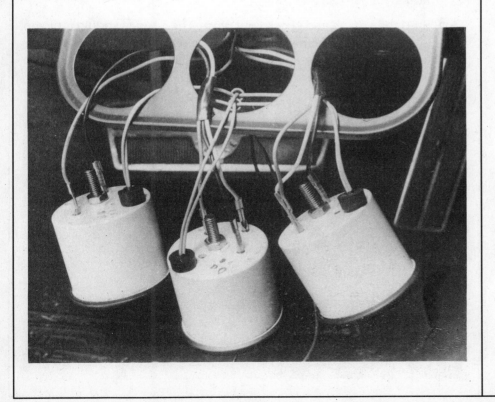

Attach the other end of each wire to its designated terminal on the back of its respective gauge (again, don't confuse the feed and ground terminals on the back of each gauge)

# Haynes electrical manual

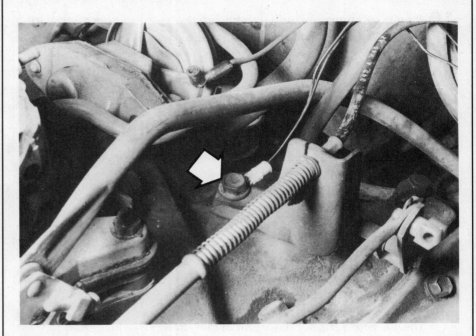

**Attach the forward end of each gauge ground lead to a good chassis ground**

**13** Attach the black wire to the negative terminal of the gauge and to a good chassis ground. If you're going to use a painted portion of the vehicle, be sure to scrape the paint off first.

**14** Attach the red wire between the positive terminal of the gauge and a suitable hot accessory wire. Make sure you pick a wire – such as a radio or blower motor lead – that has voltage *only when the ignition switch is On.*

**15** Start the engine and check your work. The gauges should indicate oil pressure and water temperature. Inspect the sending units for leaks. Turn off the engine. If either gauge fails to give a reading, check your wiring.

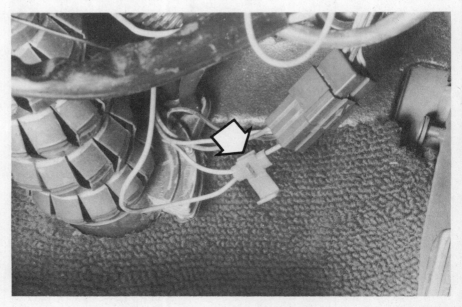

**Snap-splice the feed wire of the gauge to some power source that's hot when the ignition is turned on**

## Reusing the existing indicator light

**16** If your existing oil pressure warning light circuit is a one-wire system – and if the new sending unit has a terminal for the indicator light – simply crimp on a connector compatible with the terminal on the new sending unit and attach the warning light wire to the terminal designated for this purpose. On our new sending unit, this terminal is designated "W/L" (warning light). Your kit may use a different designation.

**17** If the existing oil pressure warning light circuit uses two wires, or the new sending unit doesn't have an extra terminal for the indicator light circuit, you'll have to obtain a T-fitting which can accomodate both the old and the new sending units. Be sure to take the dimensions of the threaded bore in the head for the old sending unit, as well as both sending units, with you when you go shopping.

**18** Most aftermarket coolant temperature sending units don't have dual terminal setups like the oil pressure sending unit shown here. So, if you still want to use the water temperature indicator warning light, you have to attach both the new sending unit and the old sending unit. Again, be sure to take the dimensions of the old threaded bore for the old sending unit and both senders with you when you look for the proper T-fitting.

**19** Start the engine and check your work. The indicator lights should come on – just as they always did – when the key is turned to On.

## Voltmeter

Hooking up a voltmeter is pretty simple, even when compared to last two gauges. There's no sending unit, so all you have to do is attach the voltmeter in parallel to any switched circuit.

**20** Attach the black wire to the negative terminal of the gauge and to a good chassis ground. If you're going to use a painted portion of the vehicle, be sure to scrape the paint off first.

**21** Attach the red wire between the positive terminal of the gauge and a suitable accessory wire. Make sure you pick a wire – such as a radio or blower motor lead – that has voltage *only when the ignition switch is On*.

**22** Turn on the engine and check the operation of the voltmeter. If the meter reads backwards, or fails to indicate anything at all, try reversing the connections. If the meter still fails to indicate properly, recheck all your connections to be sure they're clean and tight.

## Illumination bulbs

**23** Splice the red lead of each gauge illumination bulb into an existing hot wire for one of the instrument panel lights. If you're installing a multiple gauge setup like ours, splice all the hot leads of the illumination bulbs into one hot lead, then attach that single lead to the instrument panel light circuit. Make *sure* you splice the illumina-

# Haynes electrical manual

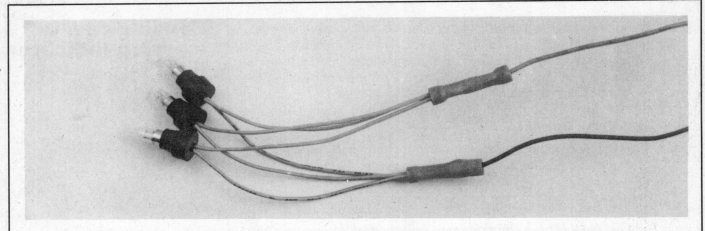

**To clean up the illumination bulb wiring, splice the feed wires of the bulbs into one feed wire and the ground wires into another**

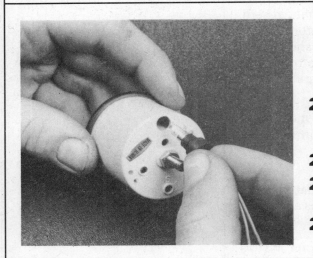

ation bulbs into a circuit controlled by the headlight switch so that it will operate only in conjunction with the regular instrument panel lights and its brightness will be controlled by the dimmer switch. Insulate the splices carefully to prevent shorts.

**24** Repeat the above procedure for the gauge illumination bulb ground leads and attach the single black lead to any convenient chassis ground.

**25** Install the bulbs in the gauges.

**26** Turn on the headlight switch and operate the dimmer to verify that the gauge illumination bulbs work properly.

**27** Install the gauges in the mounting bracket.

**Insert the illumination bulbs into the gauges**

**Install the gauges into the mounting bracket**

## Troubleshooting a gauge circuit

Because of the low voltage and light current loads to which most gauges are subjected, they seldom malfunction or require any service. Even when they do appear to be broken, the trouble is more often than not in the sending unit. Usually, replacement of the sending unit solves the problem.

If you have more than one gauge and none of them is working, check the fuse.

If the gauges are all reading high, low or oscillating in unison, check for a faulty instrument voltage regulator (most of the time, one regulator controls all gauges) or a bad ground connection for the gauge panel.

If one gauge is operating erratically, check for bad connections or a bad sending unit.

**Fuel gauges**

One easy way to test a faulty fuel gauge is to substitute a fuel level sending unit of known accuracy. It isn't necessary to install the substitute unit in the tank. Simply disconnect the wire(s) from the unit in the tank and attach them to the same terminals on the test unit. Then connect a grounding wire between the test unit body and a good chassis ground. Move the float arm through its entire range of motion and verify that this produces a consistent response from the gauge, with the needle moving from the Empty to Full positions.

If the gauge now operates properly, the old sending unit is bad. Remove it and check for a gas-logged float, binding float or lack of continuity somewhere in the operating range of the float arm. Repair the unit, or replace it, as necessary. On some fuel gauges, you can shift the float or float arm to recalibrate the sending unit and correct the gauge reading. On others, you can shift the winding poles toward or away from the armature to recalibrate the gauge. You can clean dirty contact points – which cause needle fluctuation – on a gauge with vibrating thermostatic blades by pulling a strip of clean bond paper between them. Make sure that no particles of paper are left between the points.

**Caution:** *Never use emery cloth to clean the points – particles of emery will be embedded in the points and cause erratic gauge action.*

If the fuel gauge still doesn't register properly, either the gauge unit itself, or the wiring, is faulty. Check the wire between the sending unit and the fuel gauge for continuity. Check all wiring connections too. If the wiring and connections are okay, or if fixing any problem(s) with them doesn't give accurate readings, replace the fuel gauge.

**Temperature gauges**

1   Disconnect the wire at the sending unit. The gauge should indicate Cold. Ground the sending unit wire. The gauge should move to Hot. If the gauge operates as described with the sending unit wire disconnected and grounded, but doesn't work properly when the wire is connected, replace the sending unit.

2   If the gauge indicates higher than Cold when the wire to the sending unit is disconnected, either the gauge is defective or there is a short to ground somewhere in the wiring. Disconnect the wire that goes to the sending unit at the gauge. If the gauge now reads Cold, repair the wiring. Otherwise, replace the gauge.

**3** If the gauge reads Cold when the wire is disconnected, but doesn't move to Hot when it's grounded, check the fuse (see Chapter 1). If the fuse is OK, ground the sending unit terminal of the gauge. If this causes the gauge to read Hot, repair the wire that goes to the sending unit.

**4** If there's no response from the gauge when the sending unit terminal is grounded, check for voltage at the ignition switch terminal on the gauge. If there's voltage and a good connection at the gauge, replace the gauge. If there's no voltage, the problem is in the ignition switch or the wiring between the fuse panel and the gauge.

## Oil pressure gauges

Since oil pressure gauge circuits are highly similar to temperature gauge circuits, the above procedure for temperature gauge circuits may also be used to troubleshoot oil pressure gauge circuits.

## Electronic instrumentation

All the gauge and indicator light circuits described thus far are electrical or electro-mechanical. In this section, we'll look at some typical electronic gauges.

## Electronic speedometer

Electronic speedometer circuits are basically all the same. The speedometer receives an electrical signal representing vehicle speed from an optical sensor. Output from the optical sensor is generated by a slotted wheel, which is turned by a conventional mechanical speedometer cable connected to the speedometer drive gear in the transmission. Inside the optical sensor, a light emitting diode (LED) transmits a light beam at a light-sensitive transistor. The slotted wheel rotates in a plane perpendicular to this light beam. Each time the slotted part of the wheel allows the beam to pass through to the transistor, the transistor conducts a signal to the electronic speedometer. But when the solid part of the wheel interrupts the optical beam, the transistor ceases conducting. So the spinning wheel generates a steady series of pulses to the electronic speedometer. The number of pulses generated are proportional to vehicle speed. Increasing the vehicle speed produces an increase in the pulse rate of the signal to the speedometer.

## Electronic fuel gauges

All electronic fuel gauges operate basically the same way. The voltage signal from a sending unit operates a horizontal or vertical bar display and, on most models, a low fuel warning light. The sending unit, located in the fuel tank, is similar in operation to the sending unit in thermostatic blade/variable resistor type electric gauge circuits (see above). Resistance from this sending unit varies the voltage sent to the gauge. The electronics in the gauge itself interpret the high or low voltage to display the appropriate gauge reading.

## Electronic temperature gauges

Electronic temperature gauges are similar in operation to electronic fuel gauges. A signal from a temperature sending unit immersed in engine coolant operates a horizontal bar display to indicate coolant temperature. Instead of a potentiometer in the sender unit, the temperature gauge system uses a thermistor (a resistor that changes resistance as the temperature changes). The thermistor used has a low resistance at high temperature (about 1000 ohms at 260-degrees F) and a high resistance at low temperature (about 2.5 k-ohms at 0-degrees F).

#  Accessories

## General information

In Chapters 1 and 3 we introduced you to basic circuits, troubleshooting and wiring repair. Now it's time to apply what you know to finding and correcting problems in accessory circuits.

The procedures that follow are by necessity general in nature. Whenever possible, supplement the information provided here with more specific procedures found in repair manuals written for the particular vehicle you are working on.

Before assuming an accessory circuit is faulty, be sure the battery has a reasonably good charge (see Chapter 4). Sometimes accessory circuits malfunction because they're not receiving sufficient voltage.

**Caution:** *Never test solid-state components with battery voltage, test lights/buzzers or analog multimeters. These devices may permanently damage electronic components.*

**Note:** *If the circuit in question keeps blowing fuses, check for a short (see Chapter 3).*

## Cigarette lighters

Cigarette lighter circuits are among the simplest found on modern vehicles. They consist of one wire running from the fuse panel to the lighter socket, a heating element and an electrical ground return from the socket housing to the chassis.

Visually inspect the heating element and replace it if it appears damaged. Most lighters have a replaceable element that unscrews from the handle.

**Note:** *Some vehicles have the cigarette lighter wired through the ignition switch, so, when checking a cigarette lighter, always turn the ignition ON*

*Most lighters have a replaceable heating element which unscrews from the handle*

*Probe the center terminal in the lighter socket with a test light*

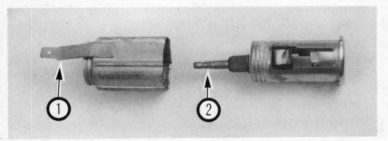

*Most lighter sockets are composed of two parts which screw together*

| 1 | Ground terminal | 2 | Positive terminal |

## Troubleshooting

**1** Insert the lighter into the socket and allow time for it to heat. If it doesn't get hot, check the fuse (see Chapter 1).

**2** If the fuse is OK, probe the center terminal in the socket with a test light, using the outer casing of the socket as a ground for the light.

**3** If the test light lights, replace the heating element.

**4** If the test light doesn't light, connect the ground wire to the ignition key (this is a good ground on almost any vehicle). If the test light comes on now, repair the ground connection on the lighter socket. Sometimes, the bad ground is from a loose connection between the two parts of the socket.

**5** If the light still doesn't come on, trace the wiring back to the fuse panel and repair as necessary.

## Cruise controls

Cruise controls all work by the same basic principles; however, the hardware used varies considerably among manufacturers. Some systems require special testers and diagnostic procedures which are beyond the scope of the home mechanic. Listed below are some general procedures that may be used to locate common problems.

**1** Locate and check the fuse (see Chapter 1).

**2** Have an assistant operate the brake lights while you check their operation (voltage from the brake light switch deactivates the cruise control).

**3** If the brake lights don't come on or don't shut off, correct the problem and retest the cruise control (see Chapter 6).

*This cruise control actuator is connected to the throttle linkage with a small chain (arrow) – note how the vacuum hose connects at the rear*

**4** Inspect the control linkage between the cruise control servo (or actuator) and the throttle linkage. This will consist of either a cable, chain or metal rod. The cruise control servo is usually fist-sized or slightly larger and is located near the carburetor or throttle body.

**5** Visually inspect the vacuum hose(s) and wires connected to the cruise control servo and transducer (if equipped) and replace as necessary.

**6** Most aftermarket cruise control units have a speed sensor mounted under the vehicle. On rear wheel drive models, these are located near the front of the driveshaft. On front wheel drive models, the sensors are located

*This cruise control servo combines the electrical control valve with the vacuum actuator – it's connected to the throttle body with a cable (arrow)*

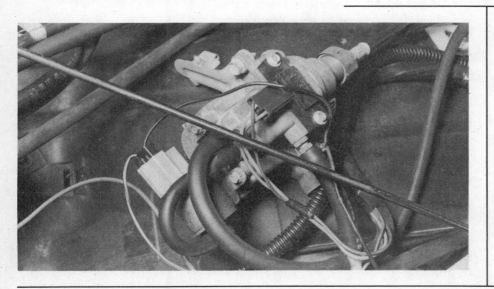

*This is a GM cruise control transducer – check all the wires, cables and hoses attached to it*

*This is a typical aftermarket drive-shaft-mounted speed sensor*

on the inner joint of a driveaxle. Raise the vehicle and support it securely on jackstands. Inspect the magnets, pickup and wiring. Frequently the magnets or wiring come loose or the pickups get damaged. Repair or replace as necessary.

**7** Factory cruise controls use a variety of speed sensing devices. Most use some form of pickup on the speedometer cable or speedometer. Disconnect the speedometer cable, rotate the speed sensor and check it with a digital ohmmeter while it's rotating. If the resistance doesn't vary as the cable rotates, the sensor is defective.

**8** Test drive the vehicle to determine if the cruise control is now working. If it isn't, take it to a dealer service department or an automotive electrical specialist for further diagnosis and repair.

*To check a cable-mounted speed sensor like this, connect an ohmmeter to the terminals (arrows); the resistance should rise and fall as the shaft is rotated*

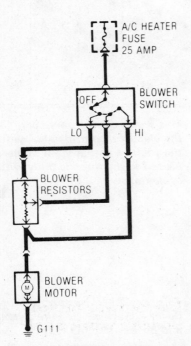

*A typical heater blower wiring diagram (three-speed shown)*

## Heater blowers

Heater circuits are relatively simple compared to the complexity of most air conditioning systems. They all have a blower motor, multi-position switch and resistor block. The blower motor is wired in series with the switch resistor block. For cooling, the resistor block is often mounted in the blower airstream.

On most systems, current flows from the fuse panel to the switch. Depending on which blower speed has been selected, current is routed through different coils in the resistor block, then through the blower motor to ground.

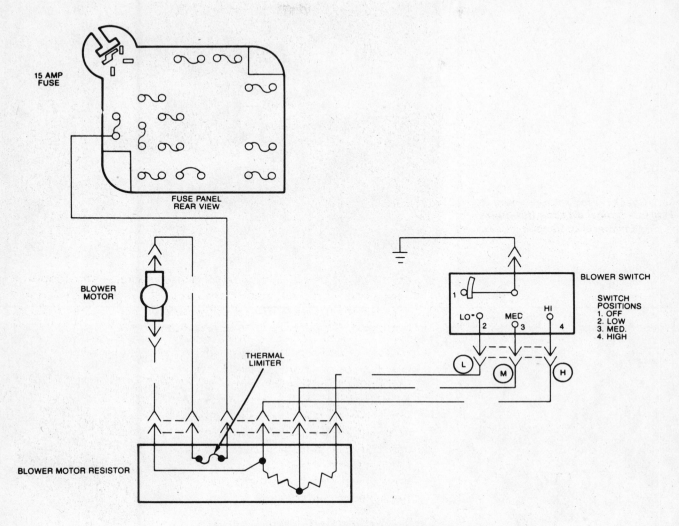

*A typical Ford ground-side switching wiring diagram*

In 1980, Ford came out with a variation known as ground-side switching. On these systems current flows from the fuse panel to the blower motor and then through the switch and resistor block to ground.

Due to the large number of different systems available, the following instructions must be general in nature. You may have to obtain the wiring diagrams for the vehicle you are working on to solve some problems.

## Vehicles with ground at the blower motor

**1**  Check the fuse (see Chapter 1).

**2**  If the fuse is OK but the motor doesn't work, turn on the motor and check for voltage at the motor's positive connector. Most blower motors are located in the engine compartment on the firewall or under

**The blower motor doesn't work at all**

*Checking for voltage going to the motor*

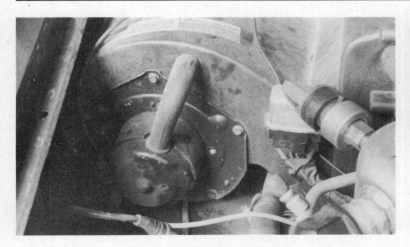

*Most larger domestic vehicles have the blowers mounted either vertically or horizontally in the engine compartment on the passenger side*

*Many compact and imported vehicles have the blower mounted under the dash, as shown here*

the dash behind the glove compartment. On some vehicles they are hidden inside the right front fender, requiring removal of the fender liner for access.

**Note:** *The ignition must be On when checking for voltage.*

**3** If there's voltage at the motor, connect a jumper wire between the motor's ground terminal (or case) and a good chassis ground. Connect a fused jumper wire between the battery positive terminal and the positive terminal on the motor. If the motor now works, remove the jumper wire. If the motor stops working when the wire is removed, check for a bad ground and retest. If the motor still doesn't work, replace it.

**4** If there's no voltage at the motor, remove the resistor block's connector and check it for voltage. If there's voltage at any of the connector terminals, check the resistor block and the wiring between the resistor block and the motor for an open or short.

**5** If there's no voltage at any of the terminals in the resistor block's connector, remove the heater control panel (if necessary) and, with the ignition On, check for voltage at the connector for the blower motor switch. If there's no voltage, check the wiring between the fuse panel and the switch for an open or a

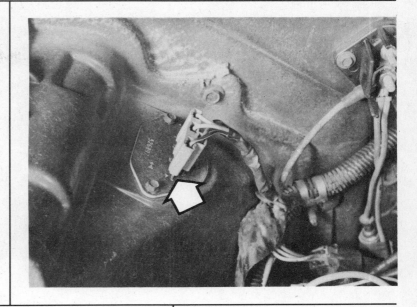

*Here's a resistor block (arrow) mounted on the blower housing – sometimes they're mounted in the housing under the dash*

*Here's a common heater control panel. You must remove it to check for power at the blower control switch. To do so, slide the ashtray out and remove the cigarette lighter socket . . .*

*. . . pull the control knobs off . . .*

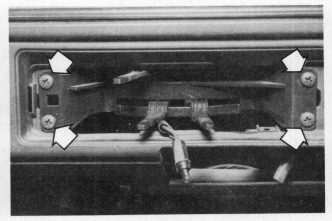

*. . . remove the mounting screws (arrows) . . .*

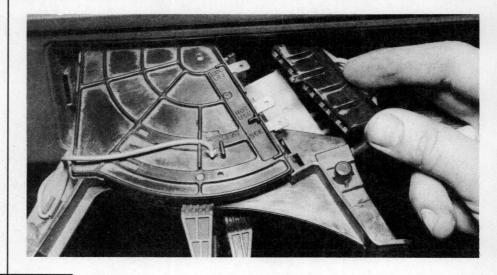

*. . . unplug the control switch and pull it out of the dash*

short. If there's voltage, connect one end of a jumper wire to the terminal of the switch's connector with voltage. Connect the other end of the jumper to each of the terminals that carry voltage to the the resistor block. If necessary, obtain the correct wiring diagram for the vehicle. If the motor now operates normally, replace the switch.

**6**   If the motor does not operate with the control switch jumpered, check for an open or short in the wiring from the switch to the resistor block.

*Checking for voltage at the blower switch connector – there should be voltage at one of the terminals*

### The motor only runs on high speed

**7**   Remove the connector at the resistor block and check the resistor block for continuity. On most vehicles, there should be continuity between all the terminals. If you doubt the condition of the resistor block, remove it and check it visually.

**8**   Test the blower motor switch as described in Step 5 above. If the motor works on other speeds when the switch is jumpered, replace the switch. If it still doesn't work on speeds other than high, check the wiring between the switch and the resistor block for opens and shorts.

### The motor runs on low speeds but *not* on high speed

**9**   Check for a blown inline fuse or a faulty high-speed relay – mostly on GM vehicles – (see Chapter 3). If the inline fuse and relay (when equipped) are OK but the motor still doesn't work, check the blower switch, as described in Step 5. If the motor operates on high speed with the switch jumpered, replace the switch. If it doesn't, check the resistor block and the wiring between the switch and resistor block for shorts and opens.

*Some vehicles use a relay (arrow) to carry current when the blower is on high*

## Vehicles with ground-side switching

Use the following procedure when the blower motor does not work at all. When the motor runs on high speed but not low speeds or on low speeds but not high speed, the procedures are the same as the ones above, except substitute Step 12 below when the procedures above refer you to Step 5.

**10** Check the fuse.

**11** With the ignition and blower motor switches on, check for voltage at the motor's positive connector. If there's no voltage, check the wiring between the fuse panel and the motor for an open or short. If there's voltage, test the motor, as described in Step 3.

**12** If the motor works when tested, remove the heater control panel (see Step 5 above) and use a jumper wire to ground each terminal of the blower motor switch's connector. Make sure the ignition switch is on. If the motor now works, check for a bad ground at the switch. If the switch's ground is good, replace the switch.

**13** If the motor still doesn't work, remove the connector from the resistor block and ground the connector terminal that leads to the ground side of the blower motor. Make sure the ignition and blower switches are on. Obtain the correct wiring diagrams for the vehicle, if necessary. If the motor doesn't work, check for an open or short in the wiring between the resistor assembly and the motor. If the motor works, check the resistor block and the wiring between the switch and resistor block for a short or open.

## Electric rear view mirrors

Most electric rear view mirrors use two motors to move the glass; one for up and down adjustments and one for left-right adjustments. In addition, some mirrors have electrically heated glass defroster circuits, which are usually powered through the rear window defogger relay.

# Haynes electrical manual

## Troubleshooting

*Mirror controls usually have a selector switch (arrow) which sends power to the left or right mirror*

**1** The control switch usually has a selector portion which sends voltage to the left or right side mirror. With the ignition ON but the engine OFF, roll down the windows and operate the mirror control switch through all functions (left-right and up-down) for both the left and right side mirrors.

**2** Listen carefully for the sound of the electric motors running in the mirrors.

**3** If the motors can be heard but the mirror glass doesn't move, there's probably a problem with the drive mechanism inside the mirror. Remove and disassemble the mirror to locate the problem.

**4** If the mirrors don't operate and no sound comes from the mirrors, check the fuse (see Chapter 1).

**5** If the fuse is OK, remove the mirror control switch from its mounting without disconnecting the wires attached to it. Turn the ignition ON and check for voltage at the switch. There should be voltage at one terminal. If there's no voltage at the switch, check for an open or short in the wiring between the fuse panel and the switch.

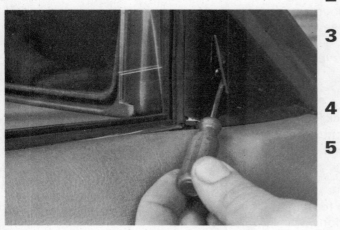

*On many modern vehicles, the mirrors are secured by screws on the inside of the door – remove the trim plate . . .*

*. . . to expose the mirror mounting screws*

*This armrest-mounted mirror switch . . .*

*. . . can be pried up with a small screwdriver (on some switches you'll have to remove screws first) . . .*

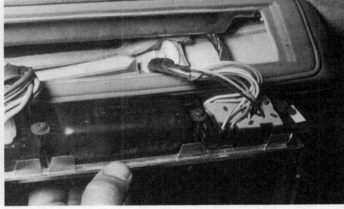

*. . . and turned over for testing with the wires still attached*

**6** If there's voltage at the switch, disconnect it. Obtain the correct wiring diagram for the vehicle and use it to check the switch for continuity in all its operating positions. If the switch does not have continuity, replace it.

**7** Re-connect the switch. Using the wiring diagram, locate the wire going from the switch to ground. Leaving the switch connected, connect a jumper wire between this wire and ground. If the mirror works normally with this wire in place, repair the faulty ground connection.

**8** If the mirror still doesn't work, remove the mirror and check the wires at the mirror for voltage. Check with ignition ON and the mirror selector switch on the appropriate side. Operate the mirror switch in all its positions. There should be voltage at one of the switch-to-mirror wires in each switch position (except the neutral "off" position).

**9** If there's not voltage in each switch position, check the wiring between the mirror and control switch for opens and shorts.

**10** If there's voltage, remove the mirror and test it off the vehicle with jumper wires. Replace the mirror if it fails this test.

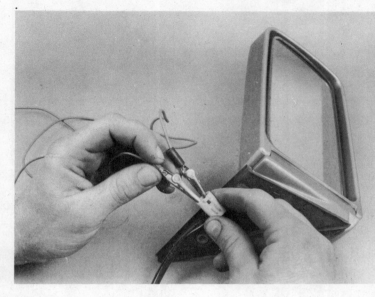

*The mirror may be tested off the vehicle with fused jumper wires connected directly to the battery*

*A typical relay-type horn, showing its single terminal and adjustment screw (arrows)*

*A typical non-relay type horn, showing its two terminals and adjustment screw (arrows)*

## Horns

There are two basic designs for electric horn circuits; relay types and non-relay types. Most American and some imported vehicles use relays to handle the heavy current required by horns. If you aren't sure which type the vehicle has, look at the horns. Relay-type systems have one electrical terminal on each horn, non-relay types have two.

## General troubleshooting

**1**   If the horn is inoperative, check the fuse (see Chapter 1).

**Note:** *Some vehicles must have the ignition switch ON for the horn to work.*

**2**   If the horn sounds weak, have an assistant operate the horn button while you listen at the front of the vehicle. Note whether the vehicle has multiple horns and determine if they are all working (touching each horn while its operating and feeling for a vibration is an easy way to do this). If the vehicle has a city-highway switch, try it both ways.

**3**   If a horn is weak or inoperative, check for a faulty ground at the horn (relay-type systems) and check for full battery voltage going to the horn (do this with a voltmeter).

**4**   If the horn tone is still poor, check for an adjustment screw and adjust for best tone.

## Relay-type circuits

**5**   When the horn button is depressed, the relay's control circuit is connected to ground, which causes the horn relay to connect the horn(s) to the battery.

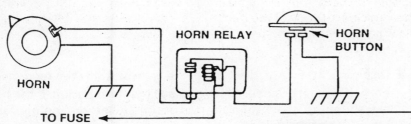

*A typical relay-type horn circuit diagram*

## The horn won't shut off

**6**   Disconnect the horn(s), then check for a stuck horn button by disconnecting the button and re-connecting the horn(s). If the horn is now silent, replace the horn button. If the horn is still blowing, disconnect the wire that goes to the horn button at the relay. If that doesn't shut it off, replace the relay. If disconnecting the wire shuts off the horn, check the horn button wire for a short to ground.

*This horn button is disconnected by first removing the steering wheel cover, then disconnecting the wire (arrow)*

# Haynes electrical manual

## The horn doesn't work

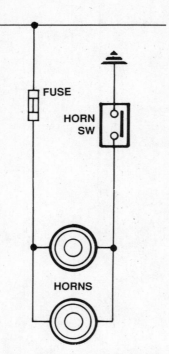

FUSE

HORN
SW

HORNS

*A typical non-relay type horn
circuit diagram*

7   Check the fuse. If it's OK, check for voltage at the terminal on each horn when the horn button is depressed. If there's voltage at each terminal, check for a bad ground at the horn(s). If the ground is good, replace the horn(s).

8   If there's no voltage at the horn(s), check the relay (see the relay check procedure in Chapter 3). Note that most horn relays are either the four-terminal or externally grounded three-terminal type.

9   If the relay is OK, check for voltage to the relay's power and control circuits. If either of the circuits is not getting voltage, inspect the wiring between the relay and the fuse panel.

10   If both relay circuits are receiving voltage, depress the horn button and check the wire that goes from the relay to the horn button for continuity to ground. If there's no continuity, check the wire for an open. If there's no open in the wire, replace the horn button.

11   If there's continuity to ground through the horn button, check for an open or short in the wire that goes from the relay to the horn(s).

## Non-relay type circuits

12   On non-relay type horn circuits, voltage is connected directly from the fuse panel to the horn. The circuit is grounded through the horn button. This type circuit is used mostly on imported cars, especially those equipped with only one horn.

## The horn won't shut off

13   Disconnect the horn, disconnect the horn button, then reconnect the horn. If the horn is now silent, replace the horn button. If the horn is still sounding, check for a short to ground in the wire going from the horn to the horn button.

## The horn doesn't work

14   If the general troubleshooting checks listed above don't find the problem, disconnect the horn and run power directly to the horn from the battery with fused jumper wires. If the horn doesn't work then, replace it.

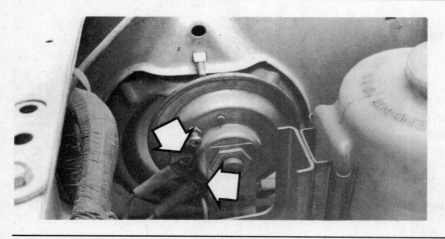

*To check a non-relay type horn, disconnect the wires from the horn (arrows) and connect fused jumper wires from the battery to the horn*

**15** If the horn works with jumpers, check the wire that runs from the fuse panel to the horn for voltage at the horn. If there's no voltage, there's a short or open between the fuse panel and the horn.

**16** If there's voltage at the horn, depress the horn button and check for continuity between ground and the wire running from the horn to the horn button, with the wire disconnected from the horn. If there's no continuity, check the wire for an open. If the wire's OK, replace the horn button.

## Electric door locks

Electric door lock systems are operated by bi-directional solenoids located in the doors. The lock switches have two operating positions: Lock and Unlock. These switches activate a relay which in turn connects voltage to the door lock solenoids. Depending on which way the relay is activated, it reverses polarity, allowing the two sides of the circuit to be used alternately as the feed (positive) and ground side.

Due to the large number of systems available, we cannot supply detailed troubleshooting procedures for all types of vehicles. Some vehicles have keyless entry, electronic control modules and anti-theft systems incorporated into the power locks. If you are unable to locate the trouble using the following general steps, consult your a dealer service department.
**Note**: *Some vehicles also have control switches connected to the key locks in the doors which unlock all the doors when one is unlocked.*

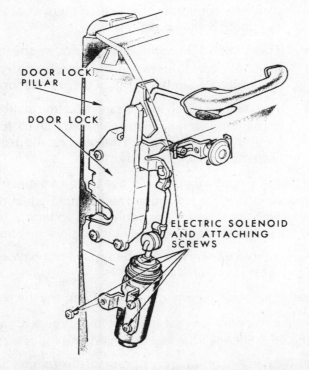

*Typical power door lock solenoid installation details (GM vehicle shown)*

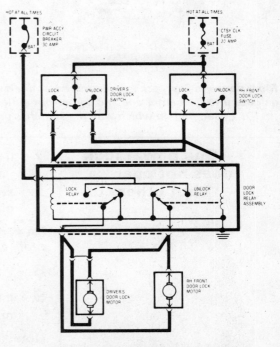

*A typical power door lock circuit*

# Haynes electrical manual

## Troubleshooting
### None of the power locks operate

**1** Always check the circuit protection first. Some vehicles use a combination of circuit breakers and fuses (see Chapter 1).

**2** Operate the door lock switches in both directions (Lock and Unlock) with the engine off. Listen for the faint click of the relay operating.

**3** If there's no click, check for voltage at the switches. If no voltage is present, check the wiring between the fuse panel and the switches for shorts and opens.

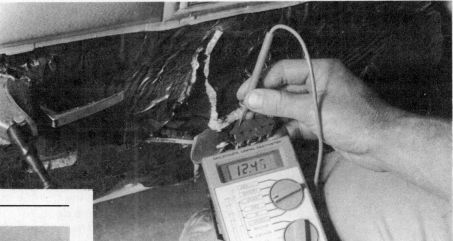

*Checking for voltage at the control switch connector – you may have to remove the door trim panel to do this*

*Most power lock switches have three terminals – voltage goes into the center one and comes out either side, depending on which way the switch is pressed*

**4** If voltage is present but no click is heard, test the switch for continuity. Replace it if there's not continuity in both switch positions.

**5** If the switch has continuity but the relay doesn't click, check the wiring between the switch and relay for continuity. Repair the wiring if there's not continuity.

**6** If the relay is receiving voltage from the switch but is not sending voltage to the solenoids, check for a bad ground at the relay case. If the relay case is grounding properly, replace the relay.

### One power lock does not operate, but others do

**7** If all but one lock solenoids operate, remove the trim panel from the affected door and check for voltage at the solenoid while the lock switch is operated. One of the wires should have voltage in the Lock position; the other should have voltage in the unlock position.

**Note:** *For information on removing the trim panel, see the Haynes Automotive Repair Manual for your particular vehicle.*

**8** If the inoperative solenoid is receiving voltage, replace the solenoid.

**9** If the inoperative solenoid isn't receiving voltage, check for an open or short in the wire between the lock solenoid and the relay.

**Note:** *It's common for wires to break in the portion of the harness between the body and door (opening and closing the door fatigues and eventually breaks the wires).*

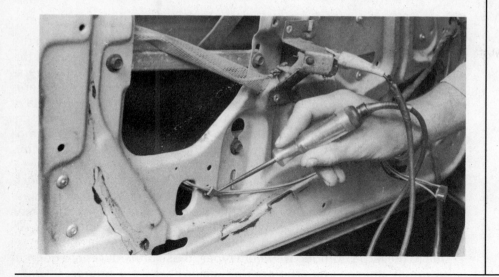

*Here a test light pierces the wire going to the solenoid, checking for voltage*

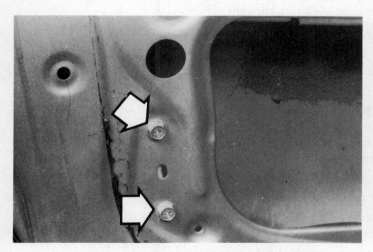

*Most door lock solenoids are bolted (arrows) to the lower rear corner of the door*

*After the bolts are removed, lift the solenoid out through the opening in the door and disconnect it*

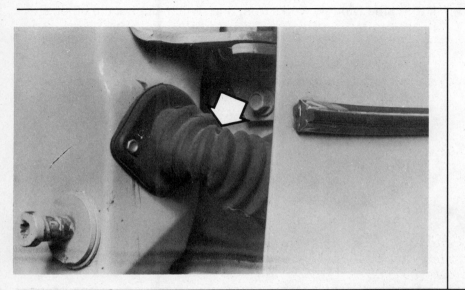

*Wires often break inside the harness between the door and body (arrow)*

## Power windows

Power windows are wired so they can be lowered and raised from the master control switch by the driver or by remote switches located at the individual windows. Each window has a separate motor which is reversible. The position of the control switch determines the polarity and therefore the direction of operation. Some systems are equipped with relays that control current flow to the motors.

Many vehicles are equipped with a separate circuit breaker for each motor in addition to the fuse or circuit breaker protecting the whole circuit. This prevents one stuck window from disabling the whole system.

Most power window systems will only operate when the ignition switch is ON. In addition, many models have a window lockout switch at the master control switch which, when activated, disables the switches at the rear windows and, sometimes, the switch at the passenger's window also. Always check these items before troubleshooting a window problem.

Due to the large number of system types, these procedures are general in nature. If you can't find the problem using these procedures, take the vehicle to a dealer service department.

## Troubleshooting

### No windows work

**1** If the power windows don't work at all, check the fuse or circuit breaker (see Chapter 1).

**2** If only the rear windows are inoperative, or if the windows only operate from the master control switch, check the rear window lockout switch for continuity in the unlocked position. Replace it if it doesn't have continuity.

**3** Check the wiring between the switches and fuse panel for continuity. Repair the wiring, if necessary.

### One window is inoperative

**4** If only one window is inoperative from the master control switch, try the other control switch at the window.

**Note:** *This doesn't apply to the drivers door window.*

**5** If the same window works from one switch, but not the other, check the switch for continuity.

*Check the switch for continuity in both directions*

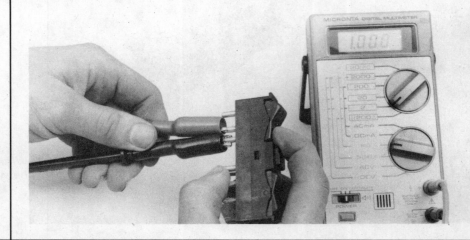

**6** If the switch tests OK, check for a short or open in the wiring between the affected switch and the window motor.

**7** If one window is inoperative from both switches, remove the trim panel from the affected door and check for voltage at the motor while the switch is operated.

**Note:** *For information on removing the trim panel, check the Haynes Automotive Repair Manual for your particular vehicle.*

**8** If voltage is reaching the motor, disconnect the glass from the regulator. Move the window up and down by hand while checking for binding and damage. Also check for binding and damage to the regulator. If the regulator is not damaged and the window moves up and down smoothly, replace the motor. If there's binding or damage, lubricate, repair or replace parts, as necessary.

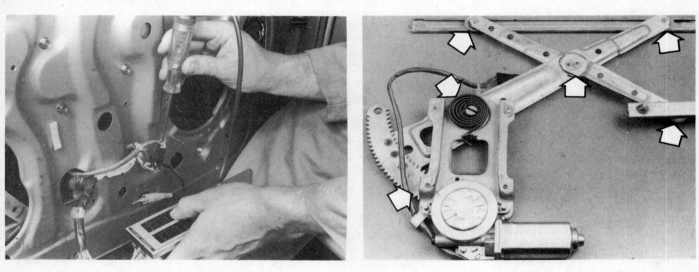

*Checking for voltage going to the power window motor*

*Here's a regulator and motor assembly removed from the vehicle – check for damage and binding at the points indicated by arrows*

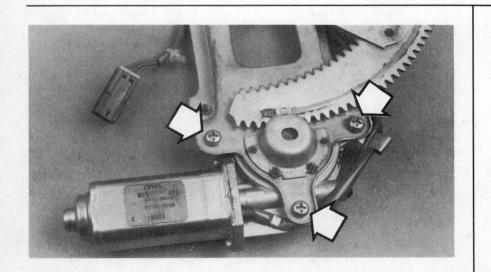

*This typical motor is secured to the regulator by three screws (arrows) – you may have to remove the regulator assembly before you can remove the motor*

**9** If voltage isn't reaching the motor, check the wiring in the circuit for continuity between the switches and motors. You'll need to obtain the wiring diagram for the vehicle. Some power window circuits are equipped with relays. If equipped, check that the relays are grounded properly and receiving voltage from the switches. Also check that each relay sends voltage to the motor when the switch is turned on. If it doesn't, replace the relay.

**10** Test the windows after you are done to confirm proper repairs.

## Power antennas

There are two basic types of power antennas: fully automatic and semi-automatic. Fully automatic antennas raise and lower when the radio is turned on or off. Semi-automatic types are raised or lowered by operating a dash-mounted switch.

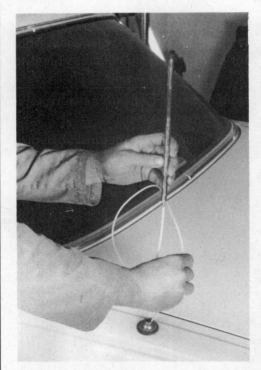

*Some antenna masts may be replaced without removing the antenna from the vehicle*

The service life of an antenna may be increased by doing a little routine maintenance. Carefully clean off any accumulated dirt and grime from the mast with a soft, lint-free cloth. Some manufacturers recommend light lubrication of the mast to prevent sticking – check your owners manual for the proper procedure.

Most antennas have a drain hose coming from the bottom – inspect the hose to make sure it's not plugged.

Before checking for an electrical problem, inspect the mast. A bent or damaged mast is the most common cause of a stuck antenna. Bent masts usually can't be straightened successfully. Some models have replaceable masts. Check with a dealer. When replacing a mast, be sure to follow the instructions provided with the new mast. If the mast isn't replaceable, the whole antenna may have to be replaced. Rebuilt antennas are sometimes available; again, check with a dealer.

If the following general procedures do not identify your antenna problem, take the vehicle to a dealer service department for further diagnosis.

### Troubleshooting

**1** If the antenna doesn't work at all, check the fuse (see Chapter 1).

**2** Operate the antenna with the ignition ON but the engine OFF. Listen for the sound of the antenna motor.

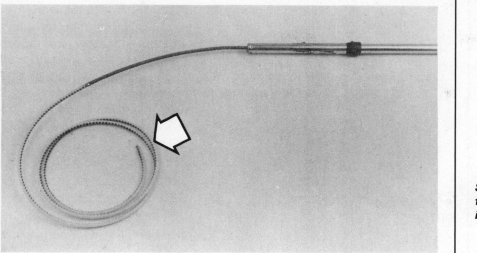

*Sometimes the plastic leader portion of the mast (arrow) breaks off inside the power antenna housing*

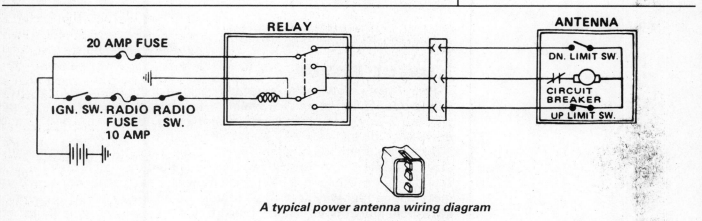

*A typical power antenna wiring diagram*

**3** If the mast doesn't move but the motor runs, remove the antenna assembly inspection cover and check for a broken mast.

**4** If the motor doesn't run, have an assistant operate the antenna control while you check for voltage and grounding at the antenna. If the antenna has a good ground and is getting voltage, it's faulty – replace it.

**5** If the antenna isn't getting voltage, check for voltage at the relay. If the relay's receiving voltage, check for a bad ground at the relay and check that the relay's sending voltage to the antenna when the antenna control is turned on. If the relay's receiving voltage but not sending it to the antenna, replace the relay.

**6** If the relay isn't getting voltage, check the wires going to the relay for a short or open.

*Checking for voltage at the antenna connector*

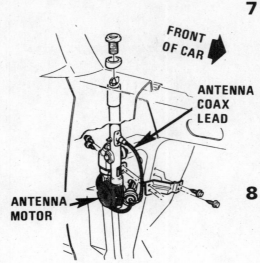

*Typical power antenna mounting details*

FRONT OF CAR

ANTENNA COAX LEAD

ANTENNA MOTOR

**7** On semi-automatic models, check for voltage at the switch and check the switch for continuity in both the UP and DOWN positions. If the switch does not have continuity in both directions, replace the switch. If there's no power to the switch, check the wiring between the fuse panel and the switch for a short or open.

**8** On fully automatic models, if there's voltage at the radio but no voltage going from the radio to the relay with the radio turned on, you'll normally have to remove the radio and have it checked by a qualified radio repair shop.

## Power seats

Power seats allow you to adjust the position of the seat with little effort. Numerous configurations are available; however, most systems are four-way or six-way. A four-way seat goes forward and backward and up and down. In addition, a six-way seat tilts forward and backward.

Two basic methods of powering the seats are employed. Some manufacturers use one motor with a solenoid-shifted transmission for all the seat functions. Others use a separate motor for each plane of travel (two motors for a four-way seat, three motors for a six-way seat). The control switch changes the direction of seat travel by reversing polarity to the drive motor.

Due to the complexity of seats with memory controls, side bolsters, lumbar supports and power head restraints, and also due to the special test equipment necessary to diagnose them, these components are beyond the scope of this manual. See your dealer service department or an automotive electrical specialist.

*This view from below of a six-way seat with one motor shows the transmission mounting details*

*1  Relay*
*2  Transmission*
*3  Drive cables*
*4  Motor (hidden by bracket)*

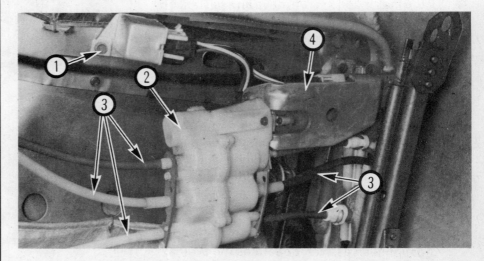

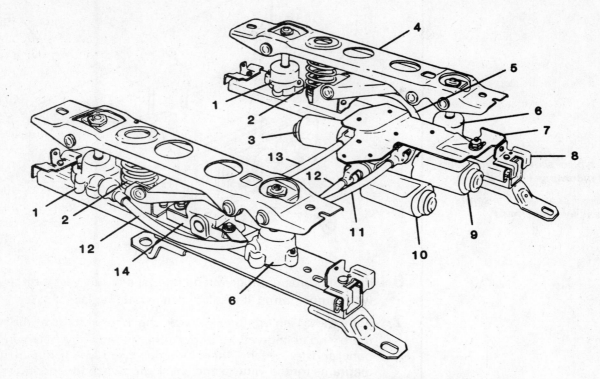

*A typical six-way power seat mechanism with three motors*

| | | |
|---|---|---|
| 1 Rear gearnut drive | 6 Front gearnut drive | 10 Rear vertical gearnut motor |
| 2 Assist springs | 7 Motor support bracket | 11 Front vertical drive cable |
| 3 Horizontal adjuster motor | 8 Lower channel stop | 12 Rear vertical drive cable |
| 4 Adjuster assembly | 9 Front vertical gearnut motor | 13 Horizontal drive cable |
| 5 Rear vertical gearnut cable | | 14 Horizontal adjuster drive |

## Troubleshooting

**1** Look under the seat for any objects which may be preventing the seat from moving.

**2** If the seat won't work at all, check the fuse or circuit breaker (see Chapter 1).

**Note:** *On some vehicles the ignition must be ON for the power seats to work.*

**3** With the engine off to reduce the noise level, operate the seat controls in all directions and listen for sound coming from the seat motor(s).

**4** If the motor runs or clicks but the seat doesn't move, check the seat drive mechanism for wear or damage and correct as necessary. If the motor runs freely on seats with a single motor and transmission, check the transmission shift mechanism for proper operation.

**5** If the motor doesn't work or make noise, check for voltage at the motor while an assistant operates the switch.

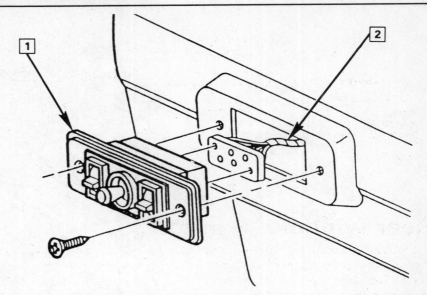

*A typical six-way power seat switch mounting – exploded view*

1   Power seat switch assembly
2   Seat switch harness

**6**   If the motor is getting voltage but doesn't run, test it off the vehicle with jumper wires. If it still doesn't work, replace it.

**7**   If the motor isn't getting voltage, check for voltage at the switch. If there's no voltage at the switch, check the wiring between the fuse panel and the switch. If there's voltage at the switch, obtain the wiring diagrams for the vehicle and check the switch for continuity in all its operating positions. Replace the switch if there's not continuity.

**8**   If the switch is OK, check for a short or open in the wiring between the switch and motor. If there's a relay between the switch and motor, check that it's grounded properly and there's voltage to the relay. Also check that there's voltage going from the relay to the motor when the when the switch is operated. If there's not, and the relay is grounded properly, replace the relay.

**9**   Test the completed repairs.

*Checking for voltage at the seat control switch*

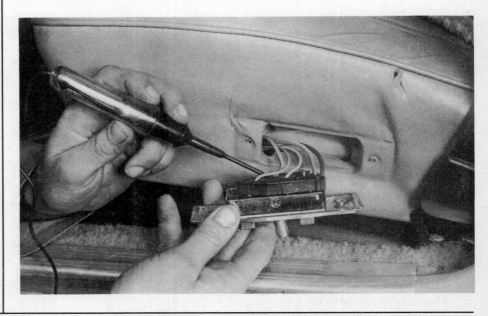

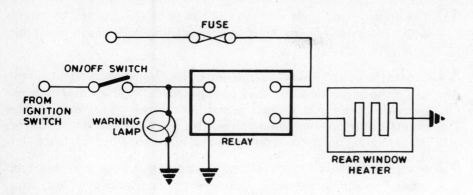

*A typical rear window defogger circuit*

# Rear window defoggers

Electric rear window defoggers function by passing an electric current through thin conductors mounted on the inner surface of the rear window glass. The defogger circuit on most vehicles includes a fuse or circuit breaker, a timer relay, switch, warning lamp, rear window grid and connecting wiring. On some vehicles, the timer relay also controls current to defoggers on the outside rear-view mirror glass.

## Troubleshooting

**1** Check the fuse and replace it, if necessary (see Chapter 1).

**2** With the ignition ON (engine OFF), switch ON the rear window defogger with the driver's door open. The interior dome (ceiling) light should dim considerably.

**3** If the dome light dims when the defogger is switched ON, check the rear window for damaged grid lines (see below).

**4** If the light doesn't dim, check for a bad connection at the window grid. If the connections are OK, trace the circuit and check continuity of the switch and of the wiring from the fuse panel to the switch/relay and from the relay to the rear window. Repair or replace as necessary.

**5** If the circuits and switch have continuity, replace the relay.

**6** The defogger should stay ON for about 10 minutes before the timer relay shuts it OFF (check your owners manual). If the defogger won't stay ON for the specified time, replace the relay.

**Note:** *The following procedure applies only to grids attached to the surface of the window. Some older vehicles have the grid **inside** the glass. On these vehicles, you must replace the window to repair a faulty grid.*

## Checking and repairing the rear window grid

**7** Visually inspect the edges of the rear window grid for missing or broken wires or bad connections.

**8** Start the engine and turn the defogger switch ON. Allow several minutes for the glass to warm up.

**9** Verify operation by holding your hand against the glass in the grid area to feel for warmth or by watching the ice or fog disappear from the window. If the glass only warms up in certain areas, the grid may have open segments.

**10** The specific grid lines that are open may be determined by noting which ones don't defog. You can normally fog the glass by breathing on it.

**11** Locate the open spot in the grid line by looking for a small gap in the line. If the gap is invisible, use a test light to find it. Starting at the positive side of the grid, touch the test light to the grid line at various points along the line. When you reach a point where the test light no longer lights, the gap lies between that point and your last test point.

**12** Mark the damaged spot with a crayon or tape on the outside of the glass. The grid lines may be repaired with a special kit such as GM no. 1052858, Loctite 15067 (or equivalent) available from dealers and auto parts stores. Follow the instructions provided in the kit.

**Note:** *Large breaks in the grid require window replacement.*

*There may be two connections on the window grid – to find out which one is positive, probe them with a test light – if it lights, you've found the positive connector*

*Rear window defogger repair kits are available from dealers and auto parts stores*

*A test light may be used to find the "dead" portions of the window grid*

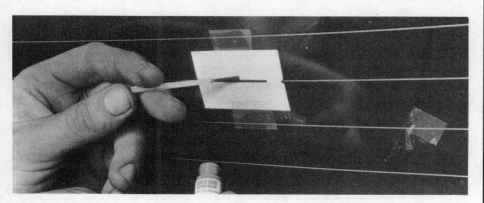

*To use a defogger repair kit, apply masking to the inside of the window at the damaged area, then brush on the special conductive coating*

## Windshield washers

Most windshield washer systems are equipped with a small electric motor-driven pump located on or adjacent to the windshield washer fluid reservoir. These are commonly known as rotary vane pumps. The main exception to this is a General Motors system which incorporates a bellows-type pump cam driven from the wiper motor.

In both types of systems, fluid is pumped through hoses and lines to one or two nozzles located on the hood, on the cowl in front of the windshield or on the windshield wipers themselves.

**1** Check the washer fluid level. If it's OK, turn on the washer pump with the the ignition switch ON, but the engine OFF. Listen for the sound of the pump operating. If you have a GM vehicle with a bellows-type pump, you should hear a clicking sound. If you have a vehicle with a vane pump, you should hear a whirring sound. If you can't hear the pump operating, proceed to the troubleshooting procedure below for your type of pump.

**2** If you can hear the pump operating but no fluid is being expelled from the washer nozzles, trace the hoses and lines between the pump and nozzles to be sure there's none kinked, damaged or disconnected.

**3** If the hoses and lines are OK, disconnect a hose as close to a nozzle as possible and operate the washer again. If a strong stream of fluid is expelled from the end of the hose, the nozzle is probably clogged. Often, nozzles can be unclogged by inserting a pin or paper clip into the hole in the end. If this doesn't unclog the nozzle, replace it.

**4** If there's no fluid being expelled from the hose, trace it back to the pump and disconnect it there. Operate the washer again. If a strong stream of fluid is expelled from the pump, there's a clog in the line between the pump and nozzle(s). If no fluid is expelled from the pump, but you can hear it operating, replace it (vane pump) or rebuild it (bellows pump – see below).

## General troubleshooting

*Washer nozzles can often be cleaned out with a pin or straightened paper clip*

## Troubleshooting rotary vane-type pumps

**5** Start with the general troubleshooting procedure above. If there's no sound coming from the pump when it's turned on, have an assistant operate the washer button (ignition ON) while you check for voltage and ground at the pump. If there's voltage and a good ground, but the pump doesn't work, replace the pump.

**6** If voltage isn't getting to the pump, check the switch and wiring for continuity and repair as necessary.

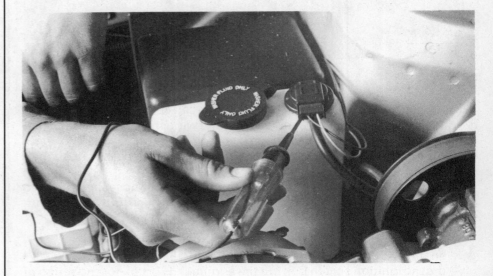

*Checking for voltage at the washer pump*

## Troubleshooting GM bellows-type pumps

**7** These systems often fail due to deterioration of the small O-rings and check valves inside the bellows housing. If the general troubleshooting procedures above reveal the pump is clicking normally but no fluid is being expelled from it, install a rebuild kit in the pump.

WASHER PUMP

PUMP MOUNTING SCREWS

*A typical GM combination wiper/washer motor assembly*

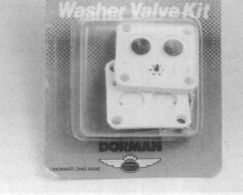

705-092

Windshield Washer Valve Kit

DORMAN

CINCINNATI, OHIO 45242

*Windshield washer valve repair kits are available for GM vehicles . . .*

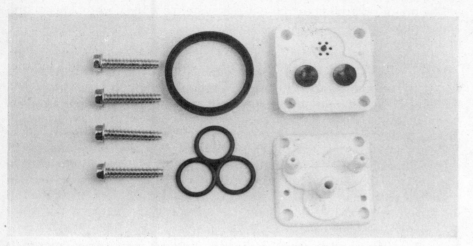

*. . . they include all the parts that commonly fail*

**8** If the pump doesn't click, the problem is in the wiper motor assembly or the switch circuit. Check the switch and the wiring between the switch and motor for continuity. If the wiring and switch check out OK, the problem is in the wiper motor assembly. Replace it.

# Windshield wipers

Wiper systems come with one, two or three speeds. In addition, some have an interval mode for light rain and drizzle. Most wiper switches also have a push button which controls the windshield washer pump. When the washer button is depressed, the wipers are switched on to clear the windshield.

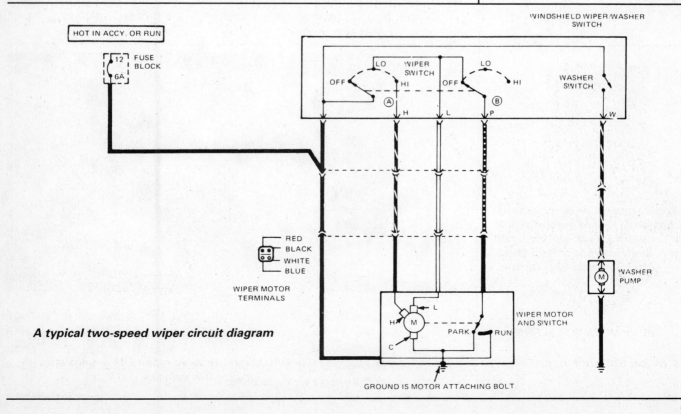

*A typical two-speed wiper circuit diagram*

# Haynes electrical manual

The major components of the wiper system are the control switch, the wiper motor assembly, washer fluid pump (see the previous Section) and interval control module or governor (on vehicles with interval wipers only).

Wiper motors have built-in limit switches that allow the wiper arms to park at the bottom of the windshield every time the wipers are shut off. The limit switch has voltage to it whenever the ignition is ON. Some vehicles have an additional function that reverses the wiper motor during the park phase to stow the wiper arms out of sight below the hoodline.

There are many variations in circuitry among the manufacturers. It is recommended that you obtain the specific wiring diagram for the vehicle you are working on. The following information is by necessity general in nature. If you are unable to locate and correct the problem using the following procedures, take the vehicle to a dealer service department or automotive electrical specialist.

**Note:** *Many auto parts stores have rebuilt wiper motors available for a fraction of the cost of new ones.*

## Troubleshooting
### The wipers work slowly

1  Make sure the battery is in good condition and has a strong charge (see Chapter 4).

2  Remove the wiper motor and operate the wiper arms by hand. Check for binding linkage and pivots. Lubricate or repair the linkage or pivots, as necessary.

### The wipers don't work at all

3  Check the fuse or circuit breaker (see Chapter 1).

4  If the fuse or circuit breaker is OK, connect a jumper wire between the wiper motor and ground, then retest. If the motor works now, repair the ground connection.

*A common cause of wipers not working is a bad ground at the wiper motor – look for corrosion or looseness around the ground connection (arrow)*

5  If the wipers still don't work, turn on the wipers and check for voltage at the motor. If there's voltage at the motor, remove the motor and check it off the vehicle with fused jumper wires from the battery. If the motor now works, check for binding linkage (see Step 2 above). If the motor still doesn't work, replace it.

*To remove a typical wiper motor, unplug the wiring connector, remove the bolts (arrows) and pull the motor out far enough to disconnect the linkage behind it*

**6** If there's no voltage at the motor, check for voltage at the switch. If there's no voltage at the switch, check the wiring between the switch and fuse panel for continuity. If there's voltage at the switch, check the wiring between the switch and motor for continuity.

**Caution:** *If the vehicle you are working on has an interval mode, use a digital ohmmeter for continuity checks – other devices may damage the solid state circuitry in the control module.*

**7** If the wiring is OK, obtain a wiring diagram for the circuit and use it to check the continuity of the switch. Replace the switch, if necessary.

**8** Check the continuity of the wires between the switch and motor. If the wires are OK, replace the switch.

**The wipers only work on one speed**

**9** Check the continuity of all the wiring between the switch and motor. If the wiring is OK, replace the interval module (governor).

**The interval function is inoperative**

**10** Check for voltage at the wiper motor when the wiper switch is OFF but the ignition is ON. If voltage is present, the limit switch in the motor is malfunctioning. Replace the wiper motor. If no voltage is present, trace and repair the limit switch wiring between the fuse panel and wiper motor.

**The wipers stop wherever they are when the switch is shut off (fail to park)**

**11** Disconnect the wiring from the wiper control switch. If the wipers stop, replace the switch. If the wipers keep running, there's a defective limit switch in the motor. Replace the motor.

**The wipers won't shut off unless the ignition is OFF**

# Haynes electrical manual

## The wipers won't retract below the hood-line (vehicles equipped with this function)

**12** Check for mechanical obstructions in the wiper linkage or on the vehicle's body which would prevent the wipers from retracting.

**13** If there are no obstructions, check the wiring between the switch and motor for continuity. If the wiring is OK, replace the wiper motor.

# Glossary

## A

**Active material** – The material on the negative and positive battery plates that interacts with the electrolyte to produce a charge.

**AC generator** – An electromechanical device that generates alternating current (AC), commonly known as an alternator. Usually belt-driven off the engine. Provides maximum output at relatively low rpm. Used on all modern vehicles. Requires a rectifier to convert AC to direct current (DC), which is used by automotive electrical system.

**Aftermarket parts** – Components that can be added to a vehicle after its manufacture. These parts are often accessories and should not be confused with original equipment manufacturer (OEM) service or replacement parts.

**Alligator clip** – A long-nosed spring-loaded metal clip with meshing teeth. Used to make temporary electrical connections.

**Alloy** – A mixture of two or more materials.

**Alternating current (AC)** – An electric current, generated through magnetism, whose polarity constantly changes back and forth from positive to negative.

**Alternator** – A device used in automobiles to produce electric current. The alternator's AC output is rectified to direct current before it reaches the vehicle's electrical system.

**Ammeter** – 1. An instrument for measuring current flow. An ammeter can be designed to measure alternating or direct current. 2. An instrument panel gauge used to measure the flow rate of current into or out of the battery. The ammeter is calibrated in amperes for both charge and discharge rates, in ranges of 20, 30 or more amperes.

**Amperage** – The total amount of current (amperes) flowing in a circuit.

**Ampere (amp)** – The unit of measurement for the flow of electrons in a circuit. The amount of current produced by one volt acting through a resistance of one ohm (1 coulomb per second).

**Ampere hour** – A unit of measurement for battery capacity, obtained by multiplying the current (in amperes) by the time (in hours) during which the current is delivered.

**Analog gauge** – see "gauge."

**Analog signal** – A signal which varies in exact proportion to a measured quantity, such as pressure, temperature, speed, etc.

**Arcing** – When electricity leaps the gap between two electrodes, it is said to be "arcing."

**Armature** – The rotating part of a generator or motor. Actually a coil of wires wrapped in a specific pattern, which rotates on a shaft.

**Atoms** – The small particles which make up all matter. Atoms are made up of a positive-charged nucleus with negative-charged electrons whirling around in orbits.

# Haynes electrical manual

## B

**Battery** – A group of two or more cells connected together for the production of an electric current by converting chemical energy into electrical energy. A battery has two poles – positive and negative. The amount of positive and negative energy is called potential.

**Battery charging** – The process of energizing a battery by passing electric current through the battery in a reverse direction.

**Battery ratings** – Performance standards conducted under laboratory conditions to describe a battery's reserve capacity and cold-crank capacities. The amphour rating is no longer in widespread use. See "cold crank rating."

**Battery state of charge** – The available amount of energy in a battery in relation to that which would ordinarily available be if the battery was fully charged.

**Battery voltage** – A figure determined by the number of cells in a battery. Because each cell generates about two volts, a six cell battery has 12 volts.

**Bendix inertia drive** – A self-engaging and releasing starter drive mechanism. The pinion gear moves into engagement when the starter motor spins and disengages when the engine starts.

**Bound electron** – An electron whose orbit is near the nucleus of an atom and is strongly attracted to it.

**Brush** – A spring-loaded block of carbon or copper that rubs against a commutator or slip ring to conduct current. A key component in all alternators and starters.

**Bulkhead connector** – An OEM device used to connect wiring inside the vehicle body with wiring outside the body. Usually located at the bulkhead or firewall.

**Butt connector** – A solderless connector used to permanently join two wire ends together.

**Bypass** – A shunt, or parallel path, around one or more elements in a circuit.

## C

**Cable** – An assembly of one or more conductors, usually individually insulated and enclosed in a protective sheath.

**Capacity** – The current output capability of a cell or battery, usually expressed in ampere hours.

**Cell** – In a storage battery, one of the sets of positive and negative plates which react with electrolyte to produce an electric current.

**Charge** – A definite quantity of electricity.

**Charge (recharge)** – To restore the active materials in a battery cell by electrically reversing the chemical action.

**Circuit** – An electrical path – from the source (battery or generator) through the load (such as a light bulb) and back to the source – through which current flows. A typical circuit consists of a battery, wire, load (light or motor) and switch. See "simple circuit" and "single-wire circuit."

**Circuit breaker** – A circuit-protection device that automatically opens or breaks an overloaded circuit. The typical circuit breaker usually consists of movable points that open if the preset ampere load is exceeded. Some circuit breakers are self-resetting; others require manual resetting.

**Closed circuit** – A circuit which is uninterrupted from the current source, through the load and back to the current source.

**Closed-end connector** – Solderless connector shaped like a hat. Used to join two, three or more wires together. Similar to wire connectors used in home wiring, but installed by crimping instead of twisting.

**Clutch interlock switch** – A switch that prevents the vehicle from starting unless the clutch is pressed.

**Coil** – Any electrical device or component consisting of wire loops wrapped around a central core. Coils depend on one of two electrical properties for operation, depending on the application (electromagnetism or induction).

**Cold-crank rating** – The minimum number of amperes a fully charged 12-volt battery can deliver for 30 seconds at 0-degrees F without falling below 7.2 battery volts.

**Commutator** – A series of copper bars insulated from each other and connected to the armature windings at the end of the armature. Provides contact with fixed brushes to draw current from (generator) or bring current to (starter) the armature.

**Conductance** – A measure of the ease with which a conductor allows electron flow. In DC circuits, conductance is the reciprocal of resistance.

**Conduction** – The transmission of heat or electricity through, or by means of, a conductor.

**Conductor** – Any material – usually a wire or other metallic object – made up of atoms whose free electrons are easily dislodged, permitting easy flow of electrons from atom to atom. Examples are copper, aluminum and steel. Conductors are all metals. The metal part of an insulated wire is often called the conductor.

**Constant voltage regulator (CVR)** – A device used to maintain a constant voltage level in a circuit, despite fluctuations in system voltage. CVRs are wired into some gauge circuits so voltage fluctuations won't affect accuracy of the gauge readings.

**Contact** – One of the contact-carrying parts of a relay or switch that engages or disengages to open or close the associated electrical circuits.

**Continuity** – A continuous path for the flow of an electrical current.

**Conventional theory** – In this theory, the direction of current flow was arbitrarily chosen to be from the positive terminal of the voltage source, through the external circuit, then back to the negative terminal of the source.

**Coulomb** – The unit of quantity of electricity or charge. The electrons that pass a given point in one second when the current is maintained at one ampere. Equal to an electrical charge of $6.25 \times 10^{18}$ electrons passing a point in one second. See "ampere."

**Current** – The movement of free electrons along a conductor. In automotive electrical work, electron flow is considered to be from positive to negative. Current flow is measured in amperes.

**Cycle** – A recurring series of events which take place in a definite order.

## D

**DC generator** – An electromechanical device that generates direct current. Usually belt-driven off the engine. Because the DC generator requires high rpm for maximum output, it's no longer used in production automobiles.

**Deep cycling** – The process of discharging a battery almost completely before recharging.

**Digital gauge** – See "gauge."

**Diode** – A semiconductor which permits current to flow in only one direction. Diodes are used to rectify current from AC to DC.

**Direct current (DC)** – An electrical current which flows steadily in only one direction.

**Discharge** – Generally, to draw electric current from the battery. Specifically, to remove more energy from a battery than is being replaced. A discharged battery is of no use until it's recharged.

**Disconnect terminal** – Solderless connectors in male and female forms, intended to be easily disconnected and connected. Typically, a blade or pin (male connector) fits into a matching receptacle or socket (female connector). Many components have built-in (blade) terminals that require a specialized female connector.

**Display** – Any device that conveys information. In a vehicle, displays are either lights, gauges or buzzers. Gauges may be analog or digital.

**DPDT** – A double-pole, double-throw switch.

**DPST** – A double-pole, single-throw switch.

**Draw** – The electric current required to operate an electrical device.

**Drive** – A device located on the starter to allow for a method of engaging the starter to the flywheel.

## E

**Electric** – A word used to describe anything having to do with electricity in any form. Used interchangeably with electrical.

**Electrical balance** – An atom or an object in which positive and negative charges are equal.

**Electricity** – The movement of electrons from one body of matter to another.

**Electrochemical** – The production of electricity from chemical reactions, as in a battery.

**Electrolyte** – A solution of sulfuric acid and water used in the cells of a battery to activate the chemical process which results in an electrical potential.

**Electromagnet** – A soft-iron core which is magnetized when an electric current is passed through a coil of wire surrounding it.

**Electromagnetic** – Having both electrical and magnetic properties.

# Haynes electrical manual

**Electromagnetism** – The magnetic field around a conductor when a current is flowing through the conductor.

**Electromechanical** – Any device which uses electrical energy to produce mechanical movement.

**Electrons** – Those parts of an atom which are negatively charged and orbit around the nucleus of the atom.

**Electron flow** – The movement of electrons from a negative to a positive point on a conductor, or through a liquid, gas or vacuum.

**Electron theory** – States that all matter is made up of atoms which are made up of a nucleus and electrons. Free electrons moving from one atom to another, in a single direction, produce what is known as electricity.

**Electronics** – The science and engineering concerned with the behavior of electrons in devices and the utilization of such devices. Especially devices utilizing electron tubes or semiconductor devices.

**Energy** – The capacity for performing work.

**EVR** – Electronic Voltage Regulator; a type of regulator that uses all solid state devices to perform the regulatory functions.

## F

**Field** – An area covered or filled with a magnetic force. Common terminology for field magnet, field winding, magnetic field, etc.

**Field coil** – A coil of insulated wire, wrapped around an iron or steel core, that creates a magnetic field when current is passed through the wire.

**Filament** – A resistance in an electric light bulb which glows and produces light when an adequate current is sent through it.

**Fluorescent** – Having the property of giving off light when bombarded by electrons or radiant energy.

**Flux** – The lines of magnetic force flowing in a magnetic field.

**Flywheel** – A large wheel attached to the crankshaft at the rear of the engine.

**Flywheel ring gear** – A large gear pressed onto the circumference of the flywheel. When the starter gear engages the ring gear, the starter cranks the engine.

**Free electron** – An electron in the outer orbit of an atom, not strongly attracted to the nucleus; it can be easily forced out of its orbit.

**Fuse** – A circuit-protection device containing a soft piece of metal which is calibrated to melt at a predetermined amp level and break the circuit.

**Fuse block** – An insulating base on which fuse clips or other contacts are mounted.

**Fuse link** – See "fusible link."

**Fuse panel** – A plastic or fiberboard assembly that permits mounting several fuses in one centralized location. Some fuse panels are part of, or contain, a terminal block (see "terminal block").

**Fuse wire** – A wire made of an alloy which melts at a low temperature.

**Fusible link** – A circuit protection device consisting of a conductor surrounded by heat-resistant insulation. The conductor is two gages smaller than the wire it protects, so it acts as the weakest link in the circuit. Unlike a blown fuse, a failed fusible link must be cut from the wire for replacement.

## G

**Gage** – A standard SAE designation of wire sizes, expressed in AWG (American Wire Gage). The larger the gage number, the smaller the wire. Metric wire sizes are expressed in cross-sectional area, which is expressed in square millimeters. Sometimes the spelling "gauge" is also used to designate wire size. Using this spelling, however, avoids confusion with instrument panel displays (see "gauge").

**Gassing** – The breakdown of water into hydrogen and oxygen gas in a battery.

**Gauge** – An instrument panel display used to monitor engine conditions. A gauge with a movable pointer on a dial or a fixed scale is an analog gauge. A gauge with a numerical readout is called a digital gauge. Also refers to measuring device used to check regulator point openings.

**Generator** – An engine-driven device that produces an electric current through magnetism by converting rotary motion into electrical potential (see "AC generator" and "DC generator").

**Grid** – A lead screen that is pasted with active materials to form a negative or positive battery plate.

**Grommet** – A donut shaped rubber or plastic part used to protect wiring that passes through a panel, firewall or bulkhead.

**Ground** – The connection made in grounding a circuit. In a single-wire system, any metal part of the car's structure that's directly or indirectly attached to the battery's negative post. Used to conduct current from a load back to the battery. Self-grounded components are attached directly to a grounded metal part through their mounting screws. Components mounted to nongrounded parts of a vehicle require a ground wire attached to a known good ground.

## H

**Halogen light** – A special bulb that produces a brilliant white light. Because of its high intensity, a halogen light is often used for fog lights and driving lights.

**Harness** – A bundle of electrical wires. For convenience in handling and for neatness, all wires going to a certain part of the vehicle are bundled together into a harness.

**Harness ties** – Self-tightening nylon straps used to bundle wires into harnesses. Available in stock lengths that can be cut to size after installation. Once tightened, they can't be removed unless they're cut from the harness.

**Harness wrap** – One of several materials used to bundle wires into manageable harnesses. See "loom," "split loom," "loom tape" and "harness ties").

**Hot** – Connected to the battery positive terminal, energized.

**Hydrogen gas** – The lightest and most explosive of all gases. Emitted from a battery during charging procedures. This gas is very dangerous and certain safety precautions must be observed.

**Hydrometer** – A syringe-like instrument used to measure the specific gravity of a battery's electrolyte.

## I

**IAR** – Integral Alternator/Regulator; a type of regulator mounted at the rear of the alternator.

**Ignition switch** – A key-operated switch that opens and closes the circuit that supplies power to the ignition and electrical system.

**Indicator light** – An instrument-panel display used to convey information or condition of the monitored circuit or system. See "warning light."

**Induced** – Produced by the influence of a magnetic or electrical field.

**Induced current** – The current generated in a conductor as it moves through a magnetic field, or as a magnetic field is moved across a conductor.

**Induced voltage** – The voltage produced as a result of an induced current flow.

**Inductance** – That property of a coil or other electrical device which opposes any change in the existing current, present only when an alternating or pulsating current is flowing. Has no effect on the flow of direct, or static, current.

**Induction** – The process by which an electrical conductor becomes charged when near another charged body. Induction occurs through the influence of the magnetic fields surrounding the conductors.

**Input** – 1. The driving force applied to a circuit or device. 2. The terminals (or other connection) where the driving force may be applied to a circuit or device.

**Instrument Voltage Regulator** – See "Constant Voltage Regulator."

**Insulator** – A material that has few or no free electrons that readily leave their orbits. A non-conducting material used for insulating wires in electrical circuits. Cloth, glass, plastic and rubber are typical examples. Wires for modern vehicles use plastic insulation.

**Integral** – Formed as a unit with another part.

**Intercell connector** – A lead strap or connector that connects the cells in a battery.

**Intermittent** – Coming or going at intervals; not continuous.

**Ion** – An atom having an imbalanced charge due to the loss of an electron or proton. An ion may be either positively charged (have a deficiency of electrons) or negatively charged (have a surplus of electrons).

## J

**Jumper** – A short length of wire used as a temporary connection between two points.

**Junction** – 1. A connection between two or more components, conductors or sections of transmission line. 2. Any point from which three or more wires branch out in a circuit.

# Haynes electrical manual

**Junction box** – A box in which connections are made between different cables.

## L

**Lead-acid battery** – A common automotive battery in which the active materials are lead, lead peroxide and a solution of sulphuric acid.

**Lead dioxide** – A combination of lead and oxygen, as found in the storage battery. Lead dioxide is reddish brown in color.

**Lead sulfate** – A combination of lead, oxygen and sulfur, as found in the storage battery.

**Light** – An electrical load designed to emit light when current flows through it. A light consists of a glass bulb enclosing a filament and a base containing the electrical contacts. Some lights, such as sealed beam headlights, also contain a built-in reflector.

**Load** – Any device that uses electrical current to perform work in a vehicle electrical system. Lights and motors are typical examples.

**Loom** – A harness covering. Older vehicles used woven-cloth loom; most modern vehicles use a corrugated-plastic loom or split loom.

**Loom tape** – A nonadhesive tape used as a harness wrap. Adhesive-type tapes, including electrical tapes, are not recommended for wrapping harnesses. Often, a piece of shrink wrap is used at tape ends to keep the tape from unraveling.

## M

**Magnet** – A material that attracts iron and steel. Temporary magnets are made by surrounding a soft-iron core with a strong electromagnetic field. Permanent magnets are made with steel.

**Magnetic field** – The field produced by a magnet or a magnetic influence. A magnetic field has force and direction.

**Magnetic poles** – The ends of a bar or horseshoe magnet.

**Magnetism** – A property of the molecules of certain materials, such as iron, that allows the substance to be magnetized.

**Meter** – An electrical or electronic measuring device.

**Module** – A combination of components packaged in a single unit with a common mounting and providing some complete function.

**Motor** – An electromagnetic apparatus used to convert electrical energy into mechanical energy.

**Multimeter** – A test instrument with the capability to measure voltage, current and resistance.

## N

**Negative charge** – The condition when an element has more than a normal quantity of electrons.

**Negative ion** – An atom with more electrons than normal. A negative ion has a negative charge.

**Negative terminal** – The terminal on a battery which has an excess of electrons. A point from which electrons flow to the positive terminal.

**Neutral** – Neither positive nor negative, or in a natural condition. Having the normal number of electrons, i.e. the same number of electrons as protons.

**Neutral start switch** – On vehicles with an automatic transmission, a switch that prevents starting if the vehicle is not in Neutral or Park.

**Neutron** – A particle within the nucleus of an atom. A neutron is electrically neutral.

**Nichrome** – A metallic compound containing nickel and chromium, used in making high resistances.

**North pole** – The pole of a magnet from which the lines of force are emitted. The lines of force travel from the north to the south pole.

**Nucleus** – The core of an atom. The nucleus contains protons and neutrons.

**Nylon ties** – See "harness ties."

## O

**OEM (Original Equipment Manufacturer)** – A designation used to describe the equipment and parts installed on a vehicle by the manufacturer, or those available from the vehicle manufacturer as replacement parts. See "aftermarket parts."

**Ohm** – The practical unit for measuring electrical resistance.

**Ohmmeter** – An instrument for measuring resistance. In automotive electrical work, it's often used to determine the resistance that various loads contribute to a circuit or system.

**Ohm's Law** – The electrical formula that describes how voltage, current and resistance are related. The basic formula is E (electrical pressure in volts) = I (current flow in amperes) X R (resistance in ohms). What does it mean? Simply put, amperage varies in direct ratio to voltage and in inverse ratio to resistance.

**Open circuit** – An electrical circuit that isn't complete because of a broken or disconnected wire.

**Open circuit voltage** – The battery voltage when the battery has no closed circuit across the posts and is not delivering or receiving voltage.

**Orbit** – The path followed by an electron around the nucleus.

**Output** – The current, voltage, power or driving force delivered by a device or circuit. The terminals or connections where the current can be measured.

**Overrunning clutch** – A device located on the starter to allow for a method of engaging the starter with the flywheel. The overrunning clutch uses a shift lever to actuate the drive pinion to provide for a positive meshing and demeshing of the pinion with the flywheel ring gear.

## P

**Parallel circuit** – A method or pattern of connecting units in an electrical circuit so that they're connected negative-to-negative and positive-to-positive. In a parallel circuit, current can flow independently through several components at the same time. See "series circuit."

**Permanent magnet** – A magnet made of tempered steel which holds its magnetism for a long period of time.

**Pinion** – A small gear that either drives or is driven by a larger gear.

**Plate** – A battery grid that's pasted with active materials and given a forming charge which results in a negative or positive charge. Plates are submerged, as elements, in the electrolyte and electricity is produced from the chemical reactions between the plates and the electrolyte.

**Polarity** – The quality or condition of a body which has two opposite properties or directions; having poles, as in an electric cell, a magnet or a magnetic field.

**Polarity-protected connector** – A multiple-cavity connector that can be connected in only one way, either to a mating connector or to a component.

**Pole** – A positive (or negative) terminal in a cell or battery; the ends of a magnet (north or south).

**Pole shoe** – The part of a starter that's used to hold the field coils in place in their proper positions; consists of a soft-iron core which is wound with heavy copper ribbons.

**Positive** – Designating or pertaining to a kind of electrical potential.

**Positive terminal** – The battery terminal to which current flows.

**Post** – A round, tapered battery terminal that serves as a connection for battery cables.

**Potential** – Latent, or unreleased, electrical energy.

**Power supply** – A unit that supplies electrical power to a unit. For example, a battery.

**Printed circuit** – An electrical conductor consisting of thin metal foil paths attached to a flexible plastic backing. Also called a PC board. PC boards are used primarily in OEM instrument clusters and other electronic devices.

**Proton** – A positively-charged particle in the nucleus of an atom.

## Q

**Quick charger** – A battery charger designed to allow the charging of a battery in a short period of time.

## R

**Rectification** – The process of changing alternating current to direct current.

**Rectifier** – A device in the electrical system used to convert alternating current to direct current.

**Regulator** – A device used to regulate the output of a generator or alternator by controlling the current and voltage.

**Relay** – An electromagnetic device that opens or closes the flow of current in a circuit.

**Resistance** – The resistance to electron flow present in an electrical circuit, expressed in ohms.

# Haynes electrical manual

**Resistor** – Any conductor that permits electron movement but retards it. Tungsten and nickel are typical resistors.

**Rheostat** – A variable resistor, operated by a knob or handle, used to vary the resistance in a circuit. A rheostat consists of a coil of resistance wire and a movable contact or wiper that creates more or less resistance in the circuit, depending on how many coil windings it allows the current to pass through. The dimmer control for instrument panel illumination is an example.

**Ring terminal** – A conductor used to attach a wire to a screw or stud terminal. The ring is sized to the mating screw. Ring terminals are the connectors least likely to vibrate loose in rugged applications. Comes in soldered and unsoldered versions.

**Rotor** – That part of an alternator which rotates inside the stator.

## S

**Schematic** – A drawing system for portraying the components and wires in a vehicle's electrical system, using standardized symbols.

**Secondary** – The output winding of a transformer, i.e. the winding in which current flow is due to inductive coupling with another coil called the primary.

**Sending unit** – Used to operate a gauge or indicator light. In indicator light circuits, contains contact points, like a switch. In gauge circuits, contains a variable resistance that modifies current flow in accordance with the condition or system being monitored.

**Separator** – A thin sheet of non-conducting material that is placed between the negative and positive plates in an element to prevent the plates from touching.

**Series circuit** – A circuit in which the units are consecutively connected or wired positive to negative and in which current has to pass through all components, one at a time.

**Series/parallel circuit** – A circuit in which some components are wired in series, others in parallel. An example: Two loads wired in parallel with each other, but in series with the switch that controls them.

**Short circuit** – An unintentional routing of a current, bypassing part of the original circuit.

**Shorted winding** – The winding of a field or armature that's grounded because of accidental or deliberate reasons.

**Shrink wrap** – An insulating material used to protect wire splices and junctions at terminals. Upon application of open flame or heat, the wrap shrinks to fit tightly on the wire or terminal.

**Shunt** – 1. Connected in parallel with some other part. 2. A precision low value resistor placed across the terminals of an ammeter to increase its range.

**Simple circuit** – The simplest circuit includes an electrical power source, a load and some wire to connect them together.

**Single-wire circuit** – Generally used in production vehicles, in which one wire brings current to the load and the vehicle's frame acts as the return path (ground).

**Slip ring** – A device for making electrical connections between stationary and rotating contacts.

**Snap-splice connector** – Solderless connector used to tap an additional wire into an existing wire without cutting the original. Often used in installing trailer wiring to a tow vehicle.

**Solder** – An alloy of lead and tin which melts at a low temperature and is used for making electrical connections.

**Solderless connector** – Any connector or terminal that can be installed to a wire without the use of solder. They're usually crimped in place using a special crimping tool. Ring terminals, spade terminals, disconnect terminals, butt connectors, closed-end connectors and snap-splice connectors are typical examples. Ring and spade terminals also come in soldered versions.

**Solenoid** – An electromechanical device consisting of a tubular coil surrounding a movable metal core, or plunger, which moves when the coil is energized. The movable core is connected to various mechanisms to accomplish work.

**Spade terminal** – A terminal used to connect a wire to a screw or stud terminal. The spade terminal has two forked ends, either straight or with upturned tips. They're more convenient to install than ring terminals, but slightly less secure for rugged applications. Comes in soldered and unsoldered versions.

**SPDT** – A single-pole, double-throw switch.

**Specific gravity** – The measure of a battery's charge, made by comparing the relative weight of a volume of its electrolyte to the weight of an equal volume of pure water, which has an assigned value of 1.0. A fully charged battery will have a specific gravity reading of 1.260. See "hydrometer."

**Split loom** – Flexible, corrugated conduit used to bundle wires into harnesses.

**SPST** – A single-pole, single-throw switch.

**Starter** – A device used to supply the required mechanical force to turn over the engine for starting.

**Stator** – In an alternator, the part which contains the conductors within which the field rotates.

**Sulfuric acid** – A heavy, corrosive, high-boiling liquid acid that is colorless when pure. Sulfuric acid is mixed with distilled water to form the electrolyte used in storage batteries.

**Supply voltage** – The voltage obtained from the power supply to operate a circuit.

**Switch** – An electrical control device used to turn a circuit on and off, or change the connections in the circuit. Switches are described by the number of poles and throws they have. See "SPST, SPDT, DPST and DPDT."

## T

**Tachometer** – A device that measures the speed of an engine in rpm.

**Terminal** – A device attached to the end of a wire or to an apparatus for convenience in making electrical connections.

**Terminal block** – A plastic or resin assembly containing two rows of terminals screws. Used to join the circuits in several wiring harnesses.

**Test light** – A test instrument consisting of an indicator light wired into the handle of a metal probe. When the probe contacts a live circuit, current flows through the light, lighting it, and to ground through an attached lead and alligator clip. Used to test for voltage in live circuits only.

**Test light (self-powered)** – A test device containing an indicator light and a built-in battery. Used to test continuity of circuits not containing voltage at the time of the test. Used to test continuity in a harness before it's installed in the vehicle. Also called a continuity tester.

**Thermal relay** – A relay actuated by the heating effect of the current flowing through it.

**Thermistor** – The electrical element in a temperature sending unit that varies its resistance in proportion to temperature. Unlike most electrical conductors, in which resistance increases as temperature rises, resistance in a thermistor decreases. Thermistors are made from the oxides of cobalt, copper, iron or nickel.

**Tracer** – A stripe of a second color applied to a wire insulator to distinguish that wire from another one with the same color insulator.

**Transformer** – An apparatus for transforming an electric current to a higher or lower voltage without changing the total energy.

## V

**Variable resistor** – A wire-wound or composition resistor with a sliding contact for changing the resistance. See "rheostat."

**Variable transformer** – An iron-core transformer with a sliding contact which moves along the exposed turns of the secondary winding to vary the output voltage.

**Volt** – A practical unit for measuring current pressure in a circuit; the force that will move a current of one ampere through a resistance of one ohm.

**Voltage drop** – The difference in voltage between two points, caused by the loss of electrical pressure as a current flows through an impedance or resistance. All wire, no matter how low the resistance, shows at least a trace of voltage drop.

**Voltage regulator** – An electromechanical or electronic device that maintains the output voltage of a device at a predetermined value.

**Voltmeter** – 1. A test instrument that measures voltage in an electrical circuit. Used to check continuity and determine voltage drop in specific circuits of vehicle electrical systems. 2. An instrument panel gauge that measures system voltage. When the engine's not running, the voltmeter indicates battery voltage, which should be 12 to 13 volts in a 12-volt system. When the engine's running, the voltmeter indicates total system voltage, or the combined voltage output of the alternator and the battery.

**VOM (Volt-Ohmmeter)** – A two-in-one test instrument. For convenience, a voltmeter and an ohmmeter are mounted in the same case and share a common readout and test leads.

# Haynes electrical manual

## W

**Warning light** – An instrument panel display used to inform the driver when something undesirable has happened in the monitored circuit or system, such as an overheated engine or a sudden loss of oil pressure.

**Watt** – The unit for measuring electrical energy or "work." Wattage is the product of amperage multiplied by voltage.

**Winding** – One or more turns of a wire, forming a coil. Also, the individual coils of a transformer.

**Wire** – A solid or stranded group of cylindrical conductors together with any associated insulation.

# Index

# Haynes electrical manual

# Haynes electrical manual

# Haynes Automotive Manuals

NOTE: New manuals are added to this list on a periodic basis. If you do not see a listing for your vehicle, consult your local Haynes dealer for the latest product information.

## ACURA
*1776   **Integra** '86 thru '89 **& Legend** '86 thru '90

## AMC
    **Jeep CJ** - see JEEP (412)
694   **Mid-size models,** Concord, Hornet, Gremlin & Spirit '70 thru '83
934   **(Renault) Alliance & Encore** '83 thru '87

## AUDI
615   **4000** all models '80 thru '87
428   **5000** all models '77 thru '83
1117   **5000** all models '84 thru '88

## AUSTIN-HEALEY
    **Sprite** - see MG Midget (265)

## BMW
*2020   **3/5 Series** not including diesel or all-wheel drive models '82 thru '92
276   **320i** all 4 cyl models '75 thru '83
632   **528i & 530i** all models '75 thru '80
240   **1500 thru 2002** except Turbo '59 thru '77

## BUICK
    **Century (front wheel drive)** - see GM (829)
*1627   **Buick, Oldsmobile & Pontiac Full-size (Front wheel drive)** all models '85 thru '95
    **Buick** Electra, LeSabre and Park Avenue; **Oldsmobile** Delta 88 Royale, Ninety Eight and Regency; **Pontiac** Bonneville
1551   **Buick Oldsmobile & Pontiac Full-size (Rear wheel drive)**
    **Buick** Estate '70 thru '90, Electra '70 thru '84, LeSabre '70 thru '85, Limited '74 thru '79
    **Oldsmobile** Custom Cruiser '70 thru '90, Delta 88 '70 thru '85,Ninety-eight '70 thru '84
    **Pontiac** Bonneville '70 thru '81, Catalina '70 thru '81, Grandville '70 thru '75, Parisienne '83 thru '86
627   **Mid-size Regal & Century** all rear-drive models with V6, V8 and Turbo '74 thru '87
    **Regal** - see GENERAL MOTORS (1671)
    **Riviera** - see GENERAL MOTORS (38030)
    **Skyhawk** - see GENERAL MOTORS (766)
    **Skylark** '80 thru '85 - see GM (38020)
    **Skylark** '86 on - see GM (1420)
    **Somerset** - see GENERAL MOTORS (1420)

## CADILLAC
*751   **Cadillac Rear Wheel Drive** all gasoline models '70 thru '93
    **Cimarron** - see GENERAL MOTORS (766)
    **Eldorado** - see GENERAL MOTORS (38030)
    **Seville** '80 thru '85 - see GM (38030)

## CHEVROLET
*1477   **Astro & GMC Safari Mini-vans** '85 thru '93
554   **Camaro V8** all models '70 thru '81
866   **Camaro** all models '82 thru '92
    **Cavalier** - see GENERAL MOTORS (766)
    **Celebrity** - see GENERAL MOTORS (829)
24017   **Camaro & Firebird** '93 thru '96
625   **Chevelle, Malibu & El Camino** all V6 & V8 models '69 thru '87
449   **Chevette & Pontiac T1000** '76 thru '87
550   **Citation** all models '80 thru '85
*1628   **Corsica/Beretta** all models '87 thru '96
274   **Corvette** all V8 models '68 thru '82
*1336   **Corvette** all models '84 thru '91
1762   **Chevrolet Engine Overhaul Manual**
704   **Full-size Sedans** Caprice, Impala, Biscayne, Bel Air & Wagons '69 thru '90
    **Lumina** - see GENERAL MOTORS (1671)
    **Lumina APV** - see GENERAL MOTORS (2035)
319   **Luv Pick-up** all 2WD & 4WD '72 thru '82
626   **Monte Carlo** all models '70 thru '88

---

241   **Nova** all V8 models '69 thru '79
*1642   **Nova and Geo Prizm** all front wheel drive models, '85 thru '92
420   **Pick-ups '67 thru '87** - Chevrolet & GMC, all V8 & in-line 6 cyl, 2WD & 4WD '67 thru '87; Suburbans, Blazers & Jimmys '67 thru '91
*1664   **Pick-ups '88 thru '95** - Chevrolet & GMC, all full-size pick-ups, '88 thru '95; Blazer & Jimmy '92 thru '94; Suburban '92 thru '95; Tahoe & Yukon '95
831   **S-10 & GMC S-15 Pick-ups** '82 thru '93
*24071   **S-10 & GMC S-15 Pick-ups** '94 thru '96
*1727   **Sprint & Geo Metro** '85 thru '94
*345   **Vans - Chevrolet & GMC,** V8 & in-line 6 cylinder models '68 thru '96

## CHRYSLER
25025   **Chrysler Concorde, New Yorker & LHS, Dodge** Intrepid, **Eagle** Vision, '93 thru '96
2114   **Chrysler Engine Overhaul Manual**
*2058   **Full-size Front-Wheel Drive** '88 thru '93
    **K-Cars** - see DODGE Aries (723)
    **Laser** - see DODGE Daytona (1140)
*1337   **Chrysler & Plymouth Mid-size** front wheel drive '82 thru '95
    **Rear-wheel Drive** - see Dodge (2098)

## DATSUN
647   **200SX** all models '80 thru '83
228   **B - 210** all models '73 thru '78
525   **210** all models '79 thru '82
206   **240Z, 260Z & 280Z** Coupe '70 thru '78
563   **280ZX** Coupe & 2+2 '79 thru '83
    **300ZX** - see NISSAN (1137)
679   **310** all models '78 thru '82
123   **510 & PL521 Pick-up** '68 thru '73
430   **510** all models '78 thru '81
372   **610** all models '72 thru '76
277   **620 Series Pick-up** all models '73 thru '79
    **720 Series Pick-up** - see NISSAN (771)
376   **810/Maxima** all gasoline models, '77 thru '84
    **Pulsar** - see NISSAN (876)
    **Sentra** - see NISSAN (982)
    **Stanza** - see NISSAN (981)

## DODGE
    **400 & 600** - see CHRYSLER Mid-size (1337)
*723   **Aries & Plymouth Reliant** '81 thru '89
1231   **Caravan & Plymouth Voyager Mini-Vans** all models '84 thru '95
699   **Challenger/Plymouth Saporro** '78 thru '83
    **Challenger** '67-'76 - see DODGE Dart (234)
610   **Colt & Plymouth Champ (front wheel drive)** all models '78 thru '87
*1668   **Dakota Pick-ups** all models '87 thru '96
234   **Dart, Challenger/Plymouth Barracuda & Valiant** 6 cyl models '67 thru '76
*1140   **Daytona & Chrysler Laser** '84 thru '89
    **Intrepid** - see CHRYSLER (25025)
*30034   **Neon** all models '94 thru '97
*545   **Omni & Plymouth Horizon** '78 thru '90
*912   **Pick-ups** all full-size models '74 thru '93
*30041   **Pick-ups** all full-size models '94 thru '96
*556   **Ram 50/D50 Pick-ups & Raider and Plymouth Arrow Pick-ups** '79 thru '93
2098   **Dodge/Plymouth/Chrysler** rear wheel drive '71 thru '89
*1726   **Shadow & Plymouth Sundance** '87 thru '94
*1779   **Spirit & Plymouth Acclaim** '89 thru '95
*349   **Vans - Dodge & Plymouth** V8 & 6 cyl models '71 thru '96

## EAGLE
    **Talon** - see Mitsubishi Eclipse (2097)
    **Vision** - see CHRYSLER (25025)

## FIAT
094   **124 Sport Coupe & Spider** '68 thru '78
273   **X1/9** all models '74 thru '80

## FORD
10355   **Ford Automatic Trans. Overhaul**
*1476   **Aerostar Mini-vans** all models '86 thru '96

---

268   **Courier Pick-up** all models '72 thru '82
2105   **Crown Victoria & Mercury Grand Marquis** '88 thru '96
1763   **Ford Engine Overhaul Manual**
789   **Escort/Mercury Lynx** all models '81 thru '90
*2046   **Escort/Mercury Tracer** '91 thru '96
*2021   **Explorer & Mazda Navajo** '91 thru '95
560   **Fairmont & Mercury Zephyr** '78 thru '83
334   **Fiesta** all models '77 thru '80
754   **Ford & Mercury Full-size,** Ford LTD & Mercury Marquis ('75 thru '82); Ford Custom 500,Country Squire, Crown Victoria & Mercury Colony Park ('75 thru '87); Ford LTD Crown Victoria & Mercury Gran Marquis ('83 thru '87)
359   **Granada & Mercury Monarch** all in-line, 6 cyl & V8 models '75 thru '80
773   **Ford & Mercury Mid-size,** Ford Thunderbird & Mercury Cougar ('75 thru '82); Ford LTD & Mercury Marquis ('83 thru '86); Ford Torino,Gran Torino, Elite, Ranchero pick-up, LTD II, Mercury Montego, Comet, XR-7 & Lincoln Versailles ('75 thru '86)
231   **Mustang II** 4 cyl, V6 & V8 models '74 thru '78
357   **Mustang V8** all models '64-1/2 thru '73
*654   **Mustang & Mercury Capri** all models Mustang, '79 thru '93; Capri, '79 thru '86
*36051   **Mustang** all models '94 thru '97
788   **Pick-ups & Bronco** '73 thru '79
*880   **Pick-ups & Bronco** '80 thru '96
649   **Pinto & Mercury Bobcat** '75 thru '80
1670   **Probe** all models '89 thru '92
*1026   **Ranger/Bronco II** gasoline models '83 thru '92
*36071   **Ranger** '93 thru '96 &
    **Mazda Pick-ups** '94 thru '96
*1421   **Taurus & Mercury Sable** '86 thru '95
*1418   **Tempo & Mercury Topaz** all gasoline models '84 thru '94
1338   **Thunderbird/Mercury Cougar** '83 thru '88
*1725   **Thunderbird/Mercury Cougar** '89 and '96
344   **Vans** all V8 Econoline models '69 thru '91
*2119   **Vans** full size '92-'95

## GENERAL MOTORS
*10360   **GM Automatic Transmission Overhaul**
*829   **Buick Century, Chevrolet Celebrity, Oldsmobile Cutlass Ciera & Pontiac 6000** all models '82 thru '96
*1671   **Buick Regal, Chevrolet Lumina, Oldsmobile Cutlass Supreme & Pontiac Grand Prix** front wheel drive models '88 thru '95
*766   **Buick Skyhawk, Cadillac Cimarron, Chevrolet Cavalier, Oldsmobile Firenza & Pontiac J-2000 & Sunbird** '82 thru '94
38020   **Buick Skylark, Chevrolet Citation, Olds Omega, Pontiac Phoenix** '80 thru '85
1420   **Buick Skylark & Somerset, Oldsmobile Achieva & Calais and Pontiac Grand Am** all models '85 thru '95
38030   **Cadillac Eldorado** '71 thru '85, **Seville** '80 thru '85, **Oldsmobile Toronado** '71 thru '85 & **Buick Riviera** '79 thru '85
*2035   **Chevrolet Lumina APV, Olds Silhouette & Pontiac Trans Sport** all models '90 thru '95
    **General Motors Full-size Rear-wheel Drive** - see BUICK (1551)

## GEO
    **Metro** - see CHEVROLET Sprint (1727)
    **Prizm** - '85 thru '92 see CHEVY Nova (1642), '93 thru '96 see TOYOTA Corolla (1642)
*2039   **Storm** all models '90 thru '93
    **Tracker** - see SUZUKI Samurai (1626)

## GMC
    **Safari** - see CHEVROLET ASTRO (1477)
    **Vans & Pick-ups** - see CHEVROLET (420, 831, 345, 1664 & 24071)

*(Continued on other side)*

---

**Haynes North America, Inc., 861 Lawrence Drive, Newbury Park, CA 91320 • (805) 498-6703**

# Haynes Automotive Manuals (continued)

*NOTE: New manuals are added to this list on a periodic basis. If you do not see a listing for your vehicle, consult your local Haynes dealer for the latest product information.*

## HONDA
| | | |
|---|---|---|
| 351 | **Accord CVCC** all models '76 thru '83 |
| 1221 | **Accord** all models '84 thru '89 |
| 2067 | **Accord** all models '90 thru '93 |
| 42013 | **Accord** all models '94 thru '95 |
| 160 | **Civic 1200** all models '73 thru '79 |
| 633 | **Civic 1300 & 1500 CVCC** all models '80 thru '83 |
| 297 | **Civic 1500 CVCC** all models '75 thru '79 |
| 1227 | **Civic** all models '84 thru '91 |
| *2118 | **Civic & del Sol** '92 thru '95 |
| *601 | **Prelude CVCC** all models '79 thru '89 |

## HYUNDAI
| | |
|---|---|
| *1552 | **Excel** all models '86 thru '94 |

## ISUZU
| | |
|---|---|
| *1641 | **Trooper & Pick-up**, all gasoline models Pick-up, '81 thru '93; Trooper, '84 thru '91 |
| | **Hombre** - see *CHEVROLET S-10 (24071)* |

## JAGUAR
| | |
|---|---|
| *242 | **XJ6** all 6 cyl models '68 thru '86 |
| *49011 | **XJ6** all models '88 thru '94 |
| *478 | **XJ12 & XJS** all 12 cyl models '72 thru '85 |

## JEEP
| | |
|---|---|
| *1553 | **Cherokee, Comanche & Wagoneer Limited** all models '84 thru '96 |
| 412 | **CJ** all models '49 thru '86 |
| 50025 | **Grand Cherokee** all models '93 thru '95 |
| 50029 | **Grand Wagoneer & Pick-up** '72 thru '91 Grand Wagoneer '84 thru '91, Cherokee & Wagoneer '72 thru '83, Pick-up '72 thru '88 |
| *1777 | **Wrangler** all models '87 thru '95 |

## LINCOLN
| | |
|---|---|
| 2117 | **Rear Wheel Drive** all models '70 thru '96 |

## MAZDA
| | |
|---|---|
| 648 | **626** (rear wheel drive) all models '79 thru '82 |
| *1082 | **626/MX-6** (front wheel drive) '83 thru '91 |
| 370 | **GLC Hatchback** (rear wheel drive) '77 thru '83 |
| 757 | **GLC** (front wheel drive) '81 thru '85 |
| *2047 | **MPV** all models '89 thru '94 |
| | **Navajo** - see *Ford Explorer (2021)* |
| 267 | **Pick-ups** '72 thru '93 |
| | **Pick-ups** '94 thru '96 - see *Ford Ranger (36071)* |
| 460 | **RX-7** all models '79 thru '85 |
| *1419 | **RX-7** all models '86 thru '91 |

## MERCEDES-BENZ
| | |
|---|---|
| *1643 | **190 Series** four-cyl gas models, '84 thru '88 |
| 346 | **230/250/280** 6 cyl sohc models '68 thru '72 |
| 983 | **280 123 Series** gasoline models '77 thru '81 |
| 698 | **350 & 450** all models '71 thru '80 |
| 697 | **Diesel 123 Series** '76 thru '85 |

## MERCURY
*See FORD Listing*

## MG
| | |
|---|---|
| 111 | **MGB** Roadster & GT Coupe '62 thru '80 |
| 265 | **MG Midget, Austin Healey Sprite** '58 thru '80 |

## MITSUBISHI
| | |
|---|---|
| *1669 | **Cordia, Tredia, Galant, Precis & Mirage** '83 thru '93 |
| *2097 | **Eclipse, Eagle Talon & Plymouth Laser** '90 thru '94 |
| *2022 | **Pick-up** '83 thru '96 & **Montero** '83 thru '93 |

## NISSAN
| | |
|---|---|
| 1137 | **300ZX** all models including Turbo '84 thru '89 |
| *72015 | **Altima** all models '93 thru '97 |
| *1341 | **Maxima** all models '85 thru '91 |
| *771 | **Pick-ups** '80 thru '96 **Pathfinder** '87 thru '95 |
| 876 | **Pulsar** all models '83 thru '86 |
| *982 | **Sentra** all models '82 thru '94 |
| *981 | **Stanza** all models '82 thru '90 |

## OLDSMOBILE
| | |
|---|---|
| | **Achieva** - see *GENERAL MOTORS (1420)* |
| | **Bravada** - see *CHEVROLET S-10 (831)* |
| | **Calais** - see *GENERAL MOTORS (1420)* |
| | **Custom Cruiser** - see *BUICK RWD (1551)* |
| *658 | **Cutlass V6 & V8** gas models '74 thru '88 |
| | **Cutlass Ciera** - see *GENERAL MOTORS (829)* |
| | **Cutlass Supreme** - see *GM (1671)* |
| | **Delta 88** - see *BUICK Full-size RWD (1551)* |
| | **Delta 88 Brougham** - see *BUICK Full-size FWD (1551), RWD (1627)* |
| | **Delta 88 Royale** - see *BUICK Full-size RWD (1551)* |
| | **Firenza** - see *GENERAL MOTORS (766)* |
| | **Ninety-eight Regency** - see *BUICK Full-size RWD (1551), FWD (1627)* |
| | **Ninety-eight Regency Brougham** - see *BUICK Full-size RWD (1551)* |
| | **Omega** - see *GENERAL MOTORS (38020)* |
| | **Silhouette** - see *GENERAL MOTORS (2035)* |
| | **Toronado** - see *GENERAL MOTORS (38030)* |

## PEUGEOT
| | |
|---|---|
| 663 | **504** all diesel models '74 thru '83 |

## PLYMOUTH
| | |
|---|---|
| | **Laser** - see *MITSUBISHI Eclipse (2097)* |
| | *For other PLYMOUTH titles, see DODGE.* |

## PONTIAC
| | |
|---|---|
| | **T1000** - see *CHEVROLET Chevette (449)* |
| | **J-2000** - see *GENERAL MOTORS (766)* |
| | **6000** - see *GENERAL MOTORS (829)* |
| | **Bonneville** - see *Buick FWD (1627), RWD (1551)* |
| | **Bonneville Brougham** - see *Buick (1551)* |
| | **Catalina** - see *Buick Full-size (1551)* |
| 1232 | **Fiero** all models '84 thru '88 |
| 555 | **Firebird** V8 models except Turbo '70 thru '81 |
| 867 | **Firebird** all models '82 thru '92 |
| | **Firebird** '93 thru '96 - see *CHEVY Camaro (24017)* |
| | **Full-size Front Wheel Drive** - see *BUICK, Oldsmobile, Pontiac Full-size FWD (1627)* |
| | **Full-size Rear Wheel Drive** - see *BUICK Oldsmobile, Pontiac Full-size RWD (1551)* |
| | **Grand Am** - see *GENERAL MOTORS (1420)* |
| | **Grand Prix** - see *GENERAL MOTORS (1671)* |
| | **Grandville** - see *BUICK Full-size (1551)* |
| | **Parisienne** - see *BUICK Full-size (1551)* |
| | **Phoenix** - see *GENERAL MOTORS (38020)* |
| | **Sunbird** - see *GENERAL MOTORS (766)* |
| | **Trans Sport** - see *GENERAL MOTORS (2035)* |

## PORSCHE
| | |
|---|---|
| *264 | **911** except Turbo & Carrera 4 '65 thru '89 |
| 239 | **914** all 4 cyl models '69 thru '76 |
| 397 | **924** all models including Turbo '76 thru '82 |
| *1027 | **944** all models including Turbo '83 thru '89 |

## RENAULT
| | |
|---|---|
| 141 | **5 Le Car** all models '76 thru '83 |
| | **Alliance & Encore** - see *AMC (934)* |

## SAAB
| | |
|---|---|
| 247 | **99** all models including Turbo '69 thru '80 |
| *980 | **900** all models including Turbo '79 thru '88 |

## SATURN
| | |
|---|---|
| 2083 | **Saturn** all models '91 thru '96 |

## SUBARU
| | |
|---|---|
| 237 | **1100, 1300, 1400 & 1600** '71 thru '79 |
| *681 | **1600 & 1800** 2WD & 4WD '80 thru '89 |

## SUZUKI
| | |
|---|---|
| *1626 | **Samurai/Sidekick & Geo Tracker** '86 thru '96 |

## TOYOTA
| | |
|---|---|
| 1023 | **Camry** all models '83 thru '91 |
| 92006 | **Camry** all models '92 thru '95 |
| 935 | **Celica Rear Wheel Drive** '71 thru '85 |
| *2038 | **Celica Front Wheel Drive** '86 thru '93 |
| 1139 | **Celica Supra** all models '79 thru '92 |
| 361 | **Corolla** all models '75 thru '79 |
| 961 | **Corolla** all rear wheel drive models '80 thru '87 |
| 1025 | **Corolla** all front wheel drive models '84 thru '92 |
| *92036 | **Corolla & Geo Prizm** '93 thru '96 |
| 636 | **Corolla Tercel** all models '80 thru '82 |
| 360 | **Corona** all models '74 thru '82 |
| 532 | **Cressida** all models '78 thru '82 |
| 313 | **Land Cruiser** all models '68 thru '82 |
| *1339 | **MR2** all models '85 thru '87 |
| 304 | **Pick-up** all models '69 thru '78 |
| *656 | **Pick-up** all models '79 thru '95 |
| *2048 | **Previa** all models '91 thru '95 |
| 2106 | **Tercel** all models '87 thru '94 |

## TRIUMPH
| | |
|---|---|
| 113 | **Spitfire** all models '62 thru '81 |
| 322 | **TR7** all models '75 thru '81 |

## VW
| | |
|---|---|
| 159 | **Beetle & Karmann Ghia** '54 thru '79 |
| 238 | **Dasher** all gasoline models '74 thru '81 |
| 96017 | **Golf & Jetta** all models '93 thru '97 |
| *884 | **Rabbit, Jetta, Scirocco, & Pick-up** gas models '74 thru '91 & Convertible '80 thru '92 |
| 451 | **Rabbit, Jetta & Pick-up** diesel '77 thru '84 |
| 082 | **Transporter 1600** all models '68 thru '79 |
| 226 | **Transporter 1700, 1800 & 2000** '72 thru '79 |
| 084 | **Type 3 1500 & 1600** all models '63 thru '73 |
| 1029 | **Vanagon** all air-cooled models '80 thru '83 |

## VOLVO
| | |
|---|---|
| 203 | **120, 130 Series & 1800 Sports** '61 thru '73 |
| 129 | **140 Series** all models '66 thru '74 |
| *270 | **240 Series** all models '76 thru '93 |
| 400 | **260 Series** all models '75 thru '82 |
| *1550 | **740 & 760 Series** all models '82 thru '88 |

## TECHBOOK MANUALS
| | |
|---|---|
| 2108 | **Automotive Computer Codes** |
| 1667 | **Automotive Emissions Control Manual** |
| 482 | **Fuel Injection Manual, 1978 thru 1985** |
| 2111 | **Fuel Injection Manual, 1986 thru 1996** |
| 2069 | **Holley Carburetor Manual** |
| 2068 | **Rochester Carburetor Manual** |
| 10240 | **Weber/Zenith/Stromberg/SU Carburetors** |
| 1762 | **Chevrolet Engine Overhaul Manual** |
| 2114 | **Chrysler Engine Overhaul Manual** |
| 1763 | **Ford Engine Overhaul Manual** |
| 1736 | **GM and Ford Diesel Engine Repair Manual** |
| 1666 | **Small Engine Repair Manual** |
| 10355 | **Ford Automatic Transmission Overhaul** |
| 10360 | **GM Automatic Transmission Overhaul** |
| 1479 | **Automotive Body Repair & Painting** |
| 2112 | **Automotive Brake Manual** |
| 2113 | **Automotive Detaiing Manual** |
| 1654 | **Automotive Eelectrical Manual** |
| 1480 | **Automotive Heating & Air Conditioning** |
| 2109 | **Automotive Reference Manual & Dictionary** |
| 2107 | **Automotive Tools Manual** |
| 10440 | **Used Car Buying Guide** |
| 2110 | **Welding Manual** |
| 10450 | **ATV Basics** |

## SPANISH MANUALS
| | |
|---|---|
| 98903 | **Reparación de Carrocería & Pintura** |
| 98905 | **Códigos Automotrices de la Computadora** |
| 98910 | **Frenos Automotriz** |
| 98915 | **Inyección de Combustible 1986 al 1994** |
| 99040 | **Chevrolet & GMC Camionetas** '67 al '87 Incluye Suburban, Blazer & Jimmy '67 al '91 |
| 99041 | **Chevrolet & GMC Camionetas** '88 al '95 Incluye Suburban '92 al '95, Blazer & Jimmy '92 al '94, Tahoe y Yukon '95 |
| 99042 | **Chevrolet & GMC Camionetas Cerradas** '68 al '95 |
| 99055 | **Dodge Caravan & Plymouth Voyager** '84 al '95 |
| 99075 | **Ford Camionetas y Bronco** '80 al '94 |
| 99077 | **Ford Camionetas Cerradas** '69 al '91 |
| 99083 | **Ford Modelos de Tamaño Grande** '75 al '87 |
| 99088 | **Ford Modelos de Tamaño Mediano** '75 al '86 |
| 99095 | **GM Modelos de Tamaño Grande** '70 al '90 |
| 99118 | **Nissan Sentra** '82 al '94 |
| 99125 | **Toyota Camionetas y 4-Runner** '79 al '95 |

*\* Listings shown with an asterisk (\*) indicate model coverage as of this printing. These titles will be periodically updated to include later model years - consult your Haynes dealer for more information.*

Over 100 Haynes motorcycle manuals also available

5-97

**Haynes North America, Inc., 861 Lawrence Drive, Newbury Park, CA 91320 • (805) 498-6703**